T0036584

PENGUIN BOOKS

The Conspiracy against the Human Race

Thomas Ligotti was born in Detroit in 1953. Considered one of the foremost authors of supernatural horror stories, he began publishing in the early 1980s. Following a tradition established by Edgar Allan Poe and perpetuated by H. P. Lovecraft, Ligotti is noted for his portrayals of characters who are outsiders to ordinary life, his depictions of otherworldly dimensions, and his uniquely dark vision of human life. His works are often praised by critics for their inventive imagination and evocative prose. Ligotti's first collection of tales, *Songs of a Dead Dreamer*, was published in 1986, and its follow-up, *Grimscribe*, in 1991. Among his other publications are the collections *Noctuary* and *Teatro Grottesco* as well as an influential philosophical work, *The Conspiracy against the Human Race: A Contrivance of Horror*. He has received several awards, including the Horror Writers Association's Bram Stoker Award for his omnibus collection *The Nightmare Factory* and his short novel *My Work Is Not Yet Done*. He lives in Florida.

ALSO BY THOMAS LIGOTTI

FICTION

Songs of a Dead Dreamer

Grimscribe

Noctuary

The Agonizing Resurrection
of Victor Frankenstein
and Other Gothic Tales

My Work Is Not Yet Done

Teatro Grottesco

The Spectral Link

OTHER WORK

Death Poems

Born to Fear: Interviews with Thomas Ligotti

The Conspiracy against the Human Race

A CONTRIVANCE OF HORROR

WITH A NEW PREFACE
BY THE AUTHOR

THOMAS LIGOTTI

PENGUIN BOOKS

PENGUIN BOOKS
An imprint of Penguin Random House LLC
375 Hudson Street
New York, New York 10014
penguinrandomhouse.com

First published in the United States of America by Hippocampus Press 2010
This edition with a new preface by Thomas Ligotti published in Penguin Books 2018

Parts of this work were published, in different form, in the following publications: "Literature Is Entertainment or It Is Nothing: An Interview with Thomas Ligotti" by Neddal Ayad, *Fantastic Metropolis* (website), October 31, 2004; "Thomas Ligotti on *Sweeney Todd*," *Horror: Another 100 Best Books*, Stephen Jones and Kim Newman, eds., 2005; Introduction by Thomas Ligotti, *The Tenant* by Roland Topor, 2006; "'It's All a Matter of Personal Pathology': An Interview with Thomas Ligotti" by Matt Cardin, *The Teeming Brain* (weblog), 2006.

All excerpts from the works of Peter Wessel Zapffe © Gisle R. Tangenes; used with permission. All excerpts from the writings of H. P. Lovecraft © Robert C. Harrall; used with permission of Lovecraft Properties LLC.

LIBRARY OF CONGRESS CATALOGING-IN-PUBLICATION DATA
Names: Ligotti, Thomas, author.
Title: The conspiracy against the human race: a contrivance of horror / Thomas Ligotti.
Description: New York : Penguin Books, 2018.
Identifiers: LCCN 2018015341 (print) | LCCN 2018015510 (ebook) |
ISBN 9780525504917 (ebook) | ISBN 9780143133148 (paperback)
Subjects: LCSH: Horror in literature. | Literature—Philosophy. | Pessimism in literature. |
BISAC: PHILOSOPHY / Ethics & Moral Philosophy. | LITERARY COLLECTIONS / Essays.
Classification: LCC PN56.H6 (ebook) | LCC PN56.H6 L54 2018 (print) |
DDC 809/.9164—dc23
LC record available at https://lccn.loc.gov/2018015341

Printed in the United States of America
13th Printing

Set in Berkeley Oldstyle   •   Designed by Elke Sigal

To Jonathan Padgett

Look at your body—
A painted puppet, a poor toy
Of jointed parts ready to collapse,
A diseased and suffering thing
With a head full of false imaginings.
  —*The Dhammapada*

Contents

Preface

To avoid all possibility of false appearances, I should disclose up front to being a writer of supernatural horror stories. Strictly speaking, then, *The Conspiracy against the Human Race* represents more than a slight exception to this practice. Nonetheless, certain readers of the present book may view it as essentially belonging to the domain of the supernatural, the weird, the uncanny, and so forth. Although a work of nonfiction, its subtitle, "A Contrivance of Horror," does seem to encourage such a conclusion. However, sometimes words have two or more meanings, and it is not unusual for writers to take advantage of this fact when giving a title to their handiwork. Thus, whether the term "contrivance" denotes my intended design for this volume or refers solely to its subject matter—the vast conspiracy I attempt to illuminate—is, for better or worse, a semantic blur.

While the proximate origin of *The Conspiracy against the Human Race* resides in an interview I gave in 2004, its true germ may be traced to a far earlier time in my life. False memories we all have, but I cannot help believing this one is true. It took place when I was nine years old. I had been engaged in an argument with my father and mother concerning some incident now forgotten. This conflict ended when I charged out the front door of our family home. Lingering outside were some friends of mine who took note of my fury and asked me what was up. The first words I spoke were derogatory of my parents.

"You shouldn't say that," admonished one of my friends. I could see that the others agreed.

"Why not?" I responded in a defiant tone. And then the answer.

"Because if it weren't for your mom and dad you wouldn't be alive."

I pondered the summary logic of this rebuke to the harsh words I had spoken about my parents. Something about it seemed flawed. Was I supposed to credit my progenitors with bringing me to life, as if I were Frankenstein's monster, a thing of inanimate parts into which they had breathed vitality? Had I been only a configuration of dead matter in another dimension prior to the success of their efforts to usher me into the realm of the living? Or had they somehow saved me, as did Jesus Christ by dying for my sins, a manner of speaking that never truly captured my imagination no matter how many times I heard it repeated during my years in Catholic school? Given that death loomed large in my religious training, such thoughts came naturally to my young mind. That heaven or hell awaited me after my demise was one article of faith I took quite seriously. But how could I have been a departed soul ahead of my coming to life? In its flight from cognitive dissonance, my childhood brain could not accept that I was just as dead before I lived as I would be when I ceased to breathe. It seemed ludicrous to me that death was a sort of vise that closed in on my life from both ends. All the same, I could not wholly dismiss the supposition. If not among the dead, then where had I existed before my parents rescued me? It must have been someplace very bad in my buddies' minds to provoke their chastisement of me for denigrating my begetters. Fortunately, my contemplation of the whole issue was quickly put aside so that I could play with my friends. Still, I remained preoccupied by the inescapable circumstance of death, especially after the assurances of religious doctrines gradually faded in me.

Not much later, of course, I came to realize that my preexistent life was not death but simply nonexistence. Yet whether that nonexistence could be definitively established as good or bad, or not good or not bad, was a concern for those trained in philosophy and beyond my ability to negotiate. During my later teenage years, however, I began to question the relative value of not existing as opposed to being alive, even if the former alternative was as unappealing a prospect for me as it is for practically everyone else. If only in principle, though, nonexistence ultimately seemed the place to be. More to the point, it seemed the place to stay. This is a conspicuously dark opinion, and such opinions, strongly held, sometimes lead individuals to express them in words. The type of expression I pursued was that of writing supernatural horror stories, which I began contriving in the 1970s.

Wisely, I destroyed almost all of the literary efforts of my apprentice years, allowing only one from the aforementioned decade to exist in a handwritten draft that I revised for more than a decade before I finally thought it fit to publish alongside others I produced throughout the 1980s. The title of my "first" story, in a chronological sense, is "The Last Feast of Harlequin." The setting of the narrative is a small town, and its plot features a strange cult that exalts nonexistence while observing a spiritual interdiction with respect to the breeding of human life. Other stories I had written and would later write were based on related themes, including "The Shadow, the Darkness," in which one character speaks of a book titled *An Investigation into the Conspiracy against the Human Race.* This book is described as being "based on the nonexistence, the imaginary nature, of everything we believe ourselves to be," a conceit I develop throughout the pages to come. I almost gave the story in question the title "The Conspiracy against the Human Race," having no idea that years later I would compose a book of that name on a similar subject.

Nothing written above is meant to suggest that the volume at hand had a destiny of some kind or followed a fated narrative. There are too many false starts and stops, derailments, and plain old complications throughout a person's life in its overarching aspects to regard it as anything but "one damn thing after another," as they say. All I may claim is that the selected events coordinated in this preface are connected in some way to the production of *The Conspiracy against the Human Race* as well as being somewhat revelatory of its author's peculiar temperament, which is left entirely for readers to judge according to their own.

Acknowledgments

I would like to express my appreciation to Tim Jeski and Scott Wetherby for supplying me with materials essential to the writing of this work; to the members of Thomas Ligotti Online and its administrator, Brian Edward Poe, for participating in a forum of commentary on an early draft of *The Conspiracy against the Human Race*; to Robert Ligotti for being a ready test subject whenever I needed an alert response from a mind akin to my own; and to Jennifer Gariepy for the encouragement and insight she has afforded me over many years. In addition, I would be more than remiss not to acknowledge the counsel and labors of S. T. Joshi and Jonathan Padgett, with special recognition reserved for Nicole Ariana Seary, who granted me the benefit of her talents and experience during the most crucial stages of this book's composition. Finally, I am indebted, as are all devotees of philosophical pessimism who are not knowledgeable of the Dano-Norwegian language, to Gisle R. Tangenes for his translations of and writings on the works of Peter Wessel Zapffe. The responsibility for the use made of these valued contributions lies entirely with the author.

Introduction:
Of Pessimism and Paradox

In his study *The Nature of Evil* (1931), Radoslav A. Tsanoff cites a terse reflection set down by the German philosopher Julius Bahnsen in 1847, when he was seventeen years old. "Man is a self-conscious Nothing," wrote Bahnsen. Whether one considers these words to be juvenile or precocious, they belong to an ancient tradition of scorn for our species and its aspirations. All the same, the reigning sentiments on the human venture normally fall between qualified approval and loudmouthed braggadocio. As a rule, anyone desirous of an audience, or even a place in society, might profit from the following motto: "If you can't say something positive about humanity, then say something equivocal."

Returning to Bahnsen, he grew up to become a philosopher who not only had nothing either positive or equivocal to say about humanity, but who also arrived at a dour assessment of all existence. Like many who have tried their hand at metaphysics, Bahnsen declared that, appearances to the contrary, all reality is the expression of a unified, unchanging force—a cosmic movement that various philosophers have characterized in various ways. To Bahnsen, this force and its movement were monstrous in nature, resulting in a universe of indiscriminate butchery and mutual slaughter among its individuated parts. Additionally, the "universe according to Bahnsen" has never had a hint of design or direction. From the beginning, it was a play with no plot and no players that were anything more than portions of a master drive of purposeless self-mutilation. In Bahnsen's philosophy, everything is engaged in a disordered fantasia of carnage. Everything tears away at everything else . . . forever. Yet all this commotion in nothingness goes unnoticed by nearly everything involved in it. In the world of nature, as an instance, nothing knows of its embroilment in a festival of massacres. Only Bahnsen's self-conscious Nothing can know what is going on and be shaken by the tremors of *chaos at feast*.

As with all pessimistic philosophies, Bahnsen's rendering of existence as something strange and awful was unwelcome by the self-conscious nothings whose validation he sought. For better or worse, pessimism without compromise lacks public appeal. In all, the few who have gone to the pains of arguing for a sullen appraisal of life might as well never have been born. As history confirms, people will change their minds about almost anything, from which god they worship to how they style their hair. But when it comes to existential judgments, human beings in general have an unfalteringly good opinion of themselves and their condition in this world and are steadfastly confident they are not a collection of self-conscious nothings.

Must all reproof of our species' self-contentment then be renounced? That would be the brilliant decision, rule number one for deviants from the norm. Rule number two: If you must open your mouth, steer away from debate. Money and love may make the world go round, but disputation with that world cannot get it to budge if it is not of a mind to do so. Thus British author and Christian apologist G. K. Chesterton: "You can only find truth with logic if you have already found truth without it." What Chesterton means to say here is that logic is irrelevant to truth, because if you can find truth without logic then logic is superfluous to any truth-finding effort. Indeed, his only motive for bringing logic into his formulation is to taunt those who find logic quite relevant to finding truth, although not the kind of truth that was pivotal to Chesterton's morale as a Christian.

Renowned for stating his convictions in the form of a paradox, as above, Chesterton, along with anyone who has something positive or equivocal to say about the human race, comes out on top in the crusade for truth. (There is nothing paradoxical about that.) Therefore, should your truth run counter to that of individuals who devise or applaud paradoxes that stiff up the status quo, you would be well advised to take your arguments, tear them up, and throw them in someone else's garbage.

To be sure, though, futile argumentation has its attractions and may act as an amusing complement to the bitter joy of spewing gut-level vituperations, personal idolatries, and rampant pontifications. To absolve such an unruly application of the rational and the irrational (not that they are ever separable), the present "contrivance of horror" has been anchored in the thesis of a philosopher who had disquieting thoughts about what it is like to be a member of the human race. But too much should not be telegraphed in this prelude to abjection. For the time being, it need only be said that the philosopher in question made much of human existence as a tragedy that need not have been were it not for the intervention in our lives of a single, calamitous event: the evolution of consciousness—parent of all horrors. He also portrayed humanity as a species of contradictory beings whose continuance only worsens their plight, which is that of mutants who embody the contorted logic of a paradox—a real-life paradox and not a bungled epigram.

Even an offhand review of the topic will show that not all paradoxes are alike. Some are merely rhetorical, an apparent contradiction of logic that, if well juggled, may be intelligibly resolved within a specific context. More intriguing are those paradoxes that torture our notions of reality. In the literature of supernatural horror, a familiar storyline is that of a character who encounters a paradox *in the flesh*, so to speak, and must face down or collapse in horror before this ontological perversion—something which should not be, and yet is. Most fabled as specimens of a living paradox are the "undead," those walking cadavers greedy for an eternal presence on earth. But whether their existence should go on unendingly or be cut short by a stake in the heart is not germane to the matter at hand. What is exceedingly material resides in the supernatural horror that such beings could exist in their impossible way for an instant. Other examples of paradox and supernatural horror congealing together are inanimate things guilty of infractions against their nature. Perhaps the most outstanding instance of this phenomenon is a puppet that breaks free of its strings and becomes *self-mobilized*.

For a brief while, let us mull over some items of interest regarding puppets. They are made as they are made by puppet makers and manipulated to behave in certain ways by a puppet master's will. The puppets under discussion here are those made in our image, though never with such fastidiousness that we would mistake them for human beings. If they were so created, their resemblance to our soft shapes would be a strange and awful thing, too strange and awful, in fact, to be countenanced without alarm. Given that alarming people has little to do with merchandising puppets, they are not created so fastidiously in our image that we would mistake them for human beings, except perhaps in the half-light of a dank cellar or cluttered attic. We need to know that puppets are puppets. Nevertheless, we may still be alarmed by them. Because if we look at a puppet in a certain way, we may sometimes feel it is looking back, not as a human being looks at us but as a puppet does. It may even seem to be on the brink of coming to life. In such moments of mild disorientation, a psychological conflict erupts, a dissonance of perception that sends through our being a convulsion of supernatural horror.

A sibling term of supernatural horror is the "uncanny." Both terms are pertinent in reference to nonhuman forms that disport human qualities. Both may also refer to seemingly animate forms that are not what they seem, as with the undead—monstrosities of paradox, things that are neither one thing nor another, or, more uncannily, and more horrifically supernatural, things that are discovered to be two things at once. Whether or not there really are manifestations of the supernatural, they are horrifying to us in concept, since we think ourselves to be living in a natural world, which may be a festival of massacres but only in a physical rather than a metaphysical purport. This is why we routinely equate the supernatural with horror. And a puppet possessed of life would exemplify just such a horror, because it would negate all conceptions of a natural physicalism and affirm a metaphysics of chaos and nightmare. It would still be a puppet, but it would be a puppet with a mind and a will, a *human* puppet—a paradox more disruptive of sanity than the undead. But that is not how *they* would see it. Human puppets could not conceive of themselves as being puppets at all, not when they are fixed with a consciousness that excites in them the unshakable sense of being singled out from all other objects in creation. Once you begin to feel you are making a go of it on your own—that you are making moves and thinking thoughts which seem to have originated within you—it is not possible for you to believe you are anything but your own master.

As effigies of ourselves, puppets are not equal partners with us in the world. They are actors in a world of their own, one that exists inside of ours and reflects back upon it. What do we see in that reflection? Only what we want to see, what we can stand to see. Through the prophylactic of self-deception, we keep hidden what we do not want to let into our heads, as if we will betray to ourselves a *secret too terrible to know*. Our lives abound with baffling questions that some attempt to answer and the rest of us let pass. Naked apes or incarnate angels we may believe ourselves to be, but not human puppets. Of a higher station than these impersonators of our species, we move freely about and can speak any time we like. We believe we are making a go of it on our own, and anyone who contradicts this belief will be taken for a madman or someone who is attempting to immerse others in a contrivance of horror. How to take seriously a puppet master who has *gone over to the other side*?

When puppets are done with their play, they go back in their boxes. They do not sit in a chair reading a book, their eyes rolling like marbles over its words. They are only objects, like a corpse in a casket. If they ever came to life, our world would be a paradox and a horror in which everything was uncertain, including whether or not we were just human puppets.

All supernatural horror derives from what we believe should be and should not be. As scientists, philosophers, and spiritual figures have testified, our heads are full of illusions; things, including human things, are not dependably what they seem. Yet one thing we know for sure: the difference between what is natural and what is not. Another thing we know is that nature makes no blunders so untoward as to allow things, including human things, to swerve into supernaturalism. Were it to make such a blunder, we would do everything in our power to bury this knowledge. But we need not resort to such measures, being as natural as we are. No one can prove that our life in this world is a supernatural horror, nor cause us to suspect that it might be. Anybody can tell you that—not least a contriver of books that premise the supernatural, the uncanny, and the frightfully paradoxical as essential to our nature.

The Conspiracy
against the Human Race

The Nightmare of Being

Psychogenesis

For ages they had been without lives of their own. The whole of their being was open to the world and nothing divided them from the rest of creation. How long they had thus flourished none of them knew. Then something began to change. It happened over unremembered generations. The signs of a revision without forewarning were being writ ever more deeply into them. As their species moved forward, they began crossing boundaries whose very existence they never imagined. After nightfall, they looked up at a sky filled with stars and felt themselves small and fragile in the vastness. Soon they began to see everything in a way they never had in older times. When they found one of their own lying still and stiff, they now stood around the body as if there were something they should do that they had never done before. It was then they began to take bodies that were still and stiff to distant places so they could not find their way back to them. But even after they had done this, some within their group did see those bodies again, often standing silent in the moonlight or loitering sad-faced just beyond the glow of a fire. Everything changed once they had lives of their own and knew they had lives of their own. It even became impossible for them to believe things had ever been any other way. They were masters of their movements now, as it seemed, and never had there been anything like them. The epoch had passed when the whole of their being was open to the world and nothing divided them from the rest of creation. Something had happened. They did not know what it was, but they did know it as that which *should not be*. And something needed to be done if they were to flourish as they once had, if the very ground beneath their feet were not to fall out from under them. For ages they had been without lives of their own. Now that they had such lives there was no turning back. The whole of their being was closed to the world, and they had been divided from the rest of creation. Nothing could be done about that, having as they did lives of their own. But something would have to be done if they were to live with that which *should not be*. And over time they discovered what could be done—what would have to be done—so that they could live the lives that were now theirs to live. This would not revive among them the way things had once been done in older times; it would only be the best they could do.[1]

Ante-Mortem

For thousands of years a debate has been going on in the shadowy background of human affairs. The issue to be resolved: "What should we say about being alive?" Overwhelmingly, people have said, "Being alive is all right." More thoughtful persons have added, "Especially when you consider the alternative," disclosing a jocularity as puzzling as it is macabre, since the alternative is here implied to be both disagreeable and, upon consideration, capable of making being alive seem more agreeable than it alternatively would, as if the alternative were only a possibility that may or may not come to pass, like getting the flu, rather than a looming inevitability. And yet this covertly portentous remark is perfectly well tolerated by anyone who says that being alive is all right. These individuals stand on one side of the debate. On the other side is an imperceptible minority of disputants. Their response to the question of what we should say about being alive will be neither positive nor equivocal. They may even fulminate about how objectionable it is to be alive, or spout off that to be alive is to inhabit a nightmare without hope of awakening to a natural world, to have our bodies embedded neck-deep in a quagmire of dread, to live as shut-ins in a house of horrors from which nobody gets out alive, and so on. Now, there are really no incisive answers as to why anyone thinks or feels one way and not another. The most we can say is that the first group of people is composed of optimists, though they may not think of themselves as such, while the contending group, that imperceptible minority, is composed of pessimists. The latter know who they are. But which group is in the right—the existentially harrowed pessimists or the life-embracing optimists—will never be resolved.

If the most contemplative individuals are sometimes dubious about the value of existence, they do not often publicize their doubts but align themselves with the optimist in the street, tacitly declaiming, in more erudite terms, "Being alive is all right." The butcher, the baker, and the crushing majority of philosophers all agree on one thing: Human life is a good thing, and we should keep our species going for as long as we can. To tout the rival side of the issue is asking for grief. But some people seem born to bellyache that being alive is not all right. Should they vent this posture in philosophical or literary works, they may do so without anxiety that their efforts will have an excess of admirers. Notable among such efforts is "The Last Messiah" (1933), an essay written by the Norwegian philosopher and man of letters Peter Wessel Zapffe (1899–1990). In this work, which to date has been twice translated into English, Zapffe elucidated why he saw human existence as a tragedy.[2]

Before discussing Zapffe's elucidation of human existence as a tragedy, however, it may be useful to muse upon a few facts whose relevance will become manifest down the line. As some may know, there exist readers who treasure philosophical and literary works of a pessimistic, nihilistic, or defeatist nature as indispensable to their existence, hyperbolically speaking. Contrary by temperament, these persons are sorely aware that nothing indispensable to their existence, hyperbolically or literally speaking, must make its way into their lives, as if by natural birthright. They do not think anything indispensable to anyone's existence may be claimed as a natural birthright, since the birthrights we toss about are all lies fabricated to a purpose, as any student of humanity can verify. For those who have given thought to this matter, the only rights we may exercise are these: to seek the survival of our individual bodies, to create more bodies like our own, and to perish from corruption or mortal trauma. Of course, possession of these rights presumes that one has been brought to term and made it to the age of being reproductively ready, neither being a natural birthright. Stringently considered, then, our only natural birthright is a *right to die*. No other right has ever been allocated to anyone except as a fabrication, whether in modern times or days past.[3] The divine right of kings may now be acknowledged as a fabrication, a falsified permit for prideful dementia and impulsive mayhem. The inalienable rights of certain people, on the other hand, seemingly remain current: somehow we believe they are not fabrications because hallowed documents declare they are real. Miserly or munificent as a given right may appear, it denotes no more than the right of way warranted by a traffic light, which does not mean you have the right to drive free of vehicular misadventures. Ask any paramedic as your dead body is taken away to the nearest hospital.

Wide-Awake

Our want of any natural birthright—except to die, in most cases without assistance—is not a matter of tragedy, but only one of truth. Coming at last to the pith of Zapffe's thought as it is contained in "The Last Messiah," what the Norwegian philosopher saw as the tragedy of human existence had its beginnings when at some stage in our evolution we acquired "a damning surplus of consciousness." (Indulgence is begged in advance for the present work's profuse entreaties for assent, or at least suspension of disbelief, in this matter.) Naturally, it must be owned that there are quarrels among cognitive psychologists, philosophers of mind, and neuroscientists about what consciousness is. The fact that this question has been around since at least the time of the ancient Greeks and early Buddhists suggests there is an assumption of consciousness in the human species and that consciousness has had an effect on the way we exist. For Zapffe, the effect was

A breach in the very unity of life, a biological paradox, an abomination, an absurdity, an exaggeration of disastrous nature. Life had overshot its target, blowing itself apart. A species had been armed too heavily—by spirit made almighty without, but equally a menace to its own well-being. Its weapon was like a sword without hilt or plate, a two-edged blade cleaving everything; but he who is to wield it must grasp the blade and turn one edge toward himself.

Despite his new eyes, man was still rooted in matter, his soul spun into it and subordinated to its blind laws. And yet he could see matter as a stranger, compare himself to all phenomena, see through and locate his vital processes. He comes to nature as an unbidden guest, in vain extending his arms to beg conciliation with his maker:

Nature answers no more; it performed a miracle with man, but later did not know him. He has lost his right of residence in the universe, has eaten from the Tree of Knowledge and been expelled from Paradise. He is mighty in the near world, but curses his might as purchased with his harmony of soul, his innocence, his inner peace in life's embrace.

Could there be anything to this pessimistic verbiage, this tirade against the evolution of consciousness? Millennia had passed without much discussion one way or the other on the subject, at least in polite society, and then suddenly comes this barrage from an obscure Norwegian philosopher. What is one to say? For contrast, here are some excerpts from an online interview with the eminent British multidisciplinary thinker Nicholas Humphrey ("A Self Worth Having: A Talk with Nicolas Humphrey," 2003):

> Consciousness—phenomenal experience—seems in many ways too good to be true. The way we experience the world seems unnecessarily beautiful, unnecessarily rich and strange. . . .
>
> Phenomenal experience, surely, can and does provide the basis for creating a self worth having. And just see what becomes possible—even natural—once this new self is in place! As subjects of something so mysterious and strange, we humans gain new confidence and interest in our own survival, a new interest in other people too. We begin to be interested in the future, in immortality, and in all sorts of issues to do with . . . how far consciousness extends around us. . . .
>
> [T]he more I try to make sense of it, the more I come back to the fact that we've evolved to regard consciousness as a wonderfully good thing in its own right—which could

just be because consciousness *is* a wonderfully good thing in its own right!

Could there be anything to this *optimistic* verbiage in which consciousness is not a "breach in the very unity of life, a biological paradox, an abomination, an absurdity, an exaggeration of disastrous nature" but something that is "unnecessarily beautiful, unnecessarily rich and strange" and "a wonderfully good thing in its own right," something that makes human existence an unbelievably desirable adventure? Think about it—a British thinker thinks so well of the evolution of consciousness that he cannot contain his gratitude for this turn of events. What is one to say? Both Humphrey and Zapffe are equally passionate about what they have to say, which is not to say that they have said anything credible. Whether you think consciousness to be a benefit or a horror, this is only what you think—and nothing else. But even though you cannot demonstrate the truth of what you think, you can at least put it on show and see what the audience thinks.

Brainwork

Over the centuries, assorted theories about the nature and workings of consciousness have been put forth. The theory Zapffe implicitly accepted is this: Consciousness is connected to the human brain in a way that makes the world appear to us as it appears and makes us appear to ourselves as we appear—that is, as "selves" or as "persons" strung together by memories, sensations, emotions, and so on. This view of a materialistic basis of consciousness with an evolutionary origin may be right or wrong. No one knows exactly what consciousness is, or even if it is, all speculation on the matter being debatable to the point of chaos. Nevertheless, most thinkers in this area agree that consciousness is a fact in some way.

Accepting consciousness as a given for a sufficiently evolved brain, Zapffe moved on from there, since he was not interested in the debates surrounding this phenomenon as such but only in the way it quite apparently functions to determine the nature of our species. This was enough for his purposes, which were wholly existential and careless of seeking the technical verities of consciousness. How consciousness "happened," since it was not always present in our species, remains as much a mystery in our time as it was in Zapffe's, just as what was going on, if anything was going on, before the universe came into being remains a mystery. The same applies to the origins of living forms, however such things may be defined. First there was no life, and then there was life—nature, as it came to be called. As nature proliferated into more complex and various shapes, human organisms eventually entered the world as part of this process. After a time, consciousness happened for these organisms (along with others at much lower amplitudes). And it kept on gaining steam as we evolved. On this nearly all theorists of consciousness agree. Billions of years after earth made a jump from being lifeless to having life, human beings made a jump from not being conscious, or very much conscious, to being conscious enough to esteem or condemn this phenomenon. No one knows either how the jump was made or how long it took, although there are theories about both, as there are theories about all mutations from one state to another.

"The mutations must be considered blind," Zapffe wrote. "They work, are thrown forth, without any contact of interest with their environment." As mentioned, how the mutation of consciousness originated was of no concern to Zapffe, who focused entirely on demonstrating the tragic effect of this aptitude. Such projects are typical among pessimistic philosophers. Non-pessimistic philosophers either have an impartial attitude about consciousness or, like Nicholas Humphrey, think of it as a marvelous endowment. When non-pessimistic philosophers even notice the pessimist's attitude, they reject it. With the world on their side in the conviction that being alive is all right, non-pessimists are not disposed to musing that human existence is a wholesale tragedy. They only argue the fine points of whatever it is about human existence that grabs their attention, which may include the tragic but not so much that they lose their commitment to the proposition that being alive is all right. And they can do this until the day they die, which is all right by them.

Mutation

Established: Consciousness is not often viewed as being an instrument of tragedy in human life. But to Zapffe, consciousness would long past have proved fatal for human beings if we did not do something about it. "Why," Zapffe asked, "has mankind not long ago gone extinct during great epidemics of madness? Why do only a fairly minor number of individuals perish because they fail to endure the strain of living—because cognition gives them more than they can carry?" Zapffe's answer: "Most people learn to save themselves by artificially limiting the content of consciousness."

From an evolutionary viewpoint, in Zapffe's observation, consciousness was a blunder that required corrections for its effects. It was an adventitious outgrowth that made us into a race of contradictory beings—uncanny things that have nothing to do with the rest of creation. Because of consciousness, parent of all horrors, we became susceptible to thoughts that were startling and dreadful to us, thoughts that have never been equitably balanced by those that are collected and reassuring. Our minds now began dredging up horrors, flagrantly joyless possibilities, enough of them to make us drop to the ground in paroxysms of self-soiling consternation should they go untrammeled. This potentiality necessitated that certain defense mechanisms be put to use to keep us balanced on the knife-edge of vitality as a species.

While a modicum of consciousness may have had survivalist properties during an immemorial chapter of our evolution—so one theory goes—this faculty soon enough became a seditious agent working against us. As Zapffe concluded, we need to hamper our consciousness for all we are worth, or it will impose upon us a too clear vision of what we do not want to see, which, as the Norwegian philosopher saw it, along with every other pessimist, is "the brotherhood of suffering between everything alive." Whether or not one agrees that there is a "brotherhood of suffering between everything alive," we can all agree that human beings are the only organisms that can have such a conception of existence, or any conception period. That we can conceive of the phenomenon of suffering, our own as well as that of other organisms, is a property unique to us as a dangerously conscious species. We know there is suffering, and we do take action against it, which includes downplaying it by "artificially limiting the content of consciousness." Between taking action against and downplaying suffering, mainly the latter, most of us do not worry that it has overly sullied our existence.

As a fact, we cannot give suffering precedence in either our individual or collective lives. We have to *get on with things*, and those who give precedence to suffering will be left behind. They fetter us with their sniveling. We have someplace to go and must believe we can get there, wherever that may be. And to conceive that there is a "brotherhood of suffering between everything alive" would disable us from getting anywhere. We are preoccupied with the good life, and step by step are working toward a better life. What we do, as a conscious species, is set markers for ourselves. Once we reach one marker, we advance to the next—as if we were playing a board game we think will never end, despite the fact that it will, like it or not. And if you are too conscious of not liking it, then you may conceive of yourself as a biological paradox that cannot live with its consciousness and cannot live without it. And in so living and not living, you take your place with the undead and the human puppet.

Undoing I

For the rest of the earth's organisms, existence is relatively uncomplicated. Their lives are about three things: survival, reproduction, death—and nothing else. But we know too much to content ourselves with surviving, reproducing, dying—and nothing else. We know we are alive and know we will die. We also know we will suffer during our lives before suffering—slowly or quickly—as we draw near to death. This is the knowledge we "enjoy" as the most intelligent organisms to gush from the womb of nature. And being so, we feel shortchanged if there is nothing else for us than to survive, reproduce, and die. We want there to be more to it than that, or to think there is. This is the tragedy: Consciousness has forced us into the paradoxical position of striving to be unselfconscious of what we are—hunks of spoiling flesh on disintegrating bones.

Nonhuman occupants of this planet are unaware of death. But we are susceptible to startling and dreadful thoughts, and we need some fabulous illusions to take our minds off them. For us, then, life is a confidence trick we must run on ourselves, hoping we do not catch on to any monkey business that would leave us stripped of our defense mechanisms and standing stark naked before the silent, staring void. To end this self-deception, to free our species of the paradoxical imperative to be and not to be conscious, our backs breaking by degrees upon a wheel of lies, *we must cease reproducing*. Nothing less will do, per Zapffe, although in "The Last Messiah" the character after whom the essay is named does all the talking about human extinction. Elsewhere Zapffe speaks for himself on the subject.

> The sooner humanity dares to harmonize itself with its biological predicament, the better. And this means to willingly withdraw in contempt for its worldly terms, just as the heat-craving species went extinct when temperatures dropped. To us, it is the moral climate of the cosmos that is intolerable, and a two-child policy could make our discontinuance a pain-free one. Yet instead we are expanding and succeeding everywhere, as necessity has taught us to mutilate the formula in our hearts. Perhaps the most unreasonable effect of such invigorating vulgarization is the doctrine that the individual "has a duty" to suffer nameless agony and a terrible death if this saves or benefits the rest of his group. Anyone who declines is subjected to doom and death, instead of revulsion being directed at the world-order engendering of the situation. To any independent observer, this plainly is to juxtapose incommensurable things; no future triumph or metamorphosis can justify the pitiful blighting of a human being against his will. It is upon a pavement of battered destinies that the survivors storm ahead to ward new bland sensations and mass deaths. ("Fragments of an Interview," *Aftenposten*, 1959)

More provocative than it is astonishing, Zapffe's thought is perhaps the most elementary in the history of philosophical pessimism. As penetrable as it is cheerless, it rests on taboo commonplaces and outlawed truisms while eschewing the recondite brain-twisters of his forerunners, all of whom engaged in the kind of convoluted cerebration that for thousands of years has been philosophy's stock in trade. For example, *The World as Will and Representation* (two volumes, 1819 and 1844) by the German philosopher Arthur Schopenhauer lays out one of the most absorbingly intricate metaphysical systems ever contrived—a quasi-mystical elaboration of a "Will-to-live" as the hypostasis of reality, a mindless and untiring master of all being, a directionless force that makes everything do what it does, an imbecilic puppeteer that sustains the ruckus of our world. But Schopenhauer's Will-to-live, commendable as it may seem as a hypothesis, is too overwrought in the proving to be anything more than another intellectual labyrinth for specialists in perplexity. Comparatively, Zapffe's principles are non-technical and could never arouse the passion of professors or practitioners of philosophy, who typically circle around the minutiae of theories and not the gross facts of our lives. If we must think, it should be done only in circles, outside of which lies the unthinkable. Evidence: While commentators on Schopenhauer's thought have seized upon it as a philosophical system ripe for academic analysis, they do not emphasize that its ideal endpoint—the denial of the Will-to-live—is a construct for the end of human existence. But even Schopenhauer himself did not push this aspect of his philosophy to its ideal endpoint, which has kept him in fair repute as a philosopher.

Zombification

As adumbrated above, Zapffe arrived at two central determinations regarding humanity's "biological predicament." The first was that consciousness had overreached the point of being a sufferable property of our species, and to minimize this problem we must minimize our consciousness. From the many and various ways this may be done, Zapffe chose to home in on four principal strategies.

(1) ISOLATION. So that we may live without going into a free-fall of trepidation, we isolate the dire facts of being alive by relegating them to a remote compartment of our minds. They are the lunatic family members in the attic whose existence we deny in a conspiracy of silence.

(2) ANCHORING. To stabilize our lives in the tempestuous waters of chaos, we conspire to anchor them in metaphysical and institutional "verities"—God, Morality, Natural Law, Country, Family—that inebriate us with a sense of being official, authentic, and safe in our beds.

(3) DISTRACTION. To keep our minds unreflective of a world of horrors, we distract them with a world of trifling or momentous trash. The most operant method for furthering the conspiracy, it is in continuous employ and demands only that people keep their eyes on the ball—or their television sets, their government's foreign policy, their science projects, their careers, their place in society or the universe, etc.

(4) SUBLIMATION. That we might annul a paralyzing stage fright at what may happen to even the soundest bodies and minds, we sublimate our fears by making an open display of them. In the Zapffean sense, sublimation is the rarest technique utilized for conspiring against the human race. Putting into play both deviousness and skill, this is what thinkers and artistic types do when they recycle the most demoralizing and unnerving aspects of life as works in which the worst fortunes of humanity are presented in a stylized and removed manner as entertainment. In so many words, these thinkers and artistic types confect products that provide an escape from our suffering by a bogus simulation of it—a tragic drama or philosophical woolgathering, for instance.

Zapffe uses "The Last Messiah" to showcase how a literary-philosophical composition cannot perturb its creator or anyone else with the severity of true-to-life horrors but only provide a pale representation of these horrors, just as a King Lear's weeping for his dead daughter Cordelia cannot rend its audience with the throes of the real thing.

By watchful practice of the above connivances, we may keep ourselves from scrutinizing too assiduously the startling and dreadful mishaps that may befall us. These must come as a surprise, for if we expected them then the conspiracy could not work its magic. Naturally, conspiracy theories seldom pique the curiosity of "right-minded" individuals and are met with disbelief and denial when they do. Best to immunize your consciousness from any thoughts that are startling and dreadful so that we can all go on conspiring to survive and reproduce as paradoxical beings—puppets that can walk and talk all by themselves. At worst keep your startling and dreadful thoughts to yourself. Hearken well: "None of us wants to hear spoken the exact anxieties we keep locked up inside ourselves. Smother that urge to go spreading news of your pain and nightmares around town. Bury your dead but don't leave a trace. And be sure to get on with things or we will get on without you."

In his 1910 doctoral dissertation, published in English as *Persuasion and Rhetoric* (2004), the twenty-three-year-old Carlo Michelstaedter audited the tactics we use to falsify human existence as we trade who we are, or might be, for a specious view of ourselves. Like Pinocchio, Michelstaedter wanted to be a "real boy" and not the product of a puppet maker who, in turn, did not make himself but was made as he was made by mutations that, as Zapffe relays to us from evolutionary theory, "must be considered blind," a series of accidents that continually structure and restructure all that exists in the workshop of the world. To Michelstaedter, nothing in this world can be anything but a puppet. And a puppet is only a plaything, a thing of parts brought together as a simulacrum of real presence. It is nothing in itself. It is not whole and individual but exists only relative to other playthings, some of them human playthings that support one another's illusion of being real. However, by suppressing thoughts of suffering and death they give themselves away as beings of paradox—prevaricators who must hide from themselves the flagrantly joyless possibilities of their lives if they are to go on living. In *Persuasion and Rhetoric*, Michelstaedter pinpoints the paradox of our division from ourselves: "man 'knows,' which is why he is always two: his *life* and his *knowing*."

Michelstaedter's biographers and critics have speculated that his despair of humanity's ability to become disentangled from its puppet strings was, in conjunction with accidental factors, the cause of his suicide by gunshot the day after he finished his dissertation. Michelstaedter could not accept a stellar fact of human life: that none of us has control over what we are—a truth that extirpates all hope if what you want to be is invulnerably self-possessed ("persuaded") and without subjection to a life that would fit you within the limits of its unrealities ("rhetoric," a word oddly used by Michelstaedter). We are defined by our limitations; without them, we cannot suffice as functionaries in the big show of conscious existence. The farther you progress toward a vision of our species without limiting conditions on your consciousness, the farther you drift away from what makes you a person among persons in the human community. In the observance of Zapffe, an unleashed consciousness would alert us to the falsity of ourselves and subject us to the pain of Pinocchio. An individual's demarcations as a being, not his trespass of them, create his identity and preserve his illusion of being something special and not a freak of chance, a product of blind mutations. Transcending all illusions and their emergent activities—having absolute control of what we are and not what we need to be so that we may survive the most unsavory facts of life and death—would untether us from the moorings of our self-limited selves.

The lesson: "Let us love our limitations, for without them nobody would be left to be somebody."

Undoing II

The second of Zapffe's two central determinations—that our species should belay reproducing itself—immediately brings to mind a cast of characters from theological history known as Gnostics. The Gnostic sect of the Cathari in twelfth-century France were so tenacious in believing the world to be an evil place engendered by an evil deity that its members were offered a dual ultimatum: sexual abstinence or sodomy. (A similar sect in Bulgaria, the Bogomils, became the etymological origin of the term "buggery" for their practice of this mode of erotic release.) Around the same period, the Catholic Church mandated abstinence for its clerics, a directive that did not halt them from betimes giving in to sexual quickening. The raison d'être for this doctrine was the attainment of grace (and in legend was obligatory for those scouring hither and yon for the Holy Grail) rather than an enlightened governance of reproductive plugs and bungholes. With these exceptions, the Church did not counsel its followers to imitate its ascetic founder but sagaciously welcomed them to breed as copiously as they could.

In another orbit from the theologies of either Gnosticism or Catholicism, the nineteenth-century German philosopher Philipp

Mainländer (born Philipp Batz) also envisaged non-coital existence as the surest path to redemption for the sin of being congregants of this world. Our extinction, however, would not be the outcome of an unnatural chastity, but would be a naturally occurring phenomenon once we had evolved far enough to apprehend our existence as so hopelessly pointless and unsatisfactory that we would no longer be subject to generative promptings. Paradoxically, this evolution toward life-sickness would be promoted by a mounting happiness among us. This happiness would be quickened by our following Mainländer's evangelical guidelines for achieving such things as universal justice and charity. Only by securing every good that could be gotten in life, Mainländer figured, could we know that they were not as good as nonexistence.

While the abolishment of human life would be sufficient for the average pessimist, the terminal stage of Mainländer's wishful thought was the full summoning of a "Will-to-die" that by his deduction resided in all matter across the universe. Mainländer diagrammed this brainstorm, along with others as riveting, in a treatise whose title has been translated into English as *The Philosophy of Redemption* (1876). Unsurprisingly, the work never set the philosophical world ablaze. Perhaps the author might have garnered greater celebrity if, like the Austrian philosopher Otto Weininger in his infamous study translated as *Sex and Character* (1903), he had devoted himself to gripping ruminations on male and female matters rather than the redemptive disappearance of everyone regardless of gender.[4]

As one who had a special plan for the human race, Mainländer was not a modest thinker. "We are not everyday people," he once wrote in the royal third-person, "and must pay dearly for dining at the table of the gods." To top it off, suicide ran in his family. On the day his *Philosophy of Redemption* was published, Mainländer killed

himself, possibly in a fit of megalomania but just as possibly in sur-
render to the extinction that for him was so attractive and that he
avouched for a most esoteric reason—Deicide.

Mainländer was confident that the Will-to-die he believed
would well up in humanity had been spiritually grafted into us by
a God who, in the beginning, masterminded His own quietus. It
seems that existence was a horror to God. Unfortunately, God was
impervious to the depredations of time. This being so, His only
means to get free of Himself was by a divine form of suicide.

God's plan to suicide Himself could not work, though, as long
as He existed as a unified entity outside of space-time and matter.
Seeking to nullify His oneness so that He could be delivered into
nothingness, He shattered Himself—Big-Bang-like—into the time-
bound fragments of the universe, that is, all those objects and organisms that have been accumulating here and there for billions of
years. In Mainländer's philosophy, "God knew that He could
change from a state of super-reality into non-being only through
the development of a real world of multiformity." Employing this
strategy, He excluded Himself from being. "God is dead," wrote
Mainländer, "and His death was the life of the world." Once the
great individuation had been initiated, the momentum of its creator's self-annihilation would continue until everything became
exhausted by its own existence, which for human beings meant
that the faster they learned that happiness was not as good as they
thought it would be, the happier they would be to die out.

So: The Will-to-live that Schopenhauer argued activates the
world to its torment was revised by his disciple Mainländer not
only as evidence of a tortured life within living beings, but also as
a cover for a clandestine will in all things to burn themselves out
as hastily as possible in the fires of becoming. In this light, human
progress is shown to be an ironic symptom that our downfall into

extinction has been progressing nicely, because the more things change for the better, the more they progress toward a reliable end. And those who committed suicide, as did Mainländer, would only be forwarding God's blueprint for bringing an end to His Creation. Naturally, those who replaced themselves by procreation were of no help: "Death is succeeded by the absolute nothing; it is the perfect annihilation of each individual in appearance and being, supposing that by him no child has been begotten or born; for otherwise the individual would live on in that." Mainländer's argument that in the long run nonexistence is superior to existence was cobbled together from his unorthodox interpretation of Christian doctrines and from Buddhism as he understood it.

As the average conscious mortal knows, Christianity and Buddhism are all for leaving this world behind, with their leave-taking being for destinations unknown and impossible to conceive. For Mainländer, these destinations did not exist. His forecast was that one day our will to survive in this life or any other will be universally extinguished by a conscious will to die and stay dead, after the example of the Creator. From the standpoint of Mainländer's philosophy, Zapffe's Last Messiah would not be an unwelcome sage but a crowning force of the post-divine era. Rather than resist our end, as Mainländer concludes, we will come to see that "the knowledge that life is worthless is the flower of all human wisdom." Elsewhere the philosopher states, "Life is hell, and the sweet still night of absolute death is the annihilation of hell."

Inhospitable to rationality as Mainländer's cosmic scenario may seem, it should nonetheless give pause to anyone who is keen to make sense of the universe. Consider this: If something like God exists, or once existed, what would He not be capable of doing, or undoing? Why should God not want to be done with Himself because, unbeknownst to us, suffering was the essence of His being? Why should He not have brought forth a universe that is one great puppet show destined by Him to be crunched or scattered until an absolute nothingness had been established? Why should He fail to see the benefits of nonexistence, as many of His lesser beings have? Revealed scripture there may be that tells a different story. But that does not mean it was revealed by a reliable narrator. Just because He asserted it was all good does not mean He meant what He said. Perhaps He did not want to leave a bad impression by telling us He had absented Himself from the ceremonies before they had begun. Alone and immortal, nothing needed Him. Per Mainländer, though, He needed to bust out into a universe to complete His project of self-extinction, passing on His horror piecemeal, so to say, to His creation.

Mainländer's first philosophy, and last, is in fact no odder than any religious or secular ethos that presupposes the worth of human life. Both are objectively insupportable and irrational. Mainländer was a pessimist, and, just as with any optimist, he needed something to support his gut feeling about being alive. No one has yet conceived an authoritative reason for why the human race should continue or discontinue its being, although some believe they have. Mainländer was sure he had an answer to what he judged to be the worthlessness and pain of existence, and none may peremptorily belie it. Ontologically, Mainländer's thought is delirious; metaphorically, it explains a good deal about human experience; practically, it may in time prove to be consistent with the idea of creation as a structure of creaking bones being eaten from within by a pestilent marrow.

That there is redemption to be found in an ecumenical nonexistence is an old idea on which Mainländer put a new face. For some it is a cherished idea, like that of a peaceful afterlife or progress toward perfection in this life. The need for such ideas comes out of the fact that existence is a condition with no redeeming qualities. If this were not so, none would need cherished ideas like an ecumenical nonexistence, a peaceful afterlife, or progress toward perfection in this life.[5]

Self-Hypnosis

Among the unpleasantries of human existence is the abashment we suffer when we feel our lives to be destitute of meaning with respect to who we are, what we do, and the general way we believe things to be in the universe. If one doubts that felt meanings are imperative to our developing or maintaining a state of good feeling, just lay your eyes on the staggering number of books and therapies for a market of individuals who suffer from a deficiency of meaning, either in a limited and localized variant ("I am satisfied that my life has meaning because I received an 'A' on my calculus exam") or one that is macrocosmic in scope ("I am satisfied that my life has meaning because God loves me"). Few are the readers of Norman Vincent Peale's *The Power of Positive Thinking* (1952) who do not feel dissatisfied with who they are, what they do, and the general way they believe things to be in the universe. Millions of copies of Peale's book and its imitations have been sold, and they are not purchased by readers well satisfied with the number or intensity of felt meanings in their lives and thus with their place on the ladder of "subjective well-being," in the vernacular of positive psychology, a movement that came into its own in the early years of the twenty-first century with a spate of books about how almost anyone could lead happily meaningful lives.[6] Martin Seligman, the architect of positive psychology, defines his brainchild as "the science of what makes life worth living" and synopsized its principles in *Authentic Happiness: Using the New Positive Psychology to Realize Your Potential for Lasting Fulfillment* (2002).

There is nothing new, of course, about people searching for a happily meaningful life in a book. With the exception of sacred texts, possibly the most successful self-help manual of all time is Émile Coué's *Self Mastery Through Conscious Autosuggestion* (1922). Coué was an advocate of self-hypnosis, and there is little doubt that he had an authentically philanthropic desire to help others lead more salutary lives. On his lecture tours, he was greeted by celebrities and dignitaries around the world. Hordes turned out for his funeral in 1926.

Coué is best known for urging believers in his method to repeat the following sentence: "Day by day, in every way, I am getting better and better." How could his readers not feel that their lives had meaning, or were proceeding toward meaningfulness, by hypnotizing themselves with these words day by day? While being alive is all right for the world's general population, some of us need to get it in writing that this is so.

Every other creature in the world is insensate to meaning. But those of us on the high ground of evolution are replete with this unnatural need which any comprehensive encyclopedia of philosophy treats under the heading LIFE, THE MEANING OF. In its quest for a sense of meaning, humanity has given countless answers to questions that were never posed to it. But though our appetite for meaning may be appeased for a time, we are deceived if we think it is ever gone for good. Years may pass during which we are unmolested by LIFE, THE MEANING OF. Some days we wake up and innocently say, "It's good to be alive." Broken down, this exclamation means that we are experiencing an acute sense of well-being. If everyone were in such elevated spirits all the time, the topic of LIFE, THE MEANING OF would never enter our minds or our philosophical reference books. But an ungrounded jubilation—or even a neutral reading on the monitor of our moods—must lapse, either intermittently or for the rest of our natural lives. Our consciousness, having snoozed awhile in the garden of incuriosity, is pricked by some thorn or other, perhaps DEATH, THE MEANING OF, or spontaneously modulates to a minor key due to the vagaries of our brain chemistry, the weather, or for causes not confirmable. Then the hunger returns for LIFE, THE MEANING OF, the emptiness must be filled again, the pursuit resumed. (There is more on meaning in the section *Unpersons* contained in the next chapter, "Who Goes There?")

Perhaps we might gain some perspective on our earthly term if we stopped thinking of ourselves as beings who enact a "life." This word is loaded with connotations to which it has no right. Instead, we should substitute "existence" for "life" and forget about how well or badly we enact it. None of us "has a life" in the narrative-biographical way we think of these words. What we have are so many years of existence. It would not occur to us to say that any man or woman is in the "prime of existence." Speaking of "existence" rather than "life" unclothes the latter word of its mystique. Who would ever claim that "existence is all right, especially when you consider the alternative"?

Cosmophobia

As heretofore noted, consciousness may have assisted our species' survival in the hard times of prehistory, but as it became ever more intense, it evolved the potential to ruin everything if not securely muzzled. This is the problem: We must either outsmart consciousness or be thrown into its vortex of doleful factuality and suffer, as Zapffe termed it, a "dread of being"—not only of our own being but of being itself, the idea that the vacancy that might otherwise have obtained is occupied like a stall in a public lavatory of infinite dimensions, that there is a universe in which things like celestial bodies and human beings are roving about, that anything exists in the way it seems to exist, that we are part of all being until we stop being, if there is anything we may understand as being other than semblances or the appearance of semblances.

On the premise that consciousness must be obfuscated so that we might go on as we have all these years, Zapffe inferred that the sensible thing would be not to go on with the paradoxical nonsense of trying to inhibit our cardinal attribute as beings, since we can tolerate existence only if we believe—in accord with a complex of illusions, a legerdemain of duplicity—that we are not what we are: unreality on legs. As conscious beings, we must hold back that divulgement lest it break us with a sense of being things without significance or foundation, anatomies shackled to a landscape of unintelligible horrors. In plain language, we cannot live except as self-deceivers who must lie to ourselves about ourselves, as well as about our unwinnable situation in this world.[7]

Accepting the preceding statements as containing some truth, or at least for the sake of moving on with the present narrative, it seems that we are zealots of Zapffe's four plans for smothering consciousness: isolation ("Being alive is all right"), anchoring ("One Nation under God with Families, Morality, and Natural Birthrights for all"), distraction ("Better to kill time than kill oneself"), and sublimation ("I am writing a book titled *The Conspiracy against the Human Race*"). These practices make us organisms with a nimble intellect that can deceive themselves "for their own good." Isolation, anchoring, distraction, and sublimation are among the wiles we use to keep ourselves from dispelling every illusion that keeps us up and running. Without this cognitive double-dealing, we would be exposed for what we are. It would be like looking into a mirror and for a moment seeing the skull inside our skin looking back at us with its sardonic smile. And beneath the skull—only blackness, nothing. Someone is there, so we feel, and yet no one is there—the uncanny paradox, all the horror in a glimpse. A little piece of our world has been peeled back, and underneath is creaking desolation—a carnival where all the rides are moving but no patrons occupy the seats. We are missing from the world we have made for ourselves. Maybe if we could resolutely gaze wide-eyed at our lives we would come to know what we really are. But that would stop the showy attraction we are inclined to think will run forever.[8]

Pessimism I

Along with every other tendentious mindset, pessimism may be construed as a fluke of temperament, a shifty word that will just have to do until a better one comes along. Without the temperament that was given to them in large portion, pessimists would not see existence as basically undesirable. Optimists may have fugitive doubts about the basic desirability of existence, but pessimists never doubt that existence is basically undesirable. If you interrupted them in the middle of an ecstatic moment, which pessimists do have, and asked if existence is basically undesirable, they would reply "Of course" before returning to their ecstasy. Why they should answer in this way is a closed book. The conclusions to which temperament lead an individual, whether or not they are conclusions refractory to those of world society, are simply not subject to analysis.

Composed of the same dross as all mortals, the pessimist cleaves to whatever seems to validate his attestations. This fact should come as a shock to no one. There is no scarcity among us of those who not only want to think they are right, but also expect others to affirm their least notion as unassailable. Pessimists are no exception. But they are few and do not show up on the radar of our race. Immune to the blandishments of religions, countries, families, and everything else that puts both average and above-average citizens in the limelight, pessimists are sideliners in both history and the media. Without belief in gods or ghosts, unmotivated by a comprehensive delusion, they could never plant a bomb, plan a revolution, or shed blood for a cause.

Identical with religions that ask of their believers more than they can possibly make good on, pessimism is a set of ideals that none can follow to the letter. Those who indict a pessimist of either pathology or intellectual recalcitrance are only faking their competence to explain what cannot be explained: the mystery of why individuals are the way they are. To some extent, however, why some individuals are the way they are is not a full-fledged mystery. There are traits that run in families—legacies lurking in the genes of one generation that may profit or impair those of another. Philosophical pessimism has been called a maladaptation by those who are concerned with such things. This call seems indisputably correct. The possibility must be considered, then, that there is a genetic marker for philosophical pessimism that nature has all but deselected from our race so that we may keep on living as we have all these years. Allowing for the theory that pessimism is weakly hereditary, and is getting weaker all the time because it is maladaptive, the genes that make up the fiber of ordinary folk may someday celebrate an everlasting triumph over those of the congenitally pessimistic, ridding nature of all worry that its protocol of survival and reproduction for its most conscious species will be challenged—unless Zapffe is right and consciousness itself is maladaptive, making philosophical pessimism the correct call despite its unpopularity among those who think, or say they think, that being alive is all right. But psycho-biographers do not often take what is adaptive or maladaptive for our species into account when writing of a chosen member of the questionably dying breed of pessimists. To them, their subject's temperament has a twofold inception: (1) life stories of tribulation, even though the pessimistic caste has no sorrows exclusive to it; (2) intractable wrongheadedness, a charge that pessimists could turn against optimists if the *argumentum ad populum* were not the world's favorite fallacy.

The major part of our species seems able to undergo any trauma without significantly re-examining its household mantras, including "everything happens for a reason," "the show must go on," "accept the things you cannot change," and any other adage that gets people to keep their chins up. But pessimists cannot give themselves over to this program, and its catchwords stick in their throats. To them, the Creation is objectionable and useless on principle—the worst possible dispatch of bad news. It seems so bad, so wrong, that, should such authority be unwisely placed into their hands, they would make it a prosecutable malfeasance to produce a being who might turn out to be a pessimist.

Disenfranchised by nature, pessimists feel that they have been impressed into this world by the reproductive liberty of positive thinkers who are ever-thoughtful of the future. At whatever point in time one is situated, the future always looks better than the present, just as the present looks better than the past. No one today would write, as did the British essayist Thomas De Quincey in the early nineteenth century: "A quarter of man's misery is toothache." Knowing what we know of the progress toward the alleviation of human misery throughout history, who would damn their children to have a piteous toothache in the early nineteenth century, or in times before it, back to the days when *Homo sapiens* with toothaches scrounged to feed themselves and shivered in the cold? To the regret of pessimists, our primitive ancestors could not see that theirs was not a time in which to produce children.

So at what time was it that people knew enough to say, "*This* is the time in which to produce children"? When did we think that enough progress had been made toward the alleviation of human misery that children could be produced without our being torn by a crisis of conscience? The easy years of the Pharaohs and Western antiquity? The lazy days of the Dark Ages? The palmy decades of the Industrial Revolution as well as the other industry-driven periods that followed? The breakthrough era in which advancements in dentistry allayed humanity of one-quarter of its misery?

But few or none have ever had a crisis of conscience about producing children, because all children have been born at the best *possible* time in human history, or at least the one in which the most progress toward the alleviation of human misery has been made, which is always the time in which we live and have lived. While we have always looked back on previous times and thought that their progress toward the alleviation of human misery was not enough for us to want to live then, we do not know any better than the earliest *Homo sapiens* about what progress toward the alleviation of human misery will be made in the future, reasonably presuming that such progress will be made. And even though we may speculate about that progress, we feel no resentment about not being able to take advantage of it, or not many of us do. Nor will those of the future resent not living in the world of *their* future because even greater progress toward the alleviation of human misery will by then have been made in medicine, social conditions, political arrangements, and other areas that are almost universally regarded as domains in which human life could be better.

Will there ever be an end of the line in our progress toward the alleviation of human misery when people can honestly say, "This is without doubt the time to produce children"? And will that really be the time? No one would say, or even want to think, that theirs is a time in which people will look back on them from the future and thank their stars that they did not live in such a barbaric age that had made so little progress toward the alleviation of human misery and still produced children. As if anyone ever cared or will ever care, this is what the pessimist would say: "There has never been and never will be a time in which to produce children. Now will forever be a bad time for doing that." Moreover, the pessimist would advise each of us not to look too far into the future or we will see the reproachful faces of the unborn looking back at us from the radiant mist of their nonexistence.

Pessimism II

In his lengthy study *Pessimism* (1877), James Sully wrote that "a just and correct estimate of life is to be looked for" in "views . . . which lean neither to the favourable nor the unfavourable pole." By this claim, Sully erred in his otherwise able dissection of his subject. People are either pessimists or optimists. They forcefully "lean" one way or the other, and there is no common ground between them. For pessimists, life is something that should not be, which means that what they believe *should be* is the absence of life, nothing, non-being, the emptiness of the uncreated. Anyone who speaks up for life as something that irrefutably should be—that we would *not* be better off unborn, extinct, or forever lazing in nonexistence—is an optimist. It is all or nothing; one is in or one is out, abstractly speaking. Practically speaking, we have been a race of optimists since the nascency of human consciousness and lean like mad toward the favorable pole.

More stylish in his examination of pessimism than Sully is the American novelist and part-time philosopher Edgar Saltus, whose *Philosophy of Disenchantment* (1885) and *The Anatomy of Negation* (1886) were written for those who treasure philosophical and literary works of a pessimistic, nihilistic, or defeatist nature as indispensable to their existence. In Saltus's estimation, a "just and correct view of human life" would justly and correctly determine human life as that which should not be.

Controverting the absolutist standards of pessimism and optimism as outlined above are "heroic" pessimists, or rather heroic "pessimists." These are self-styled pessimists who take into consideration Sully's unfavorable pole but are not committed to its entailment that life is something that should not be. In his *Tragic Sense of Life in Men and Nations* (1913), the Spanish writer Miguel de Unamuno speaks of consciousness as a disease bred by a conflict between the rational and the irrational. The rational is identified with the conclusions of consciousness, primarily that we will all die. The irrational represents all that is vital in humanity, including a universal desire for immortality in either a physical or non-physical state. The coexistence of the rational and the irrational turns the human experience into a wrangle of contradictions to which we can bow our heads in resignation or defy as heroes of futility. Unamuno's penchant was for the heroic course, with the implied precondition that one has the physical and psychological spunk for the fight. In line with Unamuno, Joshua Foa Dienstag, author of *Pessimism: Philosophy, Ethic, Spirit* (2006), is also a proselytizer for a healthy, heroic pessimism (quotes implied) that faces up to much of the dispiriting lowdown on life, all radically pessimistic visions being cropped out of the picture, and marches on toward a future believed to be personally and politically workable. Also siding with this never-say-die group is William R. Brashear, whose *The Desolation of Reality* (1995) concludes with a format for redemption, however partial and imperfect, by holding tight to what he calls "tragic humanism," which recognizes human life's "ostensible insignificance, but also the necessity of proceeding as if this were not so, . . . willfully nourishing and sustaining the underlying illusions of value and order." How we nourish and sustain illusions of value and order in our lives is explained in Zapffe's "The

Last Messiah." How we might nourish and sustain *at will* what we know to be illusions without a covenant of ignominious pretense among us is not explained by Brashear and has never been explained by anyone else who espouses this *façon de vivre*. Not in the same class of pessimism as the antinatalist Zapffe—Unamuno, Dienstag, and Brashear meet existence more than halfway, safely joined in solidarity with both ordinary and sophisticated folk, who take their lumps like grown-ups and by doing so retain their status with the status quo. Attuned as they may be to the pessimist's attitude that life is something which should not be, they do not approve of it. But Unamuno, Dienstag, and Brashear's solution to the pessimist's rejection of life puts us in the same paradoxical bind that Zapffe sees in human existence, that is, living with the pretense that being alive is all right. The only difference is that Unamuno, Dienstag, and Brashear knowingly accede to a pretense that ordinary folk shirk knowing, at least as a general rule, because even average mortals are sometimes forced to admit this pretense—they just do not linger over it long enough to make it a philosophical point of pride and sing their own praises for doing so.

A philosophical cohort of Unamuno, Dienstag, and Brashear is the French existentialist writer Albert Camus. In his essay *The Myth of Sisyphus* (1942), Camus represents the unattainable goal of the title figure as an apologetic for going on with life rather than ending it. As he insists in his discussion of this gruesome parable, "We must imagine Sisyphus as happy" as he rolls his boulder to the top of the mountain from which it always tumbles down again and again and again to his despair. The credo of the Church Father Tertullian, "I believe because it is absurd," might justly be placed in the context of Camus's belief that being alive is all right, or all right enough, though it may be absurd. Indeed, the connection has not been overlooked. Caught between the irrationality of the

Carthaginian and the intellectuality of the Frenchman, Zapffe's proposal that we put out the light of the human race extends to us an antidote for our existential infirmities that is infinitely more satisfying than that of either Tertullian or his avatar Camus, the latter of whom meditated on suicide as a philosophical issue for the individual yet did not entertain the advantages of an all-out attrition of the species. By not doing so, one might conclude that Camus was only being practical. In the end, though, his insistence that we *must* imagine Sisyphus as happy is as impractical as it is feculent. Like Unamuno, Dienstag, and Brashear, Camus believed we can *assume* a view of life that can content us with the tragedy, nightmare, and meaninglessness of human existence. Camus may have been able to assume this view of life before his life ended in a vehicular misadventure, but he *must* have been jesting to pose it as a possibility or a duty for the world.

It would be a sign of callowness to bemoan the fact that pessimistic writers do not rate and may be reprehended in both good conscience and good company. Some critics of the pessimist often think they have his back to the wall when they blithely jeer, "If that is how this fellow feels, he should either kill himself or be decried as a hypocrite." That the pessimist should kill himself in order to live up to his ideas may be counterattacked as betraying such a crass intellect that it does not deserve a response. Yet it is not much of a chore to produce one. Simply because someone has reached the conclusion that the amount of suffering in this world is enough that anyone would be better off never having been born does not mean that by force of logic or sincerity he must kill himself. It only means he has concluded that the amount of suffering in this world is enough that anyone would be better off never having been born.

Others may disagree on this point as it pleases them—*but they must accept that if they believe themselves to have a stronger case than the pessimist, they are mistaken.*

Naturally, there are pessimists who do kill themselves, but nothing obliges them to kill themselves or live with the mark of the hypocrite on their brow. Voluntary death might seem a thoroughly negative course of action, but it is not as simple as that. Every negation is adulterated or stealthily launched by an affirmative spirit. An unequivocal "no" cannot be uttered or acted upon. Lucifer's last words in heaven may have been "*Non serviam*," but none has served the Almighty so dutifully, since His sideshow in the clouds would never draw any customers if it were not for the main attraction of the devil's hell on earth. Only catatonics and coma patients can persevere in a dignified withdrawal from life's rattle and hum. Without a "yes" in our hearts, nothing would be done. And to be done with our existence en masse would be the most ambitious affirmation of all.

Most people think that vitality is betokened only by such phenomena as people in their eighties who hike mountain trails or nations that build empires. This way of thinking is simply naïve, but it keeps up our morale because we like to imagine we will be able to hike mountain trails when we are in our eighties or live as citizens of a nation that has built an empire. And so the denunciations of critics who say the pessimist should kill himself or be decried as a hypocrite make every kind of sense in a world of card-carrying or crypto optimists. Once this is understood, the pessimist can spare himself from suffering more than he need at the hands of "normal people," a confederation of upstanding creatures who in concert keep the conspiracy going. This is not to say that such individuals do not suffer so much and in such a way that they sometimes kill themselves, possibly even more per capita than do pessimists, or that because they kill themselves they are hypocrites for ever having said that anyone is better off for having been born. It is only to say that when normal individuals kill themselves, even after having said that anyone is better off for having been born, they are disqualified as normal individuals, because normal individuals do not kill themselves but until their dying day think that being alive is all right and that happiness will stand out in the existence of life's newcomers, who, it is always assumed, will be as normal as they are.

Blundering

Consciousness is an existential liability, as every pessimist agrees—a blunder of blind nature, according to Zapffe, that has taken humankind down a black hole of logic. To make it through this life, we must make believe that we are not what we are—contradictory beings whose continuance only worsens our plight as mutants who embody the contorted logic of a paradox. To correct this blunder, we should desist from procreating. What could be more judicious or more urgent, existentially speaking, than our self-administered oblivion? At the very least, we might give some regard to this theory of the blunder as a "thought experiment." All civilizations become defunct. All species die out. There is even an expiration date on the universe itself. Human beings would certainly not be the first phenomenon to go belly-up. But we could be the first to precipitate our own passing, abbreviating it before the bodies really started to stack up. Could we know to their most fine-grained details the lives of all who came before us, would we bless them for the care they took to keep the race blundering along? Could we exhume them alive, would we thankfully shake their bony, undead hands and promise to pass on the favor of living to future generations? Surely that is what they would want to hear, or at least that is what we want to think they would want to hear. And just as surely that is what we would want to hear from our descendants living in far posterity, strangers though they would be as they shook our bony, undead hands.

Nature proceeds by blunders; that is its way. It is also ours. So if we have blundered by regarding consciousness as a blunder, why make a fuss over it? Our self-removal from this planet would still be a magnificent move, a feat so luminous it would bedim the sun. What do we have to lose? No evil would attend our departure from this world, and the many evils we have known would go extinct along with us. So why put off what would be the most laudable masterstroke of our existence, and the only one?

Of course, phenomena other than consciousness have been thought to be blunders, beginning with life itself. For example, in a novel titled *At the Mountains of Madness* (1936), the American writer H. P. Lovecraft has one of his characters mention a "primal myth" about "Great Old Ones who filtered down from the stars and concocted earth life as a joke or mistake." Schopenhauer, once he had drafted his own mythology that everything in the universe is energized by a Will-to-live, shifted to a commonsense pessimism to represent life as a congeries of excruciations.

> [L]ife presents itself by no means as a gift for enjoyment, but as a task, a drudgery to be performed; and in accordance with this we see, in great and small, universal need, ceaseless cares, constant pressure, endless strife, compulsory activity, with extreme exertion of all the powers of body and mind. Many millions, united into nations, strive for the common good, each individual on account of his own; but many thousands fall as a sacrifice for it. Now senseless delusions, now intriguing politics, incite them to wars with each other; then the sweat and the blood of the great multitude must flow, to carry out the ideas of

individuals, or to expiate their faults. In peace industry and trade are active, inventions work miracles, seas are navigated, delicacies are collected from all ends of the world, the waves engulf thousands. All push and drive, others acting; the tumult is indescribable. But the ultimate aim of it all, what is it? To sustain ephemeral and tormented individuals through a short span of time in the most fortunate case with endurable want and comparative freedom from pain, which, however, is at once attended with ennui; then the reproduction of this race and its striving. In this evident disproportion between the trouble and the reward, the will to live appears to us from this point of view, if taken objectively, as a fool, or subjectively, as a delusion, seized by which everything living works with the utmost exertion of its strength for some thing that is of no value. But when we consider it more closely, we shall find here also that it is rather a blind pressure, a tendency entirely without ground or motive. (*The World as Will and Representation*, translation by R. B. Haldane and J. Kemp)

Schopenhauer is here straightforward in limning his awareness that, for human beings, existence is a state of demonic mania, with the Will-to-live as the possessing spirit of "ephemeral and tormented individuals." Elsewhere in his works, he denominates consciousness as "an accident of life." A blunder. A mistake. Is there really anything behind our smiles and tears but an evolutionary slip-up?

Analogies

Schopenhauer's is a great pessimism, not least because it reveals a signature motif of the pessimistic imagination. As indicated,

Schopenhauer's insights are yoked to a philosophical super-structure centered on the Will, or the Will-to-live—a blind, deaf, and dumb force that rouses human beings to their detriment. While Schopenhauer's system of thought is as impossible to swallow as that of any other systematic philosopher, no intelligent person can fail to see that every living thing behaves *exactly* in conformity with his philosophy in its liberal articulation. Wound up like toys by some force—call it Will, élan vital, anima mundi, physiological or psychological processes, nature, or whatever—organisms go on running as they are bidden until they run down. In pessimistic philosophies only the force is real, not the things activated by it. They are only puppets, and if they have consciousness may mistakenly believe they are self-winding persons who are making a go of it on their own.

Here, then, is the signature motif of the pessimistic imagination that Schopenhauer made discernible: *Behind the scenes of life there is something pernicious that makes a nightmare of our world.* For Zapffe, the evolutionary mutation of consciousness tugged us into tragedy. For Michelstaedter, individuals can exist only as unrealities that are made as they are made and that cannot make themselves otherwise because their hands are forced by the "god" of *philopsychia* (self-love) to accept positive illusions about themselves or not accept themselves at all. For Mainländer, a Will-to-die, not Schopenhauer's Will-to-live, plays the occult master pulling our strings, making us dance in fitful motions like marionettes caught in a turbulent wake left by the passing of a self-murdered god. For Bahnsen, a purposeless force breathes a black life into everything and feasts upon it part by part, regurgitating itself into itself, ever-renewing the throbbing forms of its repast. For all others who suspect that something is amiss in the lifeblood of being, something they cannot verbalize, there are the malformed shades of suffering and death that chase them into the false light of contenting lies.

By analogy with that pernicious "something" the pessimist senses behind the scenes of life are the baleful agencies that govern the world of supernatural horror fiction. Actually, it would be more proper to speak of the many worlds of supernatural horror, since they vary from author to author as much as the renderings of the human fiasco vary from pessimist to pessimist. Even within the writings of a single author, the source of something pernicious that makes a nightmare of our world switches about, the common link being a state of affairs that overturns our conception of reality for the worse.

In "The Willows," for instance, the twentieth-century British writer Algernon Blackwood suggests that an inimical force abides within nature. What this enormity might be is known to the characters of the story only by mysterious signs and sounds that unnerve them as they make their way in a small boat down the Danube and camp for the night on an island overgrown with willows, which become the symbolic focus of a region where nature shows its most menacing aspect. The narrator tries to explain what it is about the willows that seems particularly threatening to him, as distinct from the more immediate perils of the severe weather conditions that have developed along the Danube.

A rising river, perhaps, always suggests something of the ominous: many of the little islands I saw before me would probably have been swept away by the morning; this resistless, thundering water touched the deep sense of awe. Yet I was aware that my uneasiness lay deeper far than the emotions of awe and wonder. It was not that I felt. Nor had it directly to do with the power of the driving wind—this shouting hurricane that might almost carry up a few acres of willows into the air and scatter them like so much chaff over the landscape. The wind was simply enjoying itself, for nothing rose out of the flat landscape to stop it, and I was conscious of sharing its great game with a kind of pleasurable excitement. Yet this novel emotion had nothing to do with the wind. Indeed, so vague was the sense of distress I experienced, that it was impossible to trace it to its source and deal with it accordingly, though I was aware somehow that it had to do with our utter insignificance before this unrestrained power of the elements about me. The huge-grown river had something to do with it too—a vague, unpleasant idea that we had somehow trifled with these great elemental forces in whose power we lay helpless every hour of the day and night. For here, indeed, they were gigantically at play together, and the sight appealed to the imagination.

But my emotion, so far as I could understand it, seemed to attach itself more particularly to the willow bushes, to these acres and acres of willows, crowding, so thickly growing there, swarming everywhere the eye could reach, pressing upon the river as though to suffocate it, standing in dense array mile after mile beneath the sky, watching, waiting, listening. And, apart from the elements, the willows connected themselves subtly with my malaise, attacking the mind insidiously somehow by reason of their vast numbers, and contriving in some way or other to represent to the imagination a new and mighty power, a power, moreover, not altogether friendly to us.

The mystery of the pernicious something that the willows represent is never resolved. However, at the end of the story the two travelers see a man turning over and over in the rushing river. And he bears "their mark" in the form of indentations they had seen before in the sands of the island—funnels that formed and grew in size throughout the night the men had camped on the island. Whatever power that was not "altogether friendly to us" had procured its victim and satisfied itself. The men had been saved at the price of another's death. That which makes a nightmare of our world had revealed itself for a time and withdrawn once again behind the scenes of life.

Such is the motif of supernatural horror: Something terrible in its being comes forward and makes its claim as a shareholder in our reality, or what we think is our reality and ours alone. It may be an emissary from the grave or an esoteric monstrosity, as in the ghost stories of M. R. James. It may be the offspring of a scientific experiment with unintended consequences, as in Arthur Machen's "The Great God Pan," or the hitherto unheard-of beings in the same author's "The White People." It may be a hideous token of another dimension revealed only in a mythic tome, as in Robert W. Chambers's "The Yellow Sign." Or it may be a world unto itself of pure morbidity, one suffused with a profound sense of a doom without a name—Edgar Allan Poe's world.

Reflected in the works of many supernatural writers, the signature motif Schopenhauer made discernible in pessimism was most consistently promulgated by Lovecraft, a paragon among literary figures who have thought the unthinkable, or at least thought what most mortals do not want to think. In conceiving Azathoth, that "nuclear chaos" which "bubbles at the center of all infinity,"

Lovecraft might well have been thinking of Schopenhauer's Will. As instantiated in Lovecraft's stories, the pernicious something that makes a nightmare of our world is individuated into linguistically teratological entities from beyond or outside of our universe. Like ghosts or the undead, their very existence spooks us as a violation of what should and should not be, suggesting unknown modes of being and uncanny creations which epitomize supernatural horror.

Life-Principles

Philosophically, Lovecraft was a dyed-in-the-wool scientific materialist. Nevertheless, he is a felicitous example of someone who knew ravishments that in another context would qualify as "spiritual" or "religious." Yet from childhood he adhered to a vigorous atheism. In his lectures collected as *The Varieties of Religious Experience* (1902), William James proposes that a sense of "ontological wonder" and "cosmic emotion" argues for the legitimacy of religious faith. In both his creative writings and his letters, Lovecraft's expression of the feelings James describes form an exception to the philosopher-psychologist's argument.[9] For Lovecraft, cosmic wonder and a "tranquility tinged with terror," as the British political theorist and aesthetician Edmund Burke referred to such experiences, were basic to his interest in remaining alive. Sublimating his awareness of the universe as *nothingness in motion*, he also mitigated the boredom that plagued his life by distracting himself with reveries of "*surprise, discovery, strangeness, and the impingement of the cosmic, lawless, and mystical upon the prosaic sphere of the known*" (Lovecraft's emphasis).

From the other side of an emotional and spiritual chasm, the French scientist and Christian philosopher Blaise Pascal wrote of his sense of being "engulfed in the infinite immensity of spaces whereof I know nothing, and which know nothing of me; I am terrified. The eternal silence of these infinite spaces fills me with dread" (*Pensées*, 1670). Pascal's is not an unnatural reaction for those phobic to infinite spaces that know nothing of them. "Kenophobia" is the fear of such vast spaces and voids. Perhaps keno*philia* should be coined to describe the "ontological wonder" and "cosmic emotion" Lovecraft felt when he contemplated the outer rim of the unknown.

A complex and contradictory figure, as illustrated above, Lovecraft often seemed to be on the fence when it came to his convictions about the value of existence. In a letter to Edwin Baird, the first editor of *Weird Tales*, he penned some remarks that express a univocal stand by a pessimist who is estranged from all solace known to ordinary folk. These merit quotation at length.

Popular authors do not and apparently cannot appreciate the fact that true art is obtainable only by rejecting normality and conventionality in toto, and approaching a theme purged utterly of any usual or preconceived point of view. Wild and "different" as they may consider their quasi-weird products, it remains a fact that the bizarrerie is on the surface alone; and that basically they reiterate the same old conventional values and motives and perspectives. Good and evil, teleological illusion, sugary sentiment, anthropocentric psychology—the usual superficial stock in trade, and all shot through with the eternal and inescapable commonplace. . . . Who ever wrote a story from the point of view that man is a blemish on the cosmos, who ought to be eradicated? As an example—a young man I know lately told me that he means to write a story about a scientist who wishes to dominate the earth, and who to accomplish his ends trains and overdevelops germs . . . and leads armies of them in the manner of the Egyptian plagues. I told him that although this theme has promise, it is made utterly commonplace by assigning the scientist a normal motive. There is nothing outré about wanting to conquer the earth; Alexander, Napoleon, and Wilhelm II wanted to do that. Instead, I told my friend, he should conceive a man with a morbid, frantic, shuddering hatred of the life-principle itself, who wishes to extirpate from the planet every trace of biological organism, animal and vegetable alike, including himself. That would be tolerably original. But after all, originality lies with the author. One can't write a weird story of real power without perfect psychological detachment from the human scene, and a magic prism of imagination which suffuses theme and style alike with that grotesquerie and disquieting distortion characteristic of morbid vision. Only a cynic can create horror— for behind every masterpiece of the sort must reside a driving demonic force that despises the human race and its illusions, and longs to pull them to pieces and mock them.

The salient interest of this letter is that it shows Lovecraft as a perfectionist of cosmic disillusion. But relatively dissociated from Lovecraft the cosmic disillusionist was another Lovecraft, one who reveled in protectionist illusions that could not be more alien to the propensities of his alter ego. In this latter identity, he took refuge from what he specified as his cynicism (also "cosmic pessimism") in a world of distractions and anchorings he had amassed over the years. Among them was his sentimental immersion in the past. Especially dear to him was the traditional way of life emblemized by architectural remnants of seventeenth- and eighteenth-century New England. Old towns with winding streets, houses with semicircular fanlight doors, and other postcard images of Yankeedom conjured up for Lovecraft a picture of bygone times as an aesthetic phenomenon that often tailed into a Blood-and-Soil mysticism. A proud Novanglian, Lovecraft grew up and lived among abundant reminders of a past he idealized. His attachment to historic New England counterbalanced his infatuation with the far reaches of time and space, beside which, as he well knew, the outdated culture-streams that so enraptured him were local, fleeting, and accidental forms without immanent virtue. For Lovecraft, both quaint small-paned windows and a bracing alienage from human mores had charms that he heartily honored in his works as well as his life, even during his darkest days of cynicism and pessimism.

Like most of us, Lovecraft distracted himself with fabricated values, and he did so until death was bestowed upon him by a combination of intestinal cancer and Bright's disease. Concerned as a fiction writer with smashing to bits humanity's grand illusion about its place in the universe, Lovecraft welcomed any illusions he could accept in good faith, as did Zapffe and Schopenhauer, who also pursued gratifying diversions that took their minds off what the latter philosopher called the "vanity and suffering of life." During his later years, Lovecraft did seem to mellow considerably as he walked the plank into nonexistence. In letters to his friends and colleagues he attested that he had left his cynicism and pessimism behind and had become an "indifferentist," meaning one who sees no malice in the physical universe but only a flux of particles. To the benefit of supernatural horror aficionados, Lovecraft's indifferentist philosophy did not require him to discontinue writing about virulent phenomena that compromise the sanity of anyone who learns of their existence. Lovecraft was exhilarated by the idea of something pernicious that made a nightmare of our world, whether it was indifferent to us or quite partial to our devastation. In his indifferentism, Lovecraft did not seem to have shambled far from the cognitive style of the individual who advised his friend to write about "a man with a morbid, frantic, shuddering hatred of the life-principle itself, who wishes to extirpate from the planet every trace of biological organism, animal and vegetable alike, including himself." If only there were a man who could bring to fruition such a wish. Then the earth could finally be "cleared off," as Wilbur Whately wrote in his diary in "The Dunwich Horror."

Why anyone should be drawn to the writings of Lovecraft and his confederates is usually expounded as a natural aspect of the human temper, a healthy yearning of our souls to exceed the bounds of ordinary existence. In his lecture "On Morbidity," part of a series of brief expositions on supernatural horror, an academician known only as Professor Nobody (an ostentatiously cocky pseudonym) submits his analysis of an atypical individual who does not partake in the wholesome motivation of the majority with respect to the horrific and extraordinary, "a man with a morbid, frantic, shuddering hatred of the life-principle itself." While there is indeed something invigorating in supernatural horror for this individual, it is a negative rather than a positive activation that pleasures him by its antipathy to all that lives. The floor is now ceded to the professor.

> Isolation, mental strain, emotional exertions, visionary infatuations, well-executed fevers, repudiations of well-being: only a few of the many exercises practiced by that specimen we shall call the "morbid man." And our subject of supernatural horror is a vital part of his program. Retreating from a world of heath and sanity, or at least one that daily invests in such commodities, the morbid man seeks the shadows behind the scenes of life. He backs himself into a corner alive with cool drafts and fragrant with centuries of must. It is in that corner that he builds a world of ruins out of the battered stones of his

imagination, a rancid world rife with things smelling of the crypt.

But this world is not all a romantic sanctum for the dark in spirit. So let us condemn it for a moment, this deep-end of dejection. Although there is no name for what might be called the morbid man's "sin," it still seems in violation of some deeply ingrained morality. The morbid man does not appear to be doing himself or others any good. And while we all know that melancholic moping and lugubrious ruminating are quite palatable as side-dishes of existence, he has turned them into a house specialty! Ultimately, however, he may meet this charge of wrongdoing with a simple "What of it?"

Now, such a response assumes morbidity to be a certain class of vice, one to be pursued without apology, and one whose advantages and disadvantages must be enjoyed or endured *outside the law*. But as a sower of vice, if only in his own soul, the morbid man incurs the following censure: that he is a symptom or a cause of decay within both individual and collective spheres of being. And decay, like every other process of becoming, hurts everybody. "Good!" shouts the morbid man. "Not good!" counters the crowd. Both positions betray dubious origins: one in resentment, the other in fear. And when the moral debate on this issue eventually reaches an impasse or becomes too tangled for truth, then psychological polemics can begin. Later on we will find other angles from which this problem may be attacked, enough to keep us occupied for the rest of our lives.

Meanwhile, the morbid man keeps putting his *time on earth* to no good use, until in the end—amidst mad winds, wan moonlight, and pasty specters—he uses his exactly like everyone else uses theirs: all up.

Undoing III

When people are asked to respond to the statement "I am happy—true or false," the word "true" is spoken more often than "false," overwhelmingly so. If there is some loss of face in confessing that one is not happy, this does not mean that those who profess happiness as their dominant humor are lying through their teeth. People want to be happy. They believe they should be happy. And if some philosopher says they can never be happy because their consciousness has ensured their unhappiness, that philosopher will not be part of the dialogue, especially if he blathers about discontinuing our species by ceasing to bear children who can also never be happy even though, to extend the point, they can also never be unhappy given their inexperience of existing. Ask Zapffe.

> So you ask whether I would choose to be unborn? One must be born in order to choose, and the choice involves destruction. But ask my brother in that chair over there. Indeed, it is an empty one; my brother did not get so far. Yet ask him, as he is traveling like the wind below the sky, crashing against the beach, scenting in the grass, reveling in his strength as he pursues his living food. Do you think he is bereaved by his incapacity to fulfill his fate on the waiting list of the Oslo Housing and Savings Society? And have *you* ever missed *him*? Look around in a crowded afternoon tram and reflect whether you would allow a lottery to select one of the exhausted toilers as the one whom you put into this world. They pay no attention as one person gets off and two get on. The tram keeps rolling along. ("Fragments of an Interview," *Aftenposten*, 1959)

The point that in the absence of birth nobody exists who can be deprived of happiness is terribly conspicuous. For optimists, this fact plays no part in their existential computations. For pessimists, however, it is axiomatic. Whether a pessimist urges us to live "heroically" with a knife in our gut or denounces life as not worth living is immaterial. What matters is that he makes no bones about *hurt* being the Great Problem it is incumbent on philosophy to observe. But this problem can be solved only by establishing an imbalance between hurt and happiness that would enable us in principle to say which is more desirable—existence or nonexistence. While no airtight case has ever been made regarding the undesirability of human life, pessimists still run themselves ragged trying to make one. Optimists have no comparable mission. When they do argue for the desirability of human life it is only in reaction to pessimists arguing the opposite, even though no airtight case has ever been made regarding that desirability. Optimism has always been an undeclared policy of human culture—one that grew out of our animal instincts to survive and reproduce—rather than an articulated body of thought. It is the default condition of our blood and cannot be effectively questioned by our minds or put in grave doubt by our pains. This would explain why at any given time there are more cannibals than philosophical pessimists.

For optimists, human life never needs justification, no matter how much hurt piles up, because they can always tell themselves that things will get better. For pessimists, there is no amount of happiness—should such a thing as happiness even obtain for human beings except as a misconception—that can compensate us for life's hurt. As a worst-case example, a pessimist might refer to the hurt caused by some natural or human-made cataclysm. To adduce a hedonic counterpart to the horrors that attach to such cataclysms would require a degree of ingenuity from an optimist, but it could be done. And the reason it could be done, the reason for the eternal stalemate between optimists and pessimists, is that no possible formula can be established to measure proportions and types of hurt and happiness in the world. If such a formula could be established—on the premise that an oppositional comparison may be made between hurt and happiness, of course—then either pessimists or optimists would have to give in to their adversaries.

One formula to establish the imbalance at issue has been tendered by the South African philosopher of ethics David Benatar. In his *Better Never to Have Been: The Harm of Coming into Existence* (2006), Benatar attempts to prove that, because some amount of suffering is inevitable for all who are born, while the absence of happiness does not deprive those who would have been born but were not, the scales are tipped in favor of not bearing children. Therefore, propagators violate any conceivable system of morality and ethics because they are guilty of doing harm. To Benatar, the extent of the harm that always occurs matters not. Once harm has been ensured by the begetting of a bundle of joy, a line has been crossed from moral-ethical behavior to immoral-unethical behavior. This violation of morality and ethics holds for Benatar in all instances of childbirth.

Nevertheless, people like Benatar who argue that the world's "ideal population size is zero" are written off as being unhealthy of mind. Further accentuating this presumed unhealthiness is Benatar's argument that giving birth is not only harmful but should be seen as so egregiously harmful that there is no happiness that can counterbalance it. As harms go in this world, there are none worse than the harm that entails all others. Ask William James for a perspective on one of those great harms—to which he gives the name "melancholy"—and how it is generally passed over in the lives of healthy adults.

> The method of averting one's attention from evil, and living simply in the light of good is splendid as long as it will work. It will work with many persons; it will work far more generally than most of us are ready to suppose; and within the sphere of its successful operation there is

nothing to be said against it as a religious solution. But it breaks down impotently as soon as melancholy comes; and even though one be quite free from melancholy one's self, there is no doubt that healthy-mindedness is inadequate as a philosophical doctrine, because the evil facts which it refuses positively to account for are a genuine portion of reality; and they may after all be the best key to life's significance, and possibly the only openers of our eyes to the deepest levels of truth.

The normal process of life contains moments as bad as any of those which insane melancholy is filled with, moments in which radical evil gets its innings and takes its solid turn. The lunatic's visions of horror are all drawn from the material of daily fact. Our civilization is founded on the shambles, and every individual existence goes out in a lonely spasm of helpless agony. If you protest, my friend, wait until you arrive there yourself. (*The Varieties of Religious Experience*, 1902)

James himself suffered a brush with melancholy, but he made a full recovery and began to think positively, or at least equivocally, about being alive, answering yes to the question "Is Life Worth Living?" However, by force of his honesty of intellect he knew this opinion needed to be defended as much as any other opinion. No logic can support it. Indeed, logic defeats all feeling that life is worth living, which, James says, only a self-willed belief in a higher order of existence can instill. Then every suffering will seem worthwhile in the way that the vivisection of a living dog, to use James's example, would seem worthwhile to the animal if only it could comprehend the goodly ends its pain serves for the higher order of human existence. In his lecture "Is Life Worth Living," James opined that human beings, unlike dogs, can in fact imagine a higher order of existence than theirs, one that may legitimate the worst adversities of mortal life. James was a rare philosopher in that he put no faith in logic. And he was doubtless wise to adopt that stance, since the fortunes of those who attempt to defend their opinions with logic are not enviable.

Naturally, for those whose opinion is that it is "better to be" than "better never to have been," Benatar's logic for the latter proposition is rejected as faulty, the more so in that its conclusions are not supported by a consensus of ordinary folk. Logic notwithstanding, Benatar's moral-ethical censure of reproduction does prove that humanity's continuance is not universally accepted as a good in itself, even in a super-modern world. It also reminds us that no one can make a case that every individual's birth, or any individual's birth, is a good in itself. And *that* is the case that needs to be made, at least morally and ethically speaking as well as logically speaking. (For more on this, see the section *Pressurized* in the chapter "The Cult of Grinning Martyrs.") If most people believe that *being* alive is all right—the alternative to this belief having no appeal for them—the rectitude of causing new people to *become* alive is just a matter of opinion.

Repression

In "The Last Messiah," Zapffe wrote: "The whole of living that we see before our eyes today is from inmost to outmost enmeshed in repressional mechanisms, social and individual; they can be traced right into the tritest formulas of everyday life." The quartet of formulas that Zapffe picked out as individual and social mechanisms of repression are probably the most trite he could have chosen, which may have been deliberate on his part because they are so familiar to us and so visible in our day-to-day existence. These mechanisms are related to the psychoanalytic theory of unconscious repression, although they are also perilously accessible to the conscious mind. And when they are accessed, no one can concede them with impunity. Not overweight persons or tobacco users, who must play dumb when they are scarfing down a cupcake or smoking a cigarette. Not soldiers fighting a war, who must not be aware they are risking their lives and limbs for a rationalization—their country, their god, etc. Not anyone who is going to suffer and die (that is, everyone), who will not voluntarily confess to playing the same old games for as long as possible rather than be haunted by thoughts of mortality and the unpleasantness that may precede it. And definitely not artists, who keep their aesthetic distance for fear of being hamstrung by the realities they "bring to life."

Once the facts that repressional mechanisms hide are accessed, they must be excised from our memory—or new repressional mechanisms must replace the old—so that we may continue to be protected by our cocoon of lies. If this is not done, we will be whimpering misereres morning, noon, and night instead of chanting that day by day, in every way, we are getting better and better. Although we may sometimes admit to the guileful means we use to keep us doing what we do, this is only a higher level of self-deception and paradox, not evidence that we stand on the heights of some metareality where we are really real. We say we know what is in store for us in this life, and we do. But we do not *know*. We cannot if we are to survive and multiply.

Annotating humanity's attempt to bluff itself in the interest of the species is an extensive literature on self-deception, denial, and repression.[10] Naturally, none of those working in this area of study believe human life to be such a morass of self-deception, denial, and repression that we do not know which way is up. But in Zapffe's analysis of self-deception, denial, and repression, we cannot know which way is up without paying dearly for this knowledge. Enough of us must addle our consciousness so that we can be far less conscious than we might, which is the tragedy of the human species, for anyone who might have forgotten. Those who cannot pull off this jugglery will suffer the consequences.

Some who study self-deception, denial, etc. believe these are healthy practices if they facilitate our happiness without infringing on the happiness of our fellows. They speak of self-deception, denial, etc. as "useful fictions" or "positive illusions" and ballyhoo them as staples for both the individual and society. (For his book *Vital Lies, Simple Truths: The Psychology of Self-Deception* [1996], Daniel Goleman studied how people and groups play along with factitious designs to scotch the animus and anxiety that would be loosed if an etiquette of honesty were somehow enforced.) Others believe that self-deceptive practices are too complex to be usefully analyzed. This does not mean that self-deceptive practices do not support heinous acts by the ingenious denial of these acts (Stanley Cohen, *States of Denial: Knowing about Atrocities and Suffering*, 2001); it only means that we cannot know how self-deception works in these cases. Finally, many of those who study self-deception believe we are not capable of self-deception because we cannot both consciously know something and consciously not know it, for this would involve us in a paradox.

However, others have reasoned their way around this supposed paradox. An example of such reasoning is presented by Kent Bach ("An Analysis of Self-Deception," *Philosophy and Phenomenal Research*, 1981), who offers three means of avoiding unwanted thoughts that are nevertheless accessible to a subject's consciousness: *rationalization, evasion, and jamming*. These are identical to the methods of isolation, anchoring, and distraction spotted by Zapffe in human life. Each may keep a subject in a state of self-deception regarding what is really the case. Bach's essay does not, of course, extend his three categories of self-deception to the entire human species, as does Zapffe. To Zapffe, we remember, we are all by nature and necessity false and paradoxical beings and should terminate our existence as strangers to reality who cannot live as we are and cannot live otherwise, who must constrain our consciousness because, tragically, our sanity depends on it.

In his *Why We Lie: The Evolution of Deception and the Unconscious Mind* (2007), David Livingstone Smith examines the mechanisms of self-deception and denial, both individual and social, in terms of evolutionary psychology. This approach leads him to a conclusion about these mechanisms that is compatible with Zapffe's diagnosis of humanity as a paradox. Smith's thesis is that at some time in the remote past the human mind split into the dual levels of conscious and unconscious processes the better to deceive itself and others for the purpose of adaptation. This makes Smith's hypothesis about the process of denial tantamount to that of the psychoanalytic theory of repression, by which individuals deny unpalatable facts about themselves to themselves, and, by extension, to others. Smith is in fact a psychoanalyst, and this may be seen in his statement that the "ever-present possibility of deceit is a crucial dimension of every human relationship, even the most central: our relationship with our very selves." To practice this deceit, one must repress consciousness of the deceiving, which does not exclude self-deception concerning consciousness itself and what it discloses about human life. Effectively, then, Smith is allied with Zapffe's position that the human being

> performs . . . a more or less self-conscious *repression* [Zapffe's emphasis] of its damning surplus of consciousness. The process is virtually constant during our waking and active hours, and is a requirement of social adaptability and of

everything commonly referred to as healthy and normal living.

Psychiatry even works on the assumption that the "healthy" and viable is at one with the highest in personal terms. Depression, "fear of life," refusal of nourishment and so on are invariably taken as signs of a pathological state and treated thereafter. Often, however, such phenomena are messages from a deeper, more immediate sense of life, bitter fruits of a geniality of thought or feeling at the root of anti-biological tendencies. It is not the soul being sick, but its protection failing, or else being rejected because it is experienced—correctly—as a betrayal of ego's highest potential.

Even though Zapffe regarded psychoanalysis as another form of anchoring, whether or not a repressional mechanism is accessible to our consciousness or is wholly unconscious seems a trivial point. For both Smith and Zapffe, they lead to the same thing: occlusion of the real. Another thing Smith and Zapffe share is that their ideas about humankind are not scientifically verifiable and will not be for some time to come, if ever. And without proof on a platter, anyone whose ideas are unpalatable to scientists, philosophers, and average mortals must expect to be poorly heard. Smith does not seem to understand this, and in the closing pages of his book expresses hope that humanity will one day "get real," as the saying goes. At the end of "The Last Messiah," Zapffe expressed an unconditional pessimism that this could ever happen, which was patently the only reasonable attitude for him to take. Smith himself might consider "getting real" about his hope we will ever get real, given that humanity will always have its reasons for being repressed, self-deceptive, and unreal. A utopia in which we no longer deny the realities we presently must repress cannot be realistically hoped for. And who except a pessimist would wish for that utopia?

The effectiveness of conscious repressional mechanisms has been analyzed from many angles, particularly in relation to the fear of death. An enumeration of traditional strategies for grappling with thanatophobia appears in *Choices for Living: Coping with the Fear of Dying* (2002) by Thomas S. Langer. Although the subtitle of this book suggests that it concentrates on the fear of dying, it is more about the fear of death, not about the suffering and terror that may attend either a short-lived or a dawdling migration into death. Factually, Langer's book, like many others of its kind, is fixated on living rather than on either death or dying, which seem to be only blurry contingencies while an individual is alive.

> DOCTOR: "I'm afraid you have an inoperable tumor and haven't long to live."
> PATIENT: "That can't be. I feel in perfect health."

> POLICE OFFICER: "I'm sorry to inform you, ma'am, that your husband has been involved in a vehicular misadventure. He's dead."
> WIFE: "That can't be. He just left the house ten minutes ago."

Given a little time, of course, the cancer patient and the woman who just lost her husband come around to their respective realities. Acceptance of one's new condition, as opposed to going mad or reacting in some other pathological manner, seems to be the usual process—on the condition, naturally, that an individual lives long enough to accept it and does not die of an inoperable tumor first. In the media and all forms of entertainment, such bad breaks are exposed to us all our lives. But we still do not heed the old saw "Hope for the best, but expect the worst." Instead, we hope for the best and think we have a very good chance of getting it. If we really expected the worst, we might well go mad or react in some other pathological manner before the worst came for us and ours. And that really would be the worst.

Suffering I

For almost all philosophers who write about death, the subject is studied in the abstract, with the unsightly tangibles at its bedside either bracketed or shrugged off. If dying is even given the time of day by philosophers, it must be studied as a subcategory of SUFFERING, THE MEANING OF, which few thinkers discuss outside of moral philosophy and ethics, relatively soft cognitive pastimes when placed beside logic, epistemology, ontology, etc. Philosophies that take human suffering as their overarching subject are given short shrift by analytic types, who leave SUFFERING, THE MEANING OF to religions such as Buddhism and Christianity, or to pessimists. Unless a philosopher is prepared to go all the way with it, to take a hard line on its relevance to the whole of human life, as did Schopenhauer and a few other relics of the pre-modern era, he will balk at saying anything about suffering.

One who did not balk entirely was the Austrian-born British philosopher Karl Popper, who in *The Open Society and Its Enemies* (1945) did have a thing or two to say about human suffering. Briefly, he revamped the Utilitarianism of the nineteenth-century British philosopher John Stuart Mill, who wrote: "Actions are right in proportion as they tend to promote happiness, wrong as they tend to promote the reverse of happiness." Popper remolded this summation of a positive utilitarianism into a *negative* utilitarianism whose position he handily stated as follows: "It adds to clarity in the fields of ethics, if we formulate our demands negatively, *i.e.* if we demand the elimination of suffering rather than the promotion of happiness." Taken to its logical and most humanitarian conclusion, Popper's demand can have as its only end the elimination of those who now suffer as well as "counterfactual" beings who will suffer if they are born. What else could the "elimination of suffering" mean if not its total abolition, and ours? Naturally, Popper held his horses well before suggesting that to eliminate suffering would demand that we as a species be eliminated. But as R. N. Smart famously argued (*Mind*, 1958), this is the only conclusion to be drawn from Negative Utilitarianism.

In "The Last Messiah," Zapffe is not sanguine about eliminating suffering, nor is he so unworldly as to beseech a communal solution for its elimination by snuffing out the human race, as did the Cathari and the Bogomils. (He does lash out at the barbarism of social or religious proscription of suicide, but he is not a standard-bearer for this form of personal salvation.) To reiterate with due compunction, Zapffe's thought is foremost an addendum to that of various sects and individuals who have resolved that conscious existence is so odious that extinction is preferable to survival. It also has the value of advancing a new answer to an old question: "Why should generations unborn be spared entry into the human thresher?" But what might be called "Zapffe's Paradox," in the tradition of possessively named formulations that saturate primers of philosophy, is as useless as the propositions of any other thinker who is pro-life or anti-life or is only juggling concepts to clinch what is reality and can we ever get there. That said, we can continue as if it had not been said. The measure of a philosopher's thought is not in its answers or the problems it poses, but in how well it fiddles with these answers and problems such that they animate the minds of others. Thus the importance—and the nullity—of rhetoric. Ask any hardline pessimist, but do not expect him to expect you to take his words seriously.

Suffering II

Perhaps the greatest strike against philosophical pessimism is that its only theme is human suffering. This is the last item on the list of our species' obsessions and detracts from everything that matters to us, such as the Good, the Beautiful, and a Sparkling Clean Toilet Bowl. For the pessimist, everything considered in isolation from human suffering or any cognition that does not have as its motive the origins, nature, and elimination of human suffering is at base recreational, whether it takes the form of conceptual probing or physical action in the world—for example, delving into game theory or traveling in outer space, respectively. And by "human suffering," the pessimist is not thinking of particular sufferings and their relief, but with suffering itself. Remedies may be discovered for certain diseases and sociopolitical barbarities may be amended. But these are only stopgaps. Human suffering will remain insoluble as long as human beings exist. The one truly effective solution for suffering is that spoken of in Zapffe's "The Last Messiah." It may not be a welcome solution for a stopgap world, but it would forever put an end to suffering, should we ever care to do so. The pessimist's credo, or one of them, is that nonexistence never hurt anyone and existence hurts everyone. Although our selves may be illusory creations of consciousness, our pain is nonetheless real.

As a survival-happy species, our successes are calculated in the number of years we have extended our lives, with the reduction of suffering being only incidental to this aim. To stay alive under almost any circumstances is a sickness with us. Nothing could be more unhealthy than to "watch one's health" as a means of stalling death. The lengths we will go as procrastinators of that last gasp only demonstrate a morbid dread of that event. By contrast, our fear of suffering is deficient. So Shakespeare's Edgar when he passes on the wisdom that "the worst is not / So long as we can say 'This is the worst.'" Officially, there are no fates worse than death. Unofficially, there is a profusion of such fates. For some people, just living with the thought that they will die is a fate worse than death itself.

Longevity is without question of paramount value in our lives, and finding a corrective for mortality is our compulsive project. Anything goes insofar as lengthening our earthly tenure. And how we have cashed in on our efforts. No need to cram our lives into two or three decades now that we can cram them into seven, eight, nine, or more. The life-span of non-domesticated mammals has never changed, while ours has grown by leaps and bounds. What a coup for the human race. Unaware how long they will live, other warm-blooded life forms are sluggards by comparison. Time will run out for us as it does for all creatures, true, but at least we can dream of a day when we might *elect* our own deadline. Then perhaps we can all die of the same thing: a killing satiation with our durability in a world that is MALIGNANTLY USELESS.

"Worthless" rather than "useless" is the more familiar epithet in this context. The rationale for using "useless" in place of "worthless" in this histrionically capitalized phrase is that "worthless" is tied to the concepts of desirability and value, and *by their depreciation* introduces them into the existential mix. "Useless," on the other hand, is not so inviting of these concepts. Elsewhere in this work, "worthless" is connected to the language of pessimism and does what damage it can. But the devil of it is that "worthless" really does not go far enough when speaking pessimistically about the character of existence. Too many times the question "Is life worth living?" has been asked. This usage of "worth" excites impressions of a fair lot of experiences that are arguably desirable and valuable within limits

61

and that may follow upon one another in such a way as to suggest that life is not totally worthless. With "useless," the wispy spirits of desirability and value do not as readily rear their heads. Naturally, the *uselessness* of all that is or could ever be is subject to the same repudiations as the *worthlessness* of all that is or could ever be. For this reason, the adverb "malignantly" has been annexed to "useless" to give it a little more semantic stretch and a dose of toxicity. But to express with any adequacy a sense of the uselessness of everything, a nonlinguistic modality would be needed, some effusion out of a dream that amalgamated every gradation of the useless and wordlessly transmitted to us the inanity of existence under any possible conditions. Indigent of such means of communication, the uselessness of all that exists or could possibly exist must be spoken with a poor potency.

Not unexpectedly, no one believes that everything is useless, and with good reason. We all live within relative frameworks, and within those frameworks uselessness is far wide of the norm. A potato masher is not useless if one wants to mash potatoes. For some people, a system of being that includes an afterlife of eternal bliss may not seem useless. They might say that such a system is absolutely useful because it gives them the hope they need to make it through this life. But an afterlife of eternal bliss is not and cannot be absolutely useful simply because you need it to be. It is part of a relative framework and nothing beyond that, just as a potato masher is only part of a relative framework and is useful only if you need to mash potatoes. Once you had made it through this life to an afterlife of eternal bliss, you would have no use for that afterlife. Its job would be done, and all you would have is an afterlife of eternal bliss—a paradise for reverent hedonists and pious libertines. What is the use in that? You might as well not exist at all, either in this life or in an afterlife of eternal bliss. Any kind of existence is useless. Nothing is self-justifying. Everything is justified only in a relativistic potato-masher sense.

There are some people who do not get up in arms about potato-masher relativism, while other people do. The latter want to think in terms of absolutes that are really absolute and not just absolute potato mashers. Christians, Jews, and Muslims have a real problem with a potato-masher system of being. Buddhists have no problem with a potato-masher system because for them there are no absolutes. What they need to realize is the truth of "dependent origination," which means that everything is related to everything else in a great network of potato mashers that are always interacting with one another. So the only problem Buddhists have is *not* being able to realize that the only absolutely useful thing is the realization that everything is a great network of potato mashers. They think that if they can get over this hump, they will be eternally liberated from suffering. At least they hope they will, which is all they really need to make it through this life. In the Buddhist faith, everyone suffers who cannot see that the world is a MALIGNANTLY USELESS potato-mashing network. However, that does not make Buddhists superior to Christians, Jews, and Muslims. It only means they have a different system for making it through a life where all we can do is wait for musty shadows to call our names when they are ready for us. After that happens, there will be nobody who will need anything that is not absolutely useless. Ask any atheist.

Ecocide

Despite Zapffe's work as a philosopher, although not in an occupational role (he earned his living by writing poems, plays, stories, and humorous pieces), he is better known as an early ecologist who popularized the term "biosophy" to name a discipline that would broaden the compass of philosophy to include the interests of other living things besides human beings. In this capacity, he serves as an inspiration to environmentalists who worry about the well-being of the earth and its organisms. Here, too, we catch ourselves—and Zapffe himself, as he affirmed—in the act of conspiring to build barricades against the repugnant facts of life by signing on to a cause (in this case that of environmentalism) that snubs the real issue. Vandalism of the environment is but a sidebar to humanity's refusal to look into the jaws of existence.

In truth, we have only one foot in the natural environment of this world. Other worlds are always calling us away from nature. We live in a habitat of unrealities—not of earth, air, water, and wildlife—and cradling illusion trounces grim logic every time. Some of the more combative environmentalists, however, have concurred with Zapffe that we should retire from existence. But their advocacy of worldwide suicide as a strategy for saving the earth from being pillaged by human beings receives no mention in "The Last Messiah" and was probably not on Zapffe's mind when he wrote this essay. As appealing as a universal suicide pact may be, why take part in it just to conserve this planet, this dim bulb in the blackness of space? Nature produced us, or at least subsidized our evolution. It intruded on an inorganic wasteland and set up shop. What evolved was a global workhouse where nothing is ever at rest, where the generation and discarding of life incessantly goes on. By what virtue, then, is it entitled to receive a pardon for this original sin—a capital crime in reverse, just as reproduction makes one an accessory before the fact to an individual's death?

In its course, nature has made blunders in plenty. These are left to die out, as is nature's wont. Perhaps this will be how we will go—a natural death. It might be idly theorized, though, that nature has a special plan for human beings and devised us to serve as a way of revoking itself, much like Mainländer's self-expunging God. An offbeat idea, no protest, but not the strangest we have ever heard or lived by. We could at least take up the hypothesis and see where it leads. If it is proved unviable, then where is the harm? But until then, might we not let ourselves be drawn along by nature's plan, which includes our sacking the earth as a paradoxical means of living better in it, or at least living as *our nature* bids us to live.

We did not make ourselves, nor did we fashion a world that could not work without pain, and great pain at that, with a little pleasure, very little, to string us along—a world where all organisms are inexorably pushed by pain throughout their lives to do that which will improve their chances to survive and create more of themselves. Left unchecked, this process will last as long as a single cell remains palpitating in this cesspool of the solar system, this toilet of the galaxy. So why not lend a hand in nature's suicide? For want of a deity that could be held to account for a world in which there is terrible pain, let nature take the blame for our troubles. We did not create an environment uncongenial to our species, nature did. One would think that nature was trying to kill us off, or get us to suicide ourselves once the blunder of consciousness came upon us. What was nature thinking? We tried to anthropomorphize it, to romanticize it, to let it into our hearts. But nature kept its distance, leaving us to our own devices. So be it. Survival is a two-way street. Once we settle ourselves off-world, we can blow up this planet from outer space. It's the only way to be sure its stench will not follow us. Let it save itself if it can— the condemned are known for the acrobatics they will execute to wriggle out of their sentences. But if it cannot destroy what it has made, and what could possibly unmake it, then may it perish along with every other living thing it has introduced to pain. While no species has given in to pain to the point of giving up its existence, so far as we know, it is not a phenomenon whose praises are often sung.

Hopelessness

In Zapffe's "The Last Messiah," the titular figure appears at the end and makes the mock-Socratic, biblically parodic pronouncement, "Know yourselves—*be infertile and let the earth be silent after ye*" (Zapffe's emphasis). As Zapffe pictures the scene, the Last Messiah's words will not be well received: "And when he has spoken, they will pour themselves over him, led by the pacifier makers and the midwives, and bury him in their fingernails." Semantically speaking, the Last Messiah is not a messiah, since he saves no living soul and will be erased from human memory by a vigilante group whose kingpins are "the pacifier makers and the midwives." Moreover, a resurrection seems to be the last thing in the Last Messiah's future.

To exposit why humanity should not further tarry on earth is one thing; to believe that this proposition will be agreeable to others is quite another. Due to the note of hopelessness in the coda to Zapffe's essay, we are discouraged from imagining a world in which the self-liquidation of humanity could ever be put into effect. The Norwegian himself did not take the trouble to do so in "The Last Messiah." No reason he should, since he would first have to imagine a new humanity, which is not as a practice done outside of fiction, a medium of realism but not of reality.

Yet these new humans would not have to be super-evolved or otherwise freakish organisms living far in the future. They would only have to be like Zapffe in recognizing that a retreat from the worldly scene would be a benevolent proceeding for the good of the unborn. Becoming extinct would seem to be a tall order, but not one that would be insurmountably time-consuming. Zapffe optimistically projected that those of the new humanity could be evacuated from existence over the course of a few generations. And indeed they could. As their numbers tapered off, these dead-enders of our species could be the most privileged individuals in history and share with one another material comforts once held in trust only for the wellborn or money-getting classes of the world. Since personal economic gain would be passé as a motive for the new humanity, there would be only one defensible incitement to work: to see one another through to the finish, a project that would keep everyone busy and not just staring into space while they waited for the end. There might even be bright smiles exchanged among these selfless benefactors of those who would never be forced to exist. And how many would speed up the process of extinction once euthanasia was decriminalized and offered in humane and even enjoyable ways?

What a relief, what an unburdening to have closed the book on humankind. Yet it would not need to be slammed shut. As long as we progressed toward a thinning of the herd, couples could still introduce new faces into the human fold as billions became millions and then thousands. New generations would learn about the past, and, like those before them, feel lucky not to have been born in times of fewer conveniences and cures, although they might still play at cowboys and Indians, cops and robbers, management and labor. The last of us could be the very best of us who ever roamed the earth, the great exemplars of a humanity we used to dream of becoming before we got wise to the reality that we are just a mob always in the market for new recruits.

Quite naturally, this depiction of an end times by an extinctionist covenant will seem abhorrent to those now living in hope of a better future (not necessarily one in which glorious progress has been made toward the alleviation of human misery, but at least one that will partially exculpate them from a depraved indifference to the harm predestined for their young). It may also seem a romanticized utopia, since those who predict major readjustments in humanity's self-conception (Karl Marx, et al.) often believe that a revolution in ethics will blossom when their "truths" are instituted.

Worse, or perhaps better if the solution to human suffering is to be final, the idea of a new humanity may be a smokescreen for a tyrannical oligarchy run by militants of extinction rather than a social and psychological sanctuary for a species harboring the universal goal of delimiting its stay on earth. If Zapffe uselessly exercised himself by formulating the thesis of "The Last Messiah," he was sharp enough to give it a hopeless finale. Without an iota of uncertainty, humankind is and will always be unsuited to take charge of its own deliverance. The delusional will forever be with us, thereby making pain, fear, and denial of what is right in front of our face the preferred style of living and the one that will be passed on to countless generations.

The reception of the research of a Canadian scientist named Michael Persinger may be seen as an indication of humanity's genius for keeping itself locked into its old ways. In the 1980s, Persinger modified a motorcycle helmet to affect the magnetic fields of the brain of its wearer, inducing a variety of strange sensations. These included experiences in which subjects felt themselves proximate to supernatural phenomena that included ghosts and gods.

Atheists used Persinger's studies to nail closed their argument for the subjectivity of anyone's sense of the supernatural. Not to be left behind, believers wrote their own books in which they contended that the magnetic-field-emitting motorcycle helmet proved the existence of a god that "hard-wired" itself into our brains. A field of study called neurotheology grew up around this and other laboratory experiments. Even if you can prop up a scientific theory with a cudgel of data that should render the holy opposition unconscious, they will be standing ready to discredit you—imprisonment, torture, and public execution having gone the way of chastity belts.

For writers of supernatural horror the perquisite of this deadlock is that it ensures the larger part of humanity will remain in a state of fear, because no one can ever be certain of either his own ontological status or that of gods, demons, alien invaders, and sundry other bugbears. A Buddhist would advise that we forget about whether or not the bogeymen we have invented or divined are real. The big question is this: Are *we* real?

Debatability

Even though Zapffe's theory is perceptible in our lives, we do not actually have any sense, or any strong sense, that human beings are false and paradoxical beings, at least not yet. And if we did, why would that mean we should go extinct and not continue to live as we have all these years? One would think that neuroscientists and geneticists would have as much reason to head for the cliffs because little by little they have been finding that much of our thought and behavior is attributable to neural wiring and heredity rather than to personal control over the individuals we are, or think we are. But they do not feel suicide to be mandatory just because their laboratory experiments are informing them that human nature may be nothing but puppet nature. Not the slightest tingle of uncanniness or horror runs up and down their spines, only the thrill of discovery. Most of them reproduce and do not believe there is anything questionable in doing so. If they could get a corpse to sit up on an operating table, they would jubilantly exclaim, "It's alive!" And so would we. Who cares that human beings evolved from slimy materials? We can live with that, or most of us can. Actually, we can probably live with any conception of ourselves for quite a while longer. Although we may have phases in which the power of positive thinking peters out, no scientific discoveries or anything else can get to us for long, at least not as far as we can see into the future. As a species with consciousness, we do have our inconveniences. Yet these are of negligible importance compared to what it would be like to feel in our depths that we are nothing but human puppets—things of mistaken identity who must live with the terrible knowledge that they are *not* making a go of it on their own and are not what they once thought they were. At this time, barely anyone can conceive of this happening—of hitting bottom and finding to our despair that we can never again resurrect our repressions and denials. Not until that day of lost illusions comes, if it ever comes, will we all be competent to conceive of such a thing. But a great many more generations will pass through life before that happens, if it happens.

Who Goes There?

Uncanniness I

No philosopher has ever satisfactorily answered the following question: "Why should there be something rather than nothing?" It seems a fair enough question on its face. But that it should even be asked may seem to some of us inexplicable, even preposterous. What the question suggests is our uneasiness with Something. Alternatively, there is nothing troubling about Nothing, because we cannot give it consideration. Something, on the other hand, allows or necessitates our experience of the uncanny. Whether we are speaking of something that evolved naturally or was made by the digits and opposing thumbs of humanity, whether it is animate or inanimate, that something may become uncanny to us, a contravention of what we think should or should not be.

In the same way that most of us share a general pattern of feeling about what is right or wrong in a moral sense, we also share a general pattern of feeling about what is right or wrong with respect to the world and ourselves—an internal authority that judges entities and events as within or outside of customs of reality. In experiencing the uncanny, there is a feeling of *wrongness*. A violation has transpired that alarms our internal authority regarding how something is supposed to happen or exist or behave. An offense against our world-conception or self-conception has been committed. Of course, our internal authority may itself be in the wrong, perhaps because it is a fabrication of consciousness based on a body of laws that are written only within us and not a detector of what is right or wrong in any real sense, since nothing really is right or wrong in any real sense. That we might be wrong about something being wrong would in itself be wrong according to our internal authority, which would then send out a signal of the uncanny concerning its own wrongness that would be returned to it for another round of signaling on the principle that everything it knows is wrong, which is to say that Something is always wrong. For the welfare of our functioning, however, we are insured against the adverse effects of an ever-cycling signal of uncanny wrongness by our inability to recognize it, although it might be going on all the time, thus accounting for our uneasiness about Something. But we may still perceive other phenomena to be on the wrong side of right and wrong—things that should not happen or exist or behave in the way we feel they should.

Even the most unexceptional things may impress us in this way. In no time at all they may cease to be seen the way we usually see them and come to be seen as something else, something we may not be able to name. This unsteadiness of quality and meaning in something—a puppet doll, for instance—repels our lasting inspection of it, for the longer this inspection goes on the more we become lost in a paradoxical state of knowing and not knowing what was once known and familiar. And it is then that the question "Why should there be something rather than nothing?" may become lost in the inexplicable, even preposterous, ambition to resolve it without losing our minds to the uncanny.

Everyday objects seem curiously liable to being perceived as uncanny, because we see them every day and "know" how they should be and should not be. One day those shoes on the floor of your clothes closet may attract your eye in a way they never have before. Somehow they have become abstracted from your world, appearances you cannot place, lumps of matter without a fixed quality and meaning. You feel confused as you stare at them. What are they? What is their nature? Why should there be something rather than nothing? But before your consciousness can ask any more questions, you dial it back so that your footwear seems familiar again and not uncanny in its being. You select a pair of shoes to wear that day and sit down to put them on. It is then that you notice the pair of stockings you are wearing and think of the feet they conceal . . . and the rest of the body to which those concealed feet are connected . . . and the universe in which that body is roving about with so many other uncanny shapes. "What now?" a voice from the other side of being seems to say. And what if you should look at yourself—the most everyday object there is—and feel at a loss to attach a quality and a meaning to what is being seen or what is seeing it. What now indeed.

Uncanniness II

A sense of the uncanny can be activated in the average mortal under various conditions. Principal among these conditions are those which cause us to feel that we are not what we think we are, which was touched on at the close of the previous section. In his groundbreaking essay "On the Psychology of the Uncanny" (1906), the German physician and psychologist Ernst Jentsch analyzes this feeling and its origins. Among the examples of uncanny experience Jentsch proffers in his essay is one where individuals cease to appear integrated in their identity and take on the aspect of mechanisms, things of parts that are made as they are made and are all clockwork processes rather than immutable beings unchanging at their heart. As Jentsch explains:

[A] confirmation of the fact that the emotion being discussed [the uncanny] is caused in particular by a doubt as to the animate or inanimate nature of things—or, expressed more precisely, as to their animatedness as understood by man's traditional view—lies in the way in which the lay public is generally affected by the sight of articulations of most mental and many nervous diseases. Several patients afflicted with such troubles make a quite decidedly uncanny impression on most people.

What we can always assume from our fellow men's experience of ordinary life is the relative psychical harmony in which their mental functions generally stand in relation to each other, even if moderate deviations from this equilibrium make their appearance occasionally in almost all of us: this behavior . . . constitutes man's individuality and provides the foundation for our judgment of it. Most people do not show strong psychical peculiarities. At most, such peculiarities become apparent when strong affects make themselves felt, whereby it can suddenly become evident that not everything in the human psyche is of transcendental origin, and that much that is elementary is still present within it even for our direct perception. It is of course often in just such cases that much at present is generally accounted for quite well in terms of normal psychology.

But if this relative psychical harmony happens markedly to be disturbed in the spectator, and if the situation does not seem trivial or comic, the consequence of an unimportant incident, or if it is not quite familiar (like an alcohol intoxication, for example), then the dark knowledge dawns on the unschooled observer that mechanical processes are taking place in that which he was previously used to regarding as a unified psyche. It is not unjustly that epilepsy is therefore spoken of as the *morbus sacer* ["sacred disease"], as an illness not deriving from the human world but from foreign and enigmatic spheres, for the epileptic attack of spasms reveals the human body to the viewer— the body that under normal conditions is so meaningful, expedient, and unitary, functioning according to the directions of his consciousness—as an immensely complicated and delicate mechanism. This is an important cause of the epileptic fit's ability to produce such a demonic effect on those who see it. (Translation by Roy Sellars)

The brilliance of Jentsch's example is that it explicates the uncanny not as an objective quality of something in the outside world, but as a subjective experience of a perceiver of the outside world. This is how it is in real life: The uncanny is an effect of our minds—and nothing else. And yet, at least for the average onlooker in this case, the uncanny effectively originates in an objective stimulus, something that seems to have about it a power of its own. In the example given, the objective stimulus is an animate individual observed as behaving against "animatedness as understood by man's traditional view," the offender here being an epileptic exhibiting unusual bodily motions in the midst of a seizure. The subjective reaction to the seemingly objective stimulus of the uncanny is the gaining of "dark knowledge" about the workings of individuals, including the onlooker of the epileptic in the midst of a seizure. More expansively stated, not only is the epileptic perceived as uncanny by the onlooker (unless the onlooker is a physician who understands epileptic seizures by the lights of modern medicine and not according to a "traditional view") but the onlooker also perceives himself as uncanny because he has been made conscious of the mechanical nature of all human bodies and, by extrapolation, of the fact that "mechanical processes are taking place in that which he was previously used to regarding as a unified psyche." Neuroscientists are now familiar with some of these mechanical processes, as was Zapffe, who wrote in "The Last Messiah": "All things chain together in causes and effects, and everything [man] wants to grasp dissolves before the testing thought. Soon he sees mechanics even in the so-far whole and dear, in the smile of his beloved." The knowledge that we are not the idealized beings we thought, integral and undivided, does frighten some people, including physicians and neuroscientists. Yet even though we are not as we usually perceive ourselves to be, we can still continue in our accustomed ways if only we can quash the sense of being uncanny mechanisms in a world of things that may be transformed anytime and anywhere. Such quashing is not often a problem in the so-called real world. But it *must* be a problem in the world of supernatural horror.

Artistic invocations of horror are most successful when the phenomena they depict call up the uncanny, which, unlike Jentsch's example of seeing someone having an epileptic seizure, are genuinely threatening both from the outside and from within. This species of horror can only be provoked when the supernatural is conjoined with the uncanny, because not even physicians and neuroscientists can be comfortable with supernaturalism, either by the lights of modern medicine or by any other lights. Bloodthirsty vampires and ravenous zombies are prime examples in this context, because their intrinsic supernaturalism as the undead makes them objectively uncanny things that generate subjectively uncanny sensations. They are uncanny in themselves because they once were human but have undergone a terrible rebirth and become mechanisms with a single function—to survive for survival's sake. Necessarily, they also inspire a subjective sense of the uncanny in those who perceive them because they divulge the "dark knowledge" that human beings are also things made as they are made and may be remade because they are only clockwork processes, mechanisms, rather than immutable beings unchanging at their heart. As uncanny mechanisms, vampires and zombies usually perform the mechanical act of reproduction with no weighty deliberation, or none at all—the replication of their kind being epiphenomenal to the controlling urge that drives them. This second consequence completes the requirements of a supernatural horror story to present a phenomenon that poses an uncanny threat from both outside and from within, which is the ultimate threat to ordinary folk who only want to live in a world and in a way that is natural and familiar to them and their families, even though they are darkly aware that this familiarity is a fabrication that may be invalidated.

Both requirements of the uncanny are recognizable in such horror films as *Invasion of the Body Snatchers* (1956; remakes 1978 and 2007) and John Carpenter's *The Thing* (1982), which belong only negligibly to the genre of science fiction and solidly to that of supernatural horror as cognate with the uncanny. In the former classic of cinema, human beings are replaced by physical doubles of themselves by an alien power—something pernicious, in Jentsch's analysis of the layperson's perception of epilepsy, "not deriving from the human world but from foreign and enigmatic spheres." What business does this alien power have on our planet? It has come to protract the survival of its kind by re-creating itself in *our* image. And that says all we need to know about its mechanics and intentions: They are the same as ours, only they threaten to replace the survival and reproduction of our species with the survival and reproduction of theirs. The methodology of this alien power is to make duplicates of us after we fall asleep, so that we will never again awaken as ourselves but will be transformed into another sort of being altogether. Due to these transformations, everyone who has not been taken by the Body Snatchers suffers from two appalling uncertainties. One is that any other person may not be what they seem to be—human. The other is that they themselves will also be transformed once they go to sleep. But unlike becoming a vampire or a zombie, neither being a desirable state of being, our transformation into Body Snatchers, which, despite the pluralization in the film title, seem to be parts of a hive rather than uniquely individuated entities, does not look too bad, objectively speaking. Once absorbed by the alien power, the converted lose all the qualities they had as humans except for one—that of contentment, or happiness if you like. They become quietists in their existence, which in the film appears the last thing that human beings want, preferring the agitations of the life they know. This reaction is understandable. No one wants to be other than they are, or think they are. That is a fate worse than death: the transformation in which you stop being you. And better to die than to live in an assimilated condition, even one that is permanently collected and reassuring rather than vulnerable to the startling and dreadful. Our sense of the uncanny is too ingrained in us as beings that may not be what we think we are, but who will hold on for dear life to survive and reproduce as our own species and not that of some alien power.

John Carpenter's *The Thing* is quite similar in its ontological scheme to *Invasion of the Body Snatchers*. The motivations of the Thing are the same as those of the Body Snatchers—to survive and reproduce. Only its method is different, which results in a somewhat greater degree of uncanniness in this film than in the earlier one. Because the title creature has the ability to remake itself as any and all life forms without their knowledge, the characters in the film cannot be sure who is a "thing" and who is not, since those who are transmuted retain their former appearance, memories, and behaviors even after they have become, in their essence, uncanny monstrosities from another world. This situation leaves the members of an Antarctic research station—in the vicinity of which the Thing's spacecraft crash-landed long ago—doubtful about which of them is a thing and which are still the individuals they seem to be. Naturally, those at the Antarctic station are invested in repressing any consciousness that they are things, just as those who witness someone in the midst of an epileptic seizure are invested in thinking they are not things of parts that are made as they are made and are all clockwork processes rather than immutable beings unchanging at their heart. By isolation (putting this possibility out of their minds), the latter can maintain their sense of being idealized beings, integral and undivided, and not mechanisms—human puppets who do not know themselves as such. They can also distract themselves from any petrifying news about human beings by watching films in which all of the characters suffer an uncanny doom that could not possibly have relevance to real life, since it is represented as an invasion from "foreign and enigmatic spheres" they believe have no place in our world, where we know who we are and who everyone else is—members of a species that exists to survive and reproduce, ordinary folk who have nothing to do with supernaturalism and the uncanny and who are resistant to the pessimism of fictions like *Invasion of the Body Snatchers* and *The Thing*, whose principals all suffer death or deformation in their fight to hang on to their lives and their humanity.

In protest to the mentality of ordinary folk, let us again call on the incorrigibly pixilated Professor Nobody. In his "Pessimism and Supernatural Horror—Lecture One," he accommodates us with a rejoinder to the average, optimistic mortal and helps us recall some of the main themes of the present work.

Madness, chaos, bone-deep mayhem, devastation of innumerable souls—while we scream and perish, History licks a finger and turns the page. Fiction, unable to compete with the world for vividness of pain and lasting effects of fear, compensates in its own way. How? By inventing more bizarre means to outrageous ends. Among these means, of course, is the supernatural. In transforming natural ordeals into supernatural ones, we find the strength to affirm and deny their horror simultaneously, to savor and suffer them at the same time.

So it is that supernatural horror is a possession of a profoundly divided species of being. It is not a property held by even our closest relations in the wholly natural world. We came into it, as part of our gloomy inheritance, when we became what we are. Once awareness of the human predicament was achieved, we immediately took off in two directions, splitting ourselves down the middle. One half became dedicated to apologetics, even celebration, of our new toy of consciousness. The other half condemned and occasionally launched direct assaults on this "gift."

Supernatural horror was one of the ways we found that would allow us to live with our double selves. By its employ, we discovered how to take all the things that victimize us in our natural lives and turn them into the very stuff of demonic delight in our fantasy lives. In story and song, we could entertain ourselves with the worst we could think of, overwriting real pains with ones that were unreal and harmless to our species. We can also do this trick without trespassing on the real estate of supernatural horror, but then we risk running into miseries too close to home. While horror may make us squirm or quake, it will not make us cry at the pity of things. The vampire may symbolize our horror of both life and death, but none of us

80

has ever been uprooted by a symbol. The zombie may conceptualize our sickness of the flesh and its appetites, but no one has ever been sickened to death by a concept. By means of supernatural horror we may pull our own strings of fate without collapsing—natural-born puppets whose lips are painted with our own blood.

Actors

Within the strictures of commonsense reality and personal ability, we can choose to do anything we like in this world . . . with one exception: We cannot choose what any of our choices will be. To do that, we would have to be capable of making ourselves into self-made individuals who can choose what they choose as opposed to being individuals who simply make choices. For instance, we may want to become bodybuilders and choose to do so. But if we do not want to become bodybuilders we cannot make ourselves into someone who does want to be a bodybuilder. For that to happen, there would have to be another self inside us who made us choose to want to become bodybuilders. And inside that self, there would have to be still another self who made that self want to choose to choose to make us want to become bodybuilders. This sequence of choosing, being interminable, would result in the paradox of an infinite number of selves *beyond which* there is a self making all the choices. The foregoing position is based in a strain of philosophical thought called determinism and is here stated in one of its strongest forms. British philosopher Galen Strawson describes this position, which is his own as a determinist, as pessimistic. ("Luck Swallows Everything," *Times Literary Supplement*, June 28, 1998.) It is pessimist because it turns the human image into a puppet image. And a puppet image of humanity is one of the hallmarks of pessimism.

Those who most vehemently oppose the pessimistic form of

determinism are libertarian indeterminists. They hold that we have absolute free will and can make ourselves into individuals who can choose to want to make a certain choice and not some other. They hold that we are what Michelstaedter despaired we could ever become: individuals who are invulnerably self-possessed and not the products of an indeterminable series of events and conditions that result in our being able to make only one choice and not any number of choices, because factors beyond our control have already taken care of who we are as individuals and what choices we will finally make.

In the history of philosophical lucubration, arguments for determinism are traditionally the most argued against. Why is this so, aside from the fact that it turns the human image into a puppet image? It is so because arguments for determinism step on the sacrosanct belief in moral responsibility. Even the average atheist draws the line whenever someone says that we do not have any degree of freedom and that moral responsibility is not a reality. As die-hard unbelievers, they may reject the position that moral laws descend from a higher plane unperceived by our senses; as tax-paying citizens, however, they still need to live by sublunary standards of civility. And this can be done only if free will and moral realism are the law of the land.

Of course, there are rare cases when a wrongdoer's malfeasance is determined to be the result of determining forces. Then free will and moral responsibility are waived, and the defendant is either sent to a psychiatric hospital rather than a prison or gets off scot-free because a certain judge and jury in a certain society temporarily became strong determinists without a sense of moral realism, thereby turning the human image of a defendant into a puppet image. But this is highly irregular. In the normal course of events, both determinists and indeterminists are one in promoting some kind of operative morality. As guardians of our morale, they feel moral realism to be a necessary truth, whether it is objectively *real*, as it is to indeterminists, or subjectively "real," as it is to determinists. Without this *truth*, or "truth," we could not go on living as we always have and believe that being alive is all right.

It does not seem wildly improbable that determinations have been made in our psyches that make some people determinists and others indeterminists. If we could only know how these determinations work, we would be able to answer the only interesting question in the debate pitting free will against determinism: Why argue for one side or the other? The answer to this question would abort all rivalry in this matter, since it would bring to light the reason why any philosopher would engage in a conflict more vain than most in his discipline. But should we ever get an answer to this question, the repercussions would far override matters of moral *realism* or "realism." Really, there would only be one repercussion: to reduce all philosophical proclivities to the psychology of the individuals who exhibit them. In his *Metaphilosophy and Free Will* (1996), Richard Double speaks of analytic philosophers whose writing is protective of free will.

Although this type of free will writing pays dividends in terms of precision, it has its disadvantages. First, we may lose sight of the philosophical forest for the technical trees. Second, and following from the first, we may collect psychological consolation at the expense of candor. By submerging ourselves in the nuances of theories, we may avert our attention from the big, scary questions. An attention to detail can be an exercise in bad faith when it uses up our time and energies so that we do not bother to question whether what we are trying to do is possible. Meticulous precision can enable us to remain happy and engaged at the expense of averting our eyes from the disturbing big picture.

Perhaps one day cognitive psychologists will settle once and for all why an individual would argue for either free will or determinism. Studies might also be conducted on those who cling to one side or the other of any philosophical question. This may not advance any philosophical questions, although it might make them disappear once the argumentative motives behind them have been determined.

In the everyday world, no such thing as an out-and-out determinist ever existed, since everyday people cannot shake off a sense of having free will. The best we can do is to *reason* that we are determined based on observing the common law of causality among things in the world and applying this law to ourselves. But we cannot *feel* ourselves as determined. (One philosopher has said, and possibly more have thought to themselves: "Can one *really* believe in determinism without going insane?") Being determined in thought and deed is not experientially noticeable, only abstractly deducible. It would be impossible for someone to say "I am nothing but a human puppet." The only exception would be an individual with a psychological disease that had induced in him the sense of being controlled by an alien force. Should this individual say "I am nothing but a human puppet," he would forthwith be marched to the nearest psychiatric hospital, conceivably overtaken by the horror of feeling he was a human puppet controlled by an alien force working outside him or within him or both.

The extent to which any of us is determined in thought and deed may be logically argued but cannot be known by firsthand experience. Determinists are only too aware that if free will is illusory on paper, it is insuperable in our lives. To hate our illusions or hold them dear only lashes us to them more tautly. We cannot stand up to them without our world falling apart, for those who care. And those who really care cannot be anything but believers in some form of moral *realism* or "realism," which buttresses the optimistic reality that most people call home and braces up everything you need in order to be you—your country, your loved ones, your job or vocation, your golf clubs, and, in an all around sense, your "way of life."

Impersonation

In the free will debate, the reality, or "reality," of free will is something of an irrelevancy, since it is a parasite of the feeling we each have of being or possessing a self (often capitalized). This self is an intangible entity that is spoken of as if it were an extra internal organ, yet to every one of us it seems more than the sum of our anatomical parts. Everything comes back to the self and must come back to the self, for it is the utmost issue in our deciding whether we are something or nothing, people or puppets. Without the sense of being or possessing a self, there would be no use disputing whether or not we are free, determined, or somewhere in between. Why we have a sense of self has been variously explained. (For one explanation, see the next section in this chapter.) Having this sense is what brings the free-will-versus-determinism debate to the table. Even further, it is what brings everything to the table, or at least to the table of human existence, because nothing else that exists has a sense of being a self that can do or not do anything at will.

You can *reason* that you do not have a self and that your behavior is determined, but if you *feel* that you are or possess a self, then you will probably have a time of it denying responsibility for every thought that passes through your brain or the slightest movement of your little toe. Yet there is a problem with the feeling of responsibility, because sometimes you feel responsible for something that you cannot, by any logic or physical law, be held responsible for. When someone dies of an undiagnosed case of liver cancer not long after he punches you in the stomach, you cannot say, "That's what he gets for messing with me." Yet people do say such things in such circumstances. Nevertheless, they can usually be brought to their senses about feeling somehow responsible for the death by unrelated causes of someone who has punched them in the stomach.

More often, though, an individual cannot be brought to his senses when he feels responsible for something that he cannot, by any logic or physical law, be held responsible for. For example, you call up a friend or a relative to help you fix your toilet, and while driving over to your place to do this he is hit by an eighteen-wheel truck and dies. It would not be out of the ordinary if you felt responsible for your friend or relative's death for the reason that if you had not called him up to help fix your toilet he would not have been on the road at that time and gotten killed in a collision with an eighteen-wheel truck. Under these circumstances, your friends and relatives who are still alive may find it difficult to convince you of your non-responsibility in the death of your friend or relative who died in a vehicular misadventure. There may be any number of factors involved in that fatal collision, but you could still feel that the only factor worth consideration was your calling up your friend or relative to drive over to your place when he would otherwise have been doing something you had nothing to do with. You would be mistaken to feel this way, of course, but just because you can *reason* that you are mistaken would not in itself make you *feel* any less responsible for what happened. And you may mistakenly take that feeling of terrible responsibility to your grave, because you were the self who called another self to come to your place to help fix your toilet. You might just as well blame your toilet for going out of order when it did, or blame any number of causes back to the beginning of time as much as blame yourself. The thing is this: If you can be mistaken in attributing to yourself responsibility, or anything more than a bare trace of causal responsibility, you can also be mistaken about other things, such as being a self with free will. But if you *feel* that you are or possess a self, then you will probably have a time of it denying responsibility for every thought that passes through your brain or the slightest movement of your little toe.

Other people may try to console you for your friend or relative's death by saying that this atrocious event was not your fault. They may also surreptitiously blame you for it, as people sometimes blame those who have had a heart attack for being lax in following the unhealthy injunction to watch your health. But it is quite possible you will disbelieve anyone who says you are not to blame for your friend or relative's death in a vehicular misadventure, perhaps because you can tell that they surreptitiously blame you for it. But that is inconsequential. As someone who feels he is a self, you will likely as not feel responsible for things you could not by any logic or physical law take responsibility for, or no more than a bare trace of causal responsibility. This is not even to consider circumstances in which you may feel *morally* responsible for something that happens when by rights you should not feel this way. And here is where the feeling of being a self with free will really comes in.

Say you asked your friend or relative to help fix your toilet *not* because you needed help fixing your toilet but because you wanted to get back at him for asking you to help him move into his new house the week before when he could have called a moving company, as you did when you moved into your new house, and saved you from having your little toe broken when a heavy piece of furniture fell on it during the move. Morally, inconveniencing your friend or relative just to get back at him for the reasons stated in the previous sentence was not the right thing to do, or so you feel after your friend or relative's car crashed when it collided with an eighteen-wheel truck in an explosive vehicular misadventure. You did not mean for that to happen. You were just looking for some petty form of payback, some kind of reprisal for the pain of your broken toe—and not even a proportional reprisal, nor anything illegal or particularly immoral, as these things go. Good luck, though, if you try to feel you were not responsible in an intensely moral sense for your friend or relative's vehicular misadventure. You could *reason* that your part in this misfortune was causally determined and not your fault. But if you *feel* that you are or possess a self then you will probably have a time of it denying responsibility for what happened. If you did not feel this way, what kind of person would that make you, assuming you still felt yourself a person and not some monstrous *thing*?

What is most uncanny about the self is that no one has yet been able to present the least evidence of it. Like the soul, that figure of speech which has long since been snickered out of existence, the self may be felt but never be found. It is a spectral tapeworm that takes its reality from a host organism and grows along with the physical matter in which it is encased. It may even grow beyond its material confines. Some believe that a Big Self enfolds all our little selves. Far fewer, or none, believe that little selves can have littler selves or play host to a number of self-contained selves. Do infants have selves? Fetuses? When do we get a self and can we lose it or have it taken away from us? Putting nonsense aside, some of us are surer than others of our selves. And how many of us want nothing so badly as to be a self-made somebody?

Without a relentless sense of the self, the person, we could not live as we have all these years. Were a personal god to be excluded from everyone's universe, persons would still retain their status. Sensory perceptions, memories, aches, ecstasies: Because these phenomena occur inside the same sack of skin, we suppose that we are enduring, continuous entities, things that serve as the infrastructure for war, romance, athletic competition, and every other genre of human activity. We do not just have experiences—we *own* them. That is what it means to be a person. No quibbling, everyone who is anyone holds this article of faith, even those who, like the eighteenth-century Scottish philosopher David Hume, have done a good job of logically dismantling the reality of selves. But logic cannot exorcise that "I" (ego) which stares back at you in the mirror, just as logic cannot remove the illusion of free will. When someone says she has not been feeling her old self, our thoughts turn to psychology, not metaphysics. To reason or to hold as an article of faith that the self is an illusion may help us to step around the worst pitfalls of the ego, but mitigation is light-years from liberation.

To all human beings, or almost all (see the section *Ego-Death* in this chapter), we seem to be the most real thing going. No one can say with assurance what the world outside of us is like, but inside us we feel self-assured. How does this occur? So far, no one knows. Cognitive psychologists, philosophers of mind, and neuroscientists have their theories, of course, among them those that argue for temporary selves and selves over time, psychophysical selves, neurological selves, objective selves, subjective selves, social selves, transcendent selves, the self as a process and not a "thing," and even the simultaneous existence and nonexistence of the self. But these and many other self-concepts leave the self as we have always known and experienced it intact and unharmed. We will all, or almost all, still feel that we are or possess an old-fashioned self.

Thus, cognitive psychologists, philosophers of mind, and neuroscientists who extend theories that the self does not exist as we have always believed are not saying that the self does not exist; they are only spreading complex self-constructions that save the self from anyone's questioning its existence. And those who try to prove that selves do not look out at the world from behind our eyeballs might as well be telling us that we have been snatched by the Body Snatchers or coalesced into the Thing.

Within the hierarchy of fabrications that compose our lives—families, countries, gods—the self incontestably ranks highest. Just below the self is the family, which has proven itself more durable than national or ethnic affiliations, with these in turn outranking god-figures for their staying power. So any progress toward the salvation of humankind will probably begin from the bottom—when our gods have been devalued to the status of refrigerator magnets or lawn ornaments. Following the death rattle of deities, it would appear that nations or ethnic communities are next in line for the boneyard. Only after fealty to countries, gods, and families has been shucked off can we even think about coming to grips with the least endangered of fabrications—the self. However, this hierarchy may change in time as science makes inroads regarding the question of selfhood, which, if the findings are negative, could reverse the progression, with the extinction of the self foretelling that of families, national and ethnic affiliations, and gods. After all, the quintessential sequence by which we free ourselves from our selves and our institutions is still that depicted in the Buddha legend. Born a prince, so the story goes, the nascent Enlightened One, Siddhartha Gautama, embarked on a quest to neutralize his ego by first leaving behind his family, gods, and sociopolitical station—all in one stroke. But Buddha's way requires a near inhuman dedication, and few of us have that kind of stamina. This being so, a speedy and efficient breakdown of fabrications having a worldwide ambit seems remote without the intercession of science, which could at some future date provide a vaccination against the development of "selves" after models already in use to wipe out certain diseases.

Perhaps the only matter of interest about the self is this: Whatever makes us think that we are what we think we are lies in the fact that we have consciousness, which gives us a sense of being somebody, specifically a *human* somebody, whatever that may be, since we do not have a definition of "human" on which there is universal agreement. But we do agree that, if only in practice, we are all real live selves, since we are all self-conscious. And once we have passed through every door that qualifies our selves in some way—be it by name, nationality, occupation, gender, or shoe size—we then stand before the door of consciousness—parent of all horrors. And that is all there is to our existence.

No creature caged in a zoo even knows what it is to exist, nor does it crow about being superior to another kind of thing, whether animal, vegetable, or mineral. As for us humans, we reek of our sense of being special. Those hailed as the most conscious among us—the ones needful of a refined type of brainwashing—have made investigations into what it means to be human. Their divergent ramblings on this subject keep our brains buzzing while our bodies go the way of surviving and reproducing—being alive that is, since we do not especially consider the alternative. That being human might mean something very strange and awful, something quite uncanny, is not given a passing thought. If it were, who knows what would happen to us? We could disappear in a puff of smoke or fall through a mirror that has nothing on the other side.

Naturally, such possibilities do not lift our spirits the way we need them to be lifted if we are to continue to live as we have all these years.

Nonentities

Perhaps foremost in the investigation of selfism and egology is the field of neuroscience. Therein may be found a dense and technical literature antithetical to the everyday world of the everyday self. In *Being No One* (2004), for example, the German neurophilosopher Thomas Metzinger provides a theory of how the brain manufactures the subjective sense of our existence as discrete "selves," even though, as Metzinger explains, we would be more rigorously categorized as information-processing systems for which it is expedient in an existential sense to create the illusion of "being someone." In Metzinger's schema, a human being is not a "person" but a mechanistically functioning "phenomenal self-model" that simulates a person. The reason we cannot examine these models is that we see *through* them, and so cannot see the processes of the models themselves.[1] If we could, we would know there is nothing to us but these models. This might be called "Metzinger's Paradox": You cannot know what you really are, because then you would know there is nothing to know and nothing to know it. (What now?) So rather than be know-nothings, we exist in a condition of what Metzinger describes as "naïve realism," with things not being knowable as they really are in themselves, something every scientist and philosopher knows.

The above sketch of Metzinger's central thesis is transparently inadequate, though necessarily so in the present context. By his reasoning and intuitions concerning the nature and workings of consciousness, Metzinger has no equal in his field and impresses one as a thinker whose speculative investigations will someday prove to be the way of reality. By argument and analysis, he has taken consciousness studies as far as possible by the resources available in the early twenty-first century. The project Metzinger has taken upon himself is precisely of the kind whose import is not restricted to the halls of science but is pursued for the far-reaching implications it may have with regard to the life of the average mortal. That said, the following discussion of Metzinger has an ulterior purpose having little to do with the value of his theories.

In his essay "The Shadow of a Puppet Dance: Metzinger, Ligotti and the Illusion of Selfhood" (*Collapse IV*, May 2008), James Trafford breaks down Metzinger's Paradox as follows: "The object 'man' consists of tightly packed layers of simulation, for which naïve realism becomes a necessary prophylactic in order to ward off the terror concomitant with the destruction of our intuitions regarding ourselves and our status in the world: 'Conscious subjectivity is the case in which a single organism has learned to enslave *itself*.'" The closing quote from Metzinger's *Being No One* might be seen as an extension of Zapffe's Paradox, by dint of which we repress from our consciousness all that is startling and dreadful in our lives. For Metzinger, this repression takes the form of the aforesaid naïve realism, which masks the single most startling and dreadful revelation for human beings: that we are not what we think we are. Assuaging our qualms about such a deplorable enlightenment, Metzinger avers that it is "practically impossible" for us to attain realization of our unreality due to inbuilt manacles of human perception that keep our minds in a dream state.

An interesting fact that seems relevant to Metzinger's study of the illusion of selves is the following: Metzinger is a lucid dreamer. His treatise *Being No One* contains an entire chapter on the knack of being able to "wake up" in one's dreams and recognize that one's consciousness is operating within an illusory zone created by the brain. In that aspect of our lives where we have no say in what happens and are free to choose nothing, the lucid dreamer is no one's fool, or at least not his own. He has peeked behind the curtain of what his consciousness has made and seen through its tricks and traps. This faculty might very well explain Metzinger's inquisitiveness about the nature of waking perception and the possibility that, as Poe wrote: "All that we see or seem / Is but a dream within a dream." These lines sum up the argument of *Being No One*—that we sleep in the self and cannot awake. Yet at the close of this 699-page work, following hard upon an examination of how and why human beings evolved in such a way that we believe we are someone while actually being no one, there seems to be some hedging. "At least in principle," Metzinger writes, "one can wake up from one's biological history. One can grow up, define one's own goals, and become autonomous." So imponderably nebulous, the meaning of these sentences can only be guessed at, since Metzinger leaves them hanging in the air. One is unreservedly stymied as to how this transformation could occur in terms of Metzinger's theory and research. Did he wrap up his treatise prematurely? Does he know something he is not telling us? Or did he just want to end a disillusioning book on an up note?

The same year that he published *Being No One*, Metzinger further clouded the issue. In a lecture at the University of California, Berkeley, he referred to our captivity in the illusion of a self—even though "there is no one" to have this illusion—as "the tragedy of the ego." This phrase fits like a glove into Zapffe's theory of consciousness as a tragic blunder. Disappointingly, Metzinger goes on to say that "the tragedy of the ego dissolves because nobody is ever born and nobody ever dies." This statement is borrowed from Zen Buddhism (the Heart Sutra) and loses something when translated from a monastery to a university lecture hall. In traditions of enlightenment, the only redress for our fear of death is to wake up to our brain's manufactured sense of self and thus eliminate what we mistakenly think we are before it is too late. But Metzinger's mission as a scientist-philosopher has been to shed light on the neurological mechanisms that make this goal unfeasible. Why, then, does Metzinger speak to his auditors about the "tragedy of the ego," which in all probability none of them thought to be a tragedy before coming to his lecture, and how it "dissolves because nobody is ever born and nobody ever dies"? He seems to be trying to alleviate any fears they might have about their death at the same time he is telling them that they do not exist in the first place. Either way, something is lost that everyone cannot help wanting to hold on to, tragic as that may be. Metzinger's whole routine seems to be based in the same kind of paradoxical double-talk that the world already lives by so as to deny the suffering it must endure and to continue to believe that consciousness is not a problem and that being alive is all right.

But let us not jump to conclusions. In an online forum in which some of the most prestigious figures in consciousness studies responded to Nicholas Humphrey's "A Self Worth Having," where, as quoted earlier, Humphrey says that consciousness is a "wonderfully good thing in its own right," Metzinger sums up his own position on this subject. Here he tolls the same bell as Zapffe when he writes:

> It is not at all clear if the biological form of consciousness, as so far brought about by evolution on our planet, is a *desirable* form of experience, an actual *good in itself.* . . .
> The theoretical blind spot of current philosophy of mind is the issue of conscious suffering: Thousands of pages are being written about color qualia or the contents of thought, but almost no theoretical work is devoted to

ubiquitous phenomenal states like human suffering or simple everyday sadness ("subclinical depression"), or to the phenomenal content associated with panic, despair and melancholy—let alone to the conscious experience of mortality or of losing one's dignity. . . .

The ethical-normative issue is of greater relevance. If one dares to take a closer look at the actual phenomenology of biological systems on our planet, the many different kinds of conscious suffering are *at least* as dominant a feature as are color vision or conscious thought, both of which appeared only very recently. Evolution is not something to be glorified. One way—out of countless others—to look at biological evolution on our planet is as a process that has created an expanding ocean of suffering and confusion where there previously was none. As not only the simple number of individual conscious subjects, but also the dimensionality of their phenomenal state-spaces is continuously increasing, this ocean is also *deepening*. For me, this is also a strong argument against creating artificial consciousness: We shouldn't add to this terrible mess before we have truly understood what actually is going on here. (Metzinger's emphases)

To the relatively observant eye there seems a disparity between Metzinger's conclusion of his book and Berkeley lecture and his online exchange with his colleagues. One could speculate that he felt more comfortable expressing his misgivings about the evolution of human consciousness in a cyber-convocation of his peers than in his high-profile opus and public appearances. In the former outlet, he pulls no punches when he says, "[T]here are aspects of the scientific world-view which may be damaging to our mental well-being, and *that* is what everybody intuitively feels" (Metzinger's emphasis; quoted in Trafford). This is a breathtaking statement for a well-credentialed philosopher to make (as was his inquiry quoted earlier about whether someone could *really* believe in determinism without going insane). What else could Metzinger mean by this utterance other than that well-used caveat of horror fiction that we are in danger of *knowing things we were not meant to know*? And the worst possible thing we could know—worse than knowing of our descent from a mass of microorganisms—is that we are nobodies not somebodies, puppets not people.

In a later book, *The Ego Tunnel: The Science of the Mind and the Myth of the Self* (2009), Metzinger confronts the problems involved with breaking the news to the average mortal that he or she is actually an average phenomenal self-model and not a person. He wants to assure people that this is not a secret too terrible to know but a truth that will set us free to be better human beings—once we settle on "What *is* a human being?" (since to Metzinger we are not what we think we are) and once we decide "What *should* a human become?" which is a knotty issue in light of *how* this decision should be made and *who* should make it. One of Metzinger's fears is that some people will sink into what he contemns as "vulgar materialism" and will conclude there is nothing for them in this life but survival, reproduction, and death, with the wise guys of the world saying to themselves in Metzinger's imagined soliloquy: "I don't understand what all these neuroexperts and consciousness philosophers are talking about, but the upshot seems pretty clear to me. The cat is out of the bag: We are gene-copying bio-robots, living out here on a lonely planet in a cold and empty physical universe. . . . I get the message, and you had better believe I will adjust my behavior to it." This strategy seems to be that of "heroic pessimists" like Miguel de Unamuno (see above), Joshua Foa Dienstag (see above), William Brashear (see above), Friedrich Nietzsche (see below), and any number of others who are already *in the know*. It is surely the strategy that Zapffe observed everyone to be following, the strategy that we must follow if we are to go on living as paradoxical beings who know the score but tamp down their consciousness to keep from knowing it too well. And it works well enough to keep us living as we have all these years. But could the vulgar materialist actually say that he or she is aware of being no one *as a fact* and still go on to pretend that he or she is someone? Would this not be another version of Metzinger's asking "Can one *really* believe in determinism without going insane?" Would such a mental state not only be "practically impossible" but totally impossible, just as it would be impossible for someone to say "I am nothing but a human puppet" and continue to live as he or she had lived before? It does not seem likely that you could ever see yourself as what you are per Metzinger. You would then know the horror and know that you know it. No longer would it be impossible to believe that you are nothing but a human puppet. What now? Answers: Now we go insane; now our species goes extinct in great epidemics of madness, because now we know that behind the scenes of life there is something pernicious that makes a nightmare of our world. Now we know that we are uncanny paradoxes. We know that nature has veered into the supernatural by fabricating a creature that cannot and should not exist by natural law, and yet does.

Metzinger's derision of vulgar materialism seems to rest on his optimistic belief that a future technology of consciousness will take us places where the "biological form of consciousness, as so far brought about by evolution on our planet" has not taken us. Beautiful and wonderful places, in Metzinger's admittedly well-informed and extraordinarily humane opinion. If we do not yet know what it is to be human, we have a ballpark idea of what it is to be humane. And Metzinger's preoccupation with the suffering of sentient beings matches that of any pessimist. The only difference is in his opinion of how we may eliminate or greatly ameliorate this suffering. In any event, while Metzinger has been audacious enough to state that "there are aspects of the scientific world-view which may be damaging to our mental well-being, and *that* is what everybody intuitively feels," he himself feels that everybody may not always feel that way and that the risk-benefit calculation will add up in our favor. What else could a neurophilosopher believe—that we should give up on ourselves and go extinct? Metzinger *must* have faith that once the rest of humanity has seen through the game, we will—in all sincerity and not as pretenders—play through to a world in which day by day, in every way, we are getting better and better. But that will take time—lots of it.

Even in the twenty-first century there are people who are incapable of abiding Darwin's theory unless they can reconcile it with their Creator and His design. Losing hold of these shielding eidolons would make them honor-bound to become unhinged, so they might say, because the world as they knew it would molder away in their palsied arms. Unprepared to receive the evidence, they run from it as any dreamer runs from a horror at his heels. They think that when this horror closes in on them they will die of madness to see its shape and know the touch of what they believe should not be. No doubt they would survive the experience, as so many have done before them. We have already weathered torrents of knowledge we were not meant to know yet were doomed to know. But how much more can we take? How will the human race feel about knowing that there is no human race—that there is no one? Would this be the end of the greatest horror tale ever told? Or might it be the reinstatement of the way things had been before we had lives of our own? For now, those who cannot abide even Darwin's theory without the Creator beside them seem to be safe. To quote Lovecraft on the subject of forbidden knowledge, "The sciences, each straining in its own direction, have hitherto harmed us little." But perhaps they will one day. Then the time may come to engage Zapffe's solution for saving the future from the curse of consciousness.

While we wait breathlessly for the test results of neuroscientists, people will still be knocking on your door to hawk some gimmick that will get you into their heaven. Naturally, these salesmen of the sacred do not have a clue regarding what things are like in heaven. Are there levels of heaven? Could someone be in heaven and not know it? And how often have we heard that many who are alive today will not "taste death" but instead will proceed directly to paradise when the rapture is upon us? This means that billions have already dropped dead with the unfulfilled hope of not having to suffer the throes of the unsaved.

What disillusionment must have incommoded them as they lay in extremis. Death would not be so bad if we could just disappear into it without any irksome preliminaries. But even those who expect the doors of heaven will open for them would prefer not to make their entrance after the physical trials of fighting for the life that God gave them. For the rest of us, the carousel of consciousness spins round and round, enlightening us only to the bloodcurdling probability that the worst will likely be saved for last. And even those who experience being alive as quite all right will have to live through such tacked-on endings as dying in a vehicular misadventure or lying abed sucking tubes.

Life is like a story that is spoiled by an unsatisfactory resolution of preceding events. There are no retroactive fix-ups for the corpses we shall become. "All's well that ends well" is well enough in the short run. "In the long run," as British economist John Maynard Keynes reportedly stated, "we are all dead." This does not sit well with us by way of an ending. But it is not as if we can choose how things will end for us, or for those yet unborn.

Unpersons

In his novel translated as *Moment of Freedom*, which was published ten years before his suicide in 1976, the Norwegian author and cultural critic Jens Bjørneboe wrote that "he who hasn't experienced a full depression alone and over a long period of time—he is a child." Aside from being indemonstrable in its validity, Bjørneboe's bilious discharge is also too restrictive in esteeming his personal class of suffering as the sole rite of passage to maturity as a conscious individual. Depression is only one of the psychopathologies that could be selected to make the bombastic claim that those who have not been affected by it in full and over a long period of time belong on a playground or in a playpen. But it is serviceable as an example of a psychological disease with which most people have had some experience in one or more of its varieties.

The statistically prevailing form of this disease is "atypical depression." Less common and more deadly is "melancholic depression." But whatever family name a given case of depression goes by, it has the same effect: sabotaging the network of emotions that make it seem as if you and your world mean something in some meaningful way. It is then you discover that your "old self" is not the inviolable thing you thought it was, nor is the rest of your "old reality." Both are as frail as our bodies and may be perforated as readily, deflating all that we thought meaningful about ourselves and our world.

What meaning our lives may seem to have is the work of a relatively well-constituted emotional system. As consciousness gives us the sense of being persons, our psychophysiology is responsible for making us into personalities who believe the existential game to be worth playing. We may have memories that are unlike those of anyone else, but without the proper emotions to liven those memories they might as well reside in a computer file as disconnected bits of data that never unite into a tailor-made individual for whom things seem to mean something. You can conceptualize that your life has meaning, but if you do not *feel* that meaning then your conceptualization is meaningless and you are nobody. The only matters of weight in our lives are colored by rainbows or auroras of regulated emotion which give one a sense of that "old self." But a major depression causes your emotions to evaporate, reducing you to a shell of a person standing alone in a drab landscape. Emotions are the substrate for the illusion of being a somebody among somebodies as well as for the substance we see, or think we see, in the world. Not knowing this ground-level truth of human existence is the equivalent of knowing nothing at all.

Although varying in intensity and nature, our emotions must seem ever-stable in their concatenation, just as a mixed drink must be made with specific ingredients in the same relative amounts so that they may blend into a vodka martini or a piña colada. United, our emotions ostensibly form a master self to which anomalous secondary selves may be compared for quality. Even as they are ever trading places or running together within us, clearly cut or amorphous, the experience of these biological twitterings makes it nearly impossible to doubt that they will stay with us as far as we can see into the future. Ask any couple who cannot imagine being without each other, a vital fiction without which, besides the fact that it often leads to procreation, no society could exist. It would have no reason to do so, because reason is merely the mouthpiece of emotion. Hume, who specialized in detaining his readers with obvious but unspoken realities, wrote in his *Treatise of Human Nature* (1739–40) that "reason is and ought only to be the slave of the passions." To free reason from this slavery would mean our becoming rationalists without a cause, paralytics crippled by mentation.

In speaking of depression and its defining effect of driving its victim to the point of caring nothing for anything, the American talk-show host Dick Cavett once remarked that "when you're downed by this affliction, if there were a curative magic wand on the table eight feet away, it would be too much trouble to go over and pick it up." No better elucidation has ever been proffered vis-à-vis the uselessness of reason in the absence of emotion. In the recumbence of depression, your information-gathering system collates its intelligence and reports to you these facts: (1) there is nothing to do; (2) there is nowhere to go; (3) there is nothing to be; (4) there is no one to know. Without meaning-charged emotions keeping your brain on the straight and narrow, you would lose your balance and fall into an abyss of lucidity. And for a conscious being, lucidity is a cocktail without ingredients, a crystal clear concoction that will leave you hungover with reality. In perfect knowledge there is only perfect nothingness, which is perfectly painful if what you want is meaning in your life.

William S. Burroughs said it rightly in his journals. Using his streetwise voice, he wrote: "Love? What is it? The most natural painkiller what there is." You may become curious, though, about what happened to that painkiller should depression take hold and expose your love—whatever its object—as just one of the many intoxicants that muddled your consciousness of the human tragedy. You may also want to take a second look at whatever struck you as a person, place, or thing of "beauty," a quality that lives only in the neurotransmitters of the beholder. (Aesthetics? What is it? A matter for those not depressed enough to care nothing about anything, that is, those who determine almost everything that is supposed to matter to us. Protest as you like, neither art nor an aesthetic view of life are distractions granted to everyone.) In depression, all that once seemed beautiful, or even startling and dreadful, is nothing to you. The image of a cloud-crossed moon is not in itself a purveyor of anything mysterious or mystical; it is only an ensemble of objects represented to us by our optical apparatus and perhaps processed as a memory.

This is the great lesson the depressive learns: Nothing in the world is inherently compelling. Whatever may be really "out there" cannot project itself as an affective experience. It is all a vacuous affair with only a chemical prestige. Nothing is either good or bad, desirable or undesirable, or anything else except that it is made so by laboratories inside us producing the emotions on which we live. And to live on our emotions is to live arbitrarily, inaccurately—imparting meaning to what has none of its own. Yet what other way is there to live? Without the ever-clanking machinery of emotion, everything would come to a standstill. There would be nothing to do, nowhere to go, nothing to be, and no one to know. The alternatives are clear: to live falsely as pawns of affect, or to live factually as depressives, or as individuals who know what is known to the depressive. How advantageous that we are not coerced into choosing one or the other, neither choice being excellent. One look at human existence is proof enough that our species will not be released from the stranglehold of emotionalism that anchors it to hallucinations. That may be no way to live, but to opt for depression would be to opt out of existence as we consciously know it.

Of course, individuals may recover from depression. But in that event they had better keep their consciousness of what they went through at heel. Otherwise they might start thinking that being alive is not as all right as they once thought it was when they were being shuttled about by a relatively well-constituted emotional system. The same applies to bodily systems of any kind, such as the immune system. Because when one of your systems goes haywire, you cannot function as you think you should. You may not even be able to think about anything except how much vomit, nasal mucus, phlegm, and watery stool you are discharging from your body when your immune system cannot withstand an onslaught from a viral or bacterial infection. If that is the way you were all the time, you could not go on as a well-constituted being, which means you could not go on as your old self, whatever that might have been. But chances are you will get better after one or more of your systems has gone haywire, and as a newly well-constituted being you will probably think, "I'm back to being the real me." However, you might as truthfully think that the real you is the one who was sick, not the one with well-constituted systems working together so cooperatively that you do not even notice them. You cannot go around thinking that the sick you is the real you, though, or you would turn into someone who suffers from chronic anxiety about all the ways your systems can go haywire. And *that* would become the real you.

Freaks of Salvation

Down-Going

"Depressing" is the adjective that ordinary folk affix to the life perspectives expressed by men such as Zapffe, Schopenhauer, and Lovecraft. The doctrines of world-class religions, dolorous as they may be, will never be thus defamed, because they are perceived to be "uplifting" by ordinary folk. Panglossian falsehoods convene the crowd; discouraging truths disperse it. The reason: It is depression not madness that cows us, demoralization not insanity that we dread, disillusionment of the mind not its derangement that imperils our culture of hope. An epidemic of depression would quiet those chattering voices in our heads, stopping life dead in its tracks. Providentially, we are endowed with enough manic enthusiasm to keep us plowing onward and making more of ourselves, bragging all the while about what billions of years of evolution have bidden every species to do anyway.

Zapffe, Schopenhauer, and Lovecraft fared well enough without surrendering themselves to life-affirming hysterics. This is a risky thing for anyone to do, but it is even more risky for writers, because anti-vital convictions will demote their work to a lower archive than that of wordsmiths who capitulate to positive thinking, or at least follow the maxim of being equivocal when speaking of our species. Everyone wants to keep the door open on the possibility that our lives are not MALIGNANTLY USELESS. Even highly educated readers do not want to be told that their lives are an evolutionary contingency—and nothing else—and that meaning is not what people think it means.[1]

For Schopenhauer, the fallout from his negations has been that he takes up far less floor space in the museum of modern thought than does his fellow German and antagonist Friedrich Nietzsche. Schopenhauer promises nothing but extinction for the individual following the postmortem recall of his "true nature" as a tiny parcel of the person-less and ever-roiling Will. Nietzsche borrows from religion and sermonizes that, although we will not be delivered into the afterlives of his ecclesiastic models, we must be willing in spirit to reprise this life again and again to its tiniest detail for all eternity.[2] As unappealing as repeating our lives even once may seem to some of us, we are not the ones who make a writer's reputation. This is the bailiwick of philosophical trendsetters, who discovered in Nietzsche the most spellbinding conundrum in the history of the mind. All the better for the perseverance of his corpus, which has supplied his exegetes with lifetimes of interpretation, argumentation, and general schismatic disharmony—all the purposeful activities that any religionist, with or without a deity, goes for.

Among other things, Nietzsche is famed as a promoter of human survival, just as long as enough of the survivors follow his lead as a *perverted pessimist*—one who has consecrated himself to loving life exactly because it is the worst thing imaginable, a sado-masochistic joyride through the twists and turns of being unto death. Nietzsche had no problem with human existence as a tragedy born of consciousness—parent of all horrors. This irregular pessimism is the antinomy of the "normal" pessimism of Schopenhauer, who is philosophy's red-headed stepchild because he is unequivocally on record as having said that being alive is not—and can never be—all right. Even his most admiring commentators, who do not find the technical aspects of his output to be off-putting, pull up when he openly waxes pessimistic or descants on the Will as an unselfconsciously stern master of all being, a cretinous force that makes everything do what it does, an imbecilic puppeteer that sustains the ruckus of our world. For these offenses, his stature is rather low compared to that of other major thinkers, as is that of all philosophers who bear an unconcealed grudge against life.

Although both Schopenhauer and Nietzsche spoke only to an audience of atheists, Schopenhauer erred—from a public relations stance—by not according human beings any special status among the world of things organic and inorganic or trucking in any meaning to our existence. Contra Schopenhauer, Nietzsche not only took religious readings of life seriously enough to deprecate them at great length, but was hell-bent on replacing them with goal-oriented values and a sense of meaning that even nonbelievers beg for like dogs—some project in which individuals may lose (or find) themselves.

Key to Nietzsche's popularity with atheistic amoralists is his materialistic mysticism, a sleight of mind that makes the world's meaninglessness into something meaningful and refashions fate into freedom before our eyes. As for Schopenhauer's cattle-drive existence in which an unknowable force (the Will) herds us along—that had to go. In the form of a diverting fiction, it might well be worth its conceptual weight in shivers of uncanny horror; but as a proposed reality, it is self-evidently depressing.

In confederacy with those whom he believed himself to have surpassed in the race toward an undefined destiny, Nietzsche did what he could to keep the human pageant strolling toward . . . wherever. Even though he had the clarity of mind to recognize that values did not grow on trees nor were writ on stone tablets, he duped himself into thinking that it was possible to create them. But how these values would be created and what they would be he could not say. After demolishing the life-rejecting faith of the Crucified, Nietzsche handed down his own commandments through the Antichrist-like messiah Zarathustra, who was groomed to take over Christianity's administration of the Western world and keep it afloat with counterfeit funds. Carrying around a sackload of unrealities from here to the eternal return, perhaps no one has ever been as "normal" as Nietzsche.

Why did this naysaying yes-man believe it was so important to keep up our esprit de corps by fending off the crisis of nihilism he predicted as forthcoming? Nietzsche could not have thought that at some point people were going to turn their heads to the wall due to a paucity of values, which may run low sometimes but will never run out. Those who were supposed to have gone running into the streets in a funk of foundationlessness have survived without a hitch: nihilistic or not, they still carried home an armful of affirmations. To publish or perish is not a question that professional thinkers have to think about for long. And whatever moral crisis lies ahead will have to take place in an environment undamaged by nihilism.

As a threat to human continuance, nihilism is as dead as God. (See James E. Edwards, *The Plain Sense of Things: The Fate of Religion in the Age of Normal Nihilism*, 1997.) To do away with one's values is rather impossible, an ideal to be imagined until one is seized by a natural end. Schopenhauer, a virtuoso of life's devaluation, knew that. But Nietzsche fretted about those unborn values he imagined his work would inspire, worrying over them as would an expectant parent concerned that his name, his blood, and his codes both moral and genetic be bodied forth by generations fading over the hills of time. Leaving no values that posterity could not cook up on its own, Nietzsche was withal an admirable opponent of enslaving values from the past. In their place, he left nothing. And for that we should thank him.

Possibly stolen from Nietzsche is what has been tagged as Zapffe's Paradox—where human beings deceive themselves into thinking their lives are something they are not, namely, worth living. In his *Birth of Tragedy* (1872), Nietzsche wrote:

> It is an eternal phenomenon: The insatiable will always find a way, by means of an illusion spread over things, to detain its creatures in life and to compel them to live on. One is chained by the Socratic joy of knowing and the delusion of being able thereby to heal the eternal wound of existence; another is ensnared by art's seductive veil of beauty fluttering before his eyes; yet another by the metaphysical consolation that beneath the whirl of appearances eternal life flows on indestructibly—to say nothing of the more common and almost more forceful illusions the will has at hand at every moment. (*The Birth of Tragedy*, translation by Walter Kaufmann)

One can only rue the fact that Nietzsche did not unfold this observation into a life-negating pessimism, as did Zapffe, rather than into a pessimism that teaches us "what it means 'to be frightened'"—"a pessimism of *strength*." But by the time Nietzsche wrote these words in his "Attempt at a Self-Criticism," published as a preface to the 1886 edition of *The Birth of Tragedy*, it was too late for his conversion, or reconversion, to a purist's pessimism. He had already hit the road toward what would indeed frighten average mortals, a set of persons in which he did not include himself, or did not want to include himself. Zapffe did include himself among this set, and his analysis of those who opted out of it fits Nietzsche to a tee: "In such cases, a person may be obsessed with destructive joy, dislodging the whole artificial apparatus of his life and starting with rapturous horror to make a clean sweep of it. The horror stems from the loss of all sheltering values; the rapture from his by now ruthless identification and harmony with our nature's deepest secret—the biological unsoundness, the enduring disposition for doom." In its life-negating aspect, pessimism lost a great champion when Nietzsche became joyful about the frightful, a psychic stand that in itself is a paradox if ever there was one.

Futurephilia

After Nietzsche, pessimism was revaluated by some, rejuvenated by others, and still spurned as depressing by average mortals, who continued to recite their most activating illusion: "Today is better than yesterday and tomorrow will be better still." While being alive may be all right for the moment, the future is really the place for a person to be, at least as far as we care to see into it. Lovecraft is a figure of exceeding intrigue here because much of his fiction is based on a clutch of godlike beings whose very presence in the universe degrades the idea of betterment in human life into a cosmic miscalculation. Azathoth the Blind Idiot God, Nyarlathotep the Crawling Chaos, Cthulhu the Dead Dreamer: These are some of the entities that symbolize the Lovecraftian universe as a place without sense, meaning, or value. This perspective is memorably expressed in Lovecraft's poem "Nemesis":

> I have seen the dark universe yawning
> Where the black planets roll without aim,
> Where they roll in their horror unheeded,
> Without knowledge or lustre or name.

These lines and others like them are not cordially received by votaries of the future, who will deny the vision of this quatrain or treat it as only a literary diversion, which in effect is all that it is, along with every glyph and scribble ever recorded since Gilgamesh sojourned in the land of the dead. More popular among fans of occult fiction are the canonical texts of Theosophy, Anthroposophy, Scientology, G. I. Gurdjieff's Fourth Way, the Kabbalah, and so on.

Among this select bibliography of arcane studies should be added the curiosa of "transhumanism," a zealous type of utopian thought underwritten by the belief that day by day we are getting closer and closer to building a better human. Like defenders of libertarian free will, transhumanists believe we can make ourselves into who we are today and, should the mood strike us, remake ourselves into who we will be tomorrow. But this is impossible. Because of evolution, we *got made*. We did not bring ourselves out of the primeval ooze. And everything we have done since we became a species has been a consequence of being made. No matter what we do, it will be what we were made to do—and nothing else. We may try to make something of ourselves, but we cannot take over our own evolution. We made antibiotics because we were made to be the kind of beings who make such things as antibiotics. That changed our condition without changing us, being as we are the kind of creatures who do things and make things, yet are not in the business of getting ourselves made. Nature had plans for us and still does. One of those plans seems to be the dream of transhumanism, which may just be a plan to unmake us. If so, we are not going to alter that plan simply because we imagine we can make a new person with new evolutionary programs that we will write. We know how to survive and we know how to reproduce. We know how to do many things, but we do not know what to do with ourselves that is over and above our preset patterns. Some of us only think we do. We are not even part of the process of *getting remade*. We are following orders, as we have always done, that nature is forever barking out.

As humans conceived transhumanism, transhumanists have conceived posthumanism, a far-off condition in which none will live as we have all these years but will have evolved into something beyond our present selves. And then what? Have the transhumanists really thought this through? And how could they? We have no idea where our next thought is coming from, not excluding the thoughts of transhumanists. We do have thoughts, but we do not know what we are going to make of them. How, then, are we to know what to make of ourselves? Even posthumans would still be caught without a clue in the MALIGNANTLY USELESS rut of being. And notwithstanding the cachet of a future paradise that drifts about the scheme of a posthumanity, it is not as if this idea was first conceived in the late twentieth century. In its search for the "good," or at least the better, it recapitulates our most ancient fantasies. Like a song we feel we have heard even though we are hearing it for the first time, the machinations of transhumanists serenade us from the past, and even from a pre-historical Eden of perfect existence, depending on whether or not one likes their song or cares for a homecoming in Eden. But these machinations may also sound like something that was over the moment it began—old, stale, nothing.

By definition, transhumanists are dissatisfied with what we are as a species. Naturally, they think that being alive is all right—so much so, in fact, that they cannot stand the idea of not being alive and have envisioned strategies for staying alive forever. Their problem is that they need being alive to be vastly more all right than it is. And the power of positive thinking is not enough to get them where they want to go. They are past all that, or would like to be. They are also past believing in God or an afterlife of eternal bliss. To a believer, transhumanism would be a useless appendage to what they already believe, as well as an offense against *Him who made us as He made us*, with nature as the go-between, and long ago laid down the ways in which we can make ourselves better and better. Those ways may be hard to follow, but the alternative is the despair of living without hope of an unimaginably better future. For the believer's alternative to despair, transhumanists have substituted their own. Yet while transhumanists operate on the assumption that we will massively profit when we self-mutate into posthumans, the upshot of their program is still unknown. It could begin a dynamic new chapter in the history of our race, or it could trumpet the end of us. Either way, the prophesized leap will be jumpstarted by all manner of gadgetry and will somehow involve artificial intelligence, nanotechnology, genetic engineering, and other habiliments of high technology. These will be the instruments of the New Genesis, the Logos of tomorrow. Or so says one desperate group of scientific thinkers.

For a less desperate group of scientific thinkers, posthumanism is a chimera and will not occur: we will go on with our lives as stumblebums of the same old story. Understandably, the transhumanist view is more arousing than old-fogy humanism precisely because an apocalypse has been inserted as a wild card. (See Bill Joy's "The future doesn't need us," *Wired*, 2000.) In this sense, transhumanism is a secular retelling of the Christian rapture, and some of its true believers foresee it as happening within the lifetime of *many who are alive today*, just as the early Christians believed in an impending Judgment Day. Perhaps at some time in the future, such predictions will not have to take into account eschatological contingencies and we can all relax, secure in the knowledge that day by day, in every way, we are *getting made* better and better.

Transhumanism encapsulates a long-lived error among the headliners of science: In a world without a destination, we cannot even break ground on our Tower of Babel, and no amount of rush and hurry on our part will change that. That we are going nowhere is not a curable condition; that we must go nowhere at the fastest possible velocity just might be curable, though probably not. And what difference would it make to retard our progress to nowhere? Zapffe reviled technological advancements and the discoveries to which they led, since those interested in such things would be cheated of the distraction of finding them out for themselves at whatever pace they chose. Every human activity is a tack for killing time, and it seemed criminal to him that people should have their time already killed for them by explorers, inventors, and innovators of every stripe. Zapffe himself reserved his leisure hours for that most purposive time-killer—mountain climbing.

As we should know by now, it is as easy to make fun of religious or scientific visionaries as it is to idolize them. Which attitude is adopted depends on whether or not they tell you what you want to hear. Given the excitements promised by transhumanism, odds are that it will collect a clientele of hopefuls who want to get a foot in the future, for nobody doubts that tomorrow will be better than today. Yet one possibility transhumanists have not wrestled with is that the ideal being standing at the end of evolution may deduce that the best of all possible worlds is useless, if not malignant, and that the self-extinction of our future selves would be the optimal course to take. They have also failed to reflect upon those aspects of the scientific worldview that may be damaging to our mental well-being. In that case, transhumanists will not get as far as stage one in their mission before they must head back to the conspiracy against the human race and be reeducated in the art of self-deceptive paradox.

———

Many people in this world are always looking to science to save them from something. But just as many, or more, prefer old and reputable belief systems and their sectarian offshoots for salvation. So they trust in the deity of the Old Testament, an incontinent dotard who soiled Himself and the universe with His corruption, a low-budget divinity passing itself off as the genuine article. (Ask the Gnostics.) They trust in Jesus Christ, a historical cipher stitched together like Frankenstein's monster out of parts robbed from the graves of messiahs dead and buried—a savior on a stick. They trust in the virgin-pimping Allah and his Drum Major Mohammed, a prophet-come-lately who pioneered a new genus of humbuggery for an emerging market of believers that was not being adequately served by existing religious products. They trust in anything that authenticates their importance as persons, tribes, societies, and particularly as a species that will endure in this world and perhaps in an afterworld that may be uncertain in its reality and unclear in its layout, but which sates their craving for values *not of this earth*—that depressing, meaningless place their consciousness must sidestep every day.[3] Sure enough, then, writers such as Zapffe, Schopenhauer, and Lovecraft only wrote their ticket to marginality when they failed to affirm the worth and wonder of humanity, the validity of its values (whether eternal or provisional), and, naturally, a world without a foreseeable end, or at least a world whose end no one wants to see.

Buddhanomics

Like many faiths and philosophies that go against the Western grain, Buddhism has baited legions of those in the cognitive vanguard. This religion is to be praised both for its lack of an almighty god-figure and for its gateway teaching of the Four Noble Truths. The first of these truths is the equation between the life of the average mortal and *dukkha* (roughly "suffering," but really whatever state of ill-being you care to name). The second is that craving anything in this world—good physical or mental health, long life, happiness, or even the elimination of craving—is the provenance of all suffering. Buddhism's Two Noble Truths sit atop a religion that is incomparable for its soteriological prescriptions. These begin with the Third Noble Truth, that there is a way out of suffering, and continue with the Fourth Noble Truth—that the way to be released from the leg-irons of suffering is to follow the Noble Eightfold Path, a list of things-to-do and things-not-to-do much like the Old Testament Decalogue, except not as plainly spoken or easygoing.

By laying a heavy emphasis on human life as something that needs to be drastically reworked due to the First Noble Truth of *dukkha*, Buddhism has been disparaged as pessimistic. Naturally, Buddhists deny that their religion is any such thing. It is a system for uncovering our true nature—and nothing else. Nevertheless, Buddhism and pessimism cannot be pried loose from each other. The likeness between them is simply too pronounced to be overlooked. Buddhists claim that they are not pessimists but realists. Pessimists make the same claim. Buddhists also claim they are not pessimists because their founder's teachings showed a way out of suffering for all sentient beings. Pessimists also have their plans toward this end. Ask Zapffe. Ask Mainländer. Or ask Schopenhauer about working toward a denial of the Will, which is the cause of *dukkha*, the facets of which have been identified by the Ven. Dr. Thanat Inthisan, and many other Buddhist wise men, to include "dissatisfaction, imperfection, pain, impermanence, disharmony, discomfort, irritation, war, incompleteness, insufficiency" as well as the physical and mental suffering of "birth, decay, disease, and death." Calling oneself a realist is as much the privilege of the

Buddhist as it is that of the pessimist. But to designate Buddhism as anything but pessimism is just a matter of semantics. The only real discrepancy between the two philosophies is that hundreds of millions of Buddhists have accepted *dukkha* as the primary reality of existence. How queer that pessimists cannot boast such numbers. While it is not perceived as such by followers of this ancient religion, the disavowed fact is this: *Buddhism is pessimism.* Yet whereas the pessimism that dares speak its name is met with near universal incredulity, Buddhism may advertise as truth what no pessimist can prove—that suffering is basic to human existence and it should be the work of our lives to liberate ourselves from its grasp. This double standard is flatly an outrage of logic. Of course, one must always keep in mind the latitude religions are permitted by virtue of the fact that their beliefs cannot be objectively corroborated and must be taken on faith, pessimistic though they may be.

Unlike the practical uniformity of pessimists, not all Buddhists line up on the same side even in some of the broadest aspects of their beliefs. (Ask Stephen Batchelor, author of *Buddhism Without Beliefs*, 1998.) For instance, there are differing opinions among Buddhists regarding *anatta* ("no-self") and how it relates to reincarnation, because if there is no self, then what is it that gets reborn? To this question are loads of learned exegeses. One belief held by many Buddhists is that human beings are bits and pieces that add up to nothing, things of parts, hollow puppets—non-beings that think they are something they are not. Other Buddhists believe that this is only half the story: things both exist and do not exist; things are not what they seem nor are they other than they seem; things are many and they are one; everything is nothing, including nothing.

Along with every other religion, Buddhism is a compilation of do-it-yourself projects, and some of them, such as Pure Land Buddhism, are only lightweight versions of the faiths scantily detailed here. This principle has its parallel in every philosophy, ideology, and bag of myths that has ever been presented to the world. Because no two minds are contoured alike, no one system or collocation of systems will ever be sized to fit all. If truth is what you seek, then the examined life will only take you on a long ride to the limits of solitude and leave you by the side of the road with *your* truth and nothing else. This gives leave to believers in anything to have an opinion about whatever they like. For Buddhists, though, this is a problem, because clinging to opinions, or whatever else ordinary folk cling to, is an obstruction to becoming a right-minded practitioner of Buddhism. But you can believe that in Buddhist law, or in someone's opinion of Buddhist law, there are allowance conditions that stipulate when clinging is not really clinging. All religions must have allowance conditions or they would implode upon themselves by the pressure of their own doctrines.

Since Buddhism's only objective is attaining enlightenment, that high road to nirvana (see below), it is at one with other religions in pitching a brighter future for believers in deliverance from the woes of this world. One problem: Human beings are rarely so sensitive to the woes of this world that they feel a pressing need to reject all cravings for the pleasures of this world, as Buddhism would have them do. And it seems that any amount of pleasure is pleasure enough to get us to keep the faith that being alive is all right for everyone, or almost everyone, and will certainly be all right for any children we cause to be delivered into this world. How else could we stave off a craving to become extinct?

The good news for Buddhism as a for-profit religion is that there are more than enough people who are sensitive to the woes of this world, and who are willing to let go of their cravings for its pleasures, to seek the extinction of their everyday selves in the oasis of nirvana (absolute beatitude, permanent detachment from all attachment to a benighted way of life, a step-off from the cycle of death and rebirth, or whatever happy thing you like). Reaching this oasis may happen during an individual's lifetime or could be delayed for the next round of reincarnation, when one will have another chance to cut oneself loose from karma, a doctrine that Buddhists borrowed from the Jains and the Hindus.

Leaving aside reincarnation and the mental gymnastics it foists on the believer, the central focus of Buddhism's three-ring circus remains the state or non-state of enlightenment, which, like Jesus' ethereal theme park, is an appetizing carrot suspended in the darkness of life's suffering, if you are one of those who are sensitive enough to life's suffering. However, to get that carrot you must first kowtow to dogmatic authorities that cannot be told apart from those of Christianity, spiritual ministers who strong-arm you to do some things and not do others under pain of not becoming enlightened.

But here is the real catch: If you want to become enlightened you will never become enlightened, because in Buddhism wanting things is just the thing that keeps you from getting the thing you want. Less circuitously, if you want to end your suffering, you will never end your suffering. This is the "wanting paradox," or "paradox of desire," and Buddhists are at the ready with both rational and non-rational propositions as to why this paradox is not a paradox. How to understand these propositions is past understanding, because, per Buddhism, there is nothing to understand and no one to understand it. And as long as you think there is something to understand and someone to understand it, you are doomed. Trying for this understanding is the most trying thing of all. Yet trying *not* to try for it is just as trying. There is nothing more futile than to consciously look for something to save you. But consciousness makes this fact seem otherwise. Consciousness makes it seem as if (1) there is something to do; (2) there is somewhere to go; (3) there is something to be; (4) there is someone to know. This is what makes consciousness the parent of all horrors, the thing that makes us try to do something, go somewhere, be something, and know someone, such as ourselves, so that we can escape our MALIGNANTLY USELESS being and think that being alive is all right rather than that which *should not be*.

The Buddhist "wanting paradox" might be regarded as correlative to Zapffe's Paradox (the paradox of conscious beings attempting to disclaim their consciousness of the flagrantly joyless possibilities of their lives). The difference between Buddhism's Paradox and Zapffe's Paradox is that the latter is not amenable to being resolved, explained away, or denied, either rationally or non-rationally. It can only be left unacknowledged so that we can continue to live as we have all these years, or at least as long as we can before the paradox demands acknowledgment to the extent that we cannot live with ourselves as beings whose existence is terribly false and paradoxical, things so uncanny that we can no longer even look at one another or hold our heads steady. Until that day, we will keep living as obstinate selves who affirm that being conscious is an enlightened way to be and that being alive is all right.

In the marketplace of salvation, enlightenment seems the best buy ever offered, if only at first blush. Rather than floundering in a world that is not worth the emptiness it is written on, you may sign up to attain a conclusive vision of what's what and what's not. Broadly speaking, enlightenment is the correction of our consciousness and the establishment of a state of being in which muddy illusion is washed away and a diamond of understanding shines through. This is the supreme desert . . . if it may be had, if it has any reality outside the pat or cryptic locutions that advert to it.

Millions of people have spent their lives, and some have even lost their minds, trying to win enlightenment without ever comprehending, as they sucked their last breath, what it was they had gambled to get. Had they attained enlightenment without being aware of it? Are there stages of enlightenment (maybe, depending on the type of Buddhism to which one subscribes) and how far had they gotten? In his *One Taste: Daily Reflections on Integral Spirituality*, Ken Wilber, a widely known and highly influential multidisciplinary scholar and theorist of spiritual traditions, reported that he asked one Zen Buddhist master "how many truly enlightened—deeply enlightened—Japanese Zen masters there were alive today." The master replied, "Not more than a dozen." Another Zen master put the number of fully enlightened individuals in the East at one thousand throughout Zen Buddhism's history. Wilber's conclusion: "Thus, without in any way belittling the truly stunning contributions of the glorious Eastern traditions, the point is fairly straightforward: radical transformative spirituality is extremely rare, anywhere in history, and anywhere in the world. (The numbers for the West are even more depressing. I rest my case.)" Indeed, enlightenment by Buddhism truly seems to be a well-defended redoubt whose location cannot be triangulated by speech, the only rule being that if you have to ask yourself if you have arrived, then it is certain you have not.

Ego-Death

As we have seen, Buddhism's ways and means to illumination are full of shortcomings and vexations. Nevertheless, it does seem that some have reached a state corresponding to that of Buddhist enlightenment as delineated in scads of scriptures, diaries, copyrighted publications, and public depositions. Curiously, these charmed individuals appear to have come to this state unwarned, sometimes as a result of physical trauma or a Near-Death Experience (NDE).

Perhaps the capital instance of *enlightenment by accident* is that of U. G. Krishnamurti. Although U. G. gave no credence to any doctrine of awakening, he claimed to have experienced "clinical death" at the age of forty-nine, after which he returned to life as the kind of being glorified in the literature of enlightenment. Through his clinical death and its aftermath, which he called a "calamity" due to the pain and confusion he felt during this process, U. G. was transformed.

For decades prior to his calamity, U. G. was an earnest seeker who sought enlightenment by effort rather than by accident. But his efforts got him nowhere, and he ended up financially drained. By chance he met a woman who was willing to support him, and for years he was something of a layabout. It was while living with this woman that his calamity struck. Upon recovering from his calamity, he had what he once looked for and in disgust had given up trying to find. U. G. was no longer the person he once was, for now he was someone whose ego had been erased. In this state, he had all the self-awareness of a tree frog. To his good fortune, he had no problem with his new way of functioning. He did not need to accept it, since by his report he had lost all sense of having an ego that needed to accept or reject anything. How could someone who had ceased to participate in the commerce of selves, who had inadvertently forfeited his personhood, believe or not believe in anything so outlandish as enlightenment . . . or any other spiritual vendibles, none of which are evident in the least and all of which are as outmoded as the gods of antiquity or tribal deities with names that sound comical to believers in "real" religions?[4]

While it may seem that U. G. had become a zombie, in a nonphilosophical sense, his post-calamity life was nothing like that.

Until his death in 2007, he spent much of his time berating people who came to him for spiritual succor. Cantankerous and opinionated as some of the more famous masters of Zen Buddhism, U. G. arrestingly and often humorously told those who had made the pilgrimage to his door that everything they believed about anything was wrong. Few of them could get a word in edgewise as he assassinated all that humanity has ever held sacred. Some would view U. G.'s disrespect for spirituality to be in happy rapport with the nature of enlightenment, which they have been taught cannot be pinned down by doctrines of any kind. Others would deny this assertion, perhaps because they have been indoctrinated to believe that both irreverence and deference toward the transcendent are off the mark once one has "awakened." Neither side of this squabble would have tempted U. G. What he enunciated in interviews is the near impossibility of human beings, except perhaps one in a billion, to think of themselves only as animals born to survive and reproduce.

As Zapffe had written long before U. G. began slurring every belief in the world, mental activity beyond the basic programs of our animalism has led only to suffering. ("In the beast, suffering is self-confined; in man, it knocks holes into a fear of the world and a despair of life.") U. G. never spoke of a solution for what consciousness has made of our lives. We are captured by illusions and there is *no way out*. That U. G. came upon a way out, as he told his countless interrogators, was nothing but luck, nothing he knew anything about or could pass on to others. Yet they still came to him and asked for his help. To their pleas he immediately replied he could not help them, nor could they help themselves. No help could be had from any sector in which they searched. They could seek deliverance their entire lives and make it all the way to their deathbeds with nothing but the same useless questions and useless answers with which they began. U. G. had his, but they would never get theirs.

So why should they go on living? Naturally, no one bluntly posed this question to U. G. But they had his answer: There is no "you" that lives, only a body going about its business of being alive and obeying biology. Whenever someone asked U. G. how they could become like him, he always replied it would be impossible for them even to desire to become like him, because their motive for wanting to be like him was self-interested, and as long as they believed in a self that was interested in canceling itself, that self would want to keep itself alive and thus would not want to know ego-death. Whatever people did with their lives was of no concern to U. G., as he tirelessly recapitulated to those who engaged him in conversation. He did not see his himself as a sage with spiritual merchandise to sell. That was for the mountebanks of salvation who infested the world with their codified sects, each baring its teeth to defend some trademarked trumpery.

U. G. is not the only known case of enlightenment by accident. A quite singular instance of the experience in question is that of the Australian physicist John Wren-Lewis, a non-religious man who nearly died of poisoning and woke up in a hospital in a state of enlightenment he never requested or pained himself to earn. Both U. G. and Wren-Lewis publicly emphasized the unsought nature of their illumination. Both also warned against gurus with recipes for enlightenment. In talks with interviewers, U. G., who did not write books, lambasted every religious figure known to humanity as a fraud. After his own awakening, Wren-Lewis became overtaken by the possible connection between enlightenment phenomena and NDEs. His way of thinking, for what it might be worth, parallels

Zapffe's in that it identifies ordinary consciousness as a "basic malfunction" that "is some kind of inflation or hyperactivity of the psychological survival-system" ("Aftereffects of Near-Death Experience: A Survival Mechanism Hypothesis," *The Journal of Transpersonal Psychology*, 1994). He derived hope that this malfunction could be repaired from the fact that NDE-ers are sometimes relieved from death anxiety by having their egoistic consciousness commuted into an "impersonal consciousness" of an enlightened sort. None of this is to say that reports of NDE experience are any more believable than, let us say, those of alien abductions. Leniently interpreted, however, they may foretell that our species has an outside chance at a future without extinction-fearing egos. Since the human race will never do the honorable thing and abort itself, perhaps someday we will be individually fixed to die without an unbecoming fight to the death.

A stereotypical report of an NDE is related by businessman and author Tem Horwitz in his essay "My Death: Reflections on My Journey into Non-Being" (*Death and Philosophy*, ed. Jeff Malpas and Robert C. Solomon, 1998). In the course of describing his transformation following his death as a result of anaphylactic shock in September 1995, Horwitz wrote: "There was no vestige of self-importance left. It felt like death had obliterated my ego, the attachments I had, my history, and who I had been. Death had been very democratic. It had eliminated innumerable distinctions. With one bold stroke my past had been erased. I had no identity in death. It didn't stay erased—some would say that this was the real tragedy—but it was erased for a time. Gone was my personal history with all of its little vanities. The totality of myself was changed. The 'me' was much smaller and much more compact than it had been. All that there was, was right in front of me. I felt incredibly light. Personality was a vanity, an elaborate delusion, a ruse." Compared with U. G. Krishnamurti and John Wren-Lewis, Horwitz had only a slight case of ego-death following his clinical death. Soon afterward he was "cured" of the erasure of his identity.

Another statistic of long-term ego-death was Suzanne Segal, who one day found she had become bereft of herself. After years of seeking a cure to the unease this experience had set off in her—it would seem that not everybody is at peace with being nobody—she wrote *Collision with the Infinite: A Life Beyond the Personal Self* (1996). The following year she died of a brain tumor at the age of forty-two. Although no link was established between her diseased brain and the disappearance of her ego, cerebral tumors causing altered states of consciousness and changes in personality are not unknown.[5]

Unlike U. G. but similar to Wren-Lewis, Segal sought answers to her transformation in spiritual traditions that addressed egoless experience. Unlike Wren-Lewis but similar to U. G., Segal had pursued a spiritual practice, Transcendental Meditation, before she became the beneficiary of enlightenment by accident. Segal lost her ego two years after discontinuing TM, which she performed for eight years. In an interview, she stated that she did not feel meditation played a role in the loss of her self-identity. U. G. was in agreement with Segal. After years of pursuing ego-death through meditation, he railed against this procedure as pointless and perhaps harmful.

For most of humanity, including that part which studies consciousness, the phenomenon of ego-death is not enthralling, or even well marked as a human experience. Ordinary folk have all their big questions answered to their satisfaction by some big book. And cognitive psychologists, philosophers of mind, and neuroscientists have their reputations to consider as high priests of the noosphere. Quite naturally, then, almost no one figures their time to be ill spent in bickering about some point of scripture or a psycho-philosophical poser rather than in sizing up some superlative individuals who have called into question what we are or what we might be aside from slaves of our egos. Regardless of the life stories of U. G., Wren-Lewis, and Suzanne Segal, ego-death is a state that has nothing but anecdotal evidence to support it, which groups this phenomenon with mystical experiences and revealed religions. As one might imagine, though, ego-death is laden with about as much mass appeal as physical death. It has been eyeballed as an ideal only by a minuscule number of our species who feel there is something wrong with ego-life, which they conceive as an uncanny masquerade where things they would rather not see are behind every false face. To everyone else, life is life and death is death. We are not sold on impersonal survival. It would negate all that we are, or think we are, for what are we but egos itching to survive? And once our egos have been deposed, what would be left of us? By all recorded accounts, everything would be left except what Horwitz called "a vanity, an elaborate delusion, a ruse."

Some would say that if human beings must exist, the condition in which U. G., Wren-Lewis, and Segal found themselves is the optimum model, one in which everyone's ego has been overthrown and our consciousness of ourselves as persons goes up in smoke. As Segal tried to explain what had happened to her:

> The experience of living without a personal identity, without an experience of being somebody, an "I" or a "me," is exceedingly difficult to describe, but it is absolutely unmistakable. It can't be confused with having a bad day or coming down with the flu or feeling upset or angry or spaced out. When the personal self disappears, there is no one inside who can be located as being you. The body is

only an outline, empty of everything of which it had previously felt so full.

The mind, body, and emotions no longer referred to anyone—there was no one who thought, no one who felt, no one who perceived. Yet the mind, body, and emotions continued to function unimpaired; apparently they did not need an "I" to keep doing what they always did. Thinking, feeling, perceiving, speaking, all continued as before, functioning with a smoothness that gave no indication of the emptiness behind them. No one suspected that such a radical change had occurred. All conversations were carried on as before; language was employed in the same manner. Questions could be asked and answered, cars driven, meals cooked, books read, phones answered, and letters written. (*Collision with the Infinite*)

As the ego-dead, so we might imagine, we would continue to know pain in its various forms—that is the essence of existence—but we would not be cozened by our egos to take it personally, an attitude that converts an individual's pain into conscious suffering. Naturally, we would still have to feed, but we would not be omnivorous gourmands who eat for amusement, gorging down everything in nature and turning to the laboratory for more. As for reproduction, who can say? Animals are driven to copulate, and even as the ego-dead we would not be severed from biology, although we would not be unintelligently ruled by it, as we are now. As a corollary of not being unintelligently ruled by biology, neither would we sulk over our extinction, as we do now. Why raise another generation destined to climb aboard the evolutionary treadmill? But then, why not raise another generation of the ego-dead? For those who do not perceive either their pleasures or their pains as belonging to them, neither life nor death would be objectionable or not objectionable, desirable or not desirable, all right or not all right. We would be the ego-dead, the self-less, and, dare we say, the enlightened.

A depiction of what our lives might be like in such a state would seem to have been recorded in the eightieth section of the *Tao Te Ching*, perhaps to show up humankind's modus vivendi by daydreaming about one not of this earth.

> Let all lands be small
> And their people few,
> So they have no need
> For time-saving machines.
>
> Let them keep their minds
> On the coming of death
> And never stray far
> From where they were born.
>
> Should they have boats
> Or carts to go traveling,
> Let there be nothing
> They would want to see.
>
> Should they have weapons,
> Let them be put someplace
> Out of everyone's sight
> To rust and grow useless.
>
> Let each person's duties
> Be no more than may be
> Kept track of by tying knots
> On a short piece of string.

Let their food be enough
And their clothes drab,
Their homes decent shelter
And their lives unremarkable.

If the next land is so close
That they can hear its
Dogs barking at night and its
Roosters crowing at dawn . . .

Let them get old and die
Rather than be troubled
By the least curiosity
To have a look over there.

One might think of this not as a description of an ego-dead society but of one that is dead all the way. But one would be wrong. Wherever there are those who "get old and die," there are also those who live in wait for age and for death—youths and infants and infants-to-be. And because none of them should take his fate personally in the Taoist scripture quoted above, why not take it as it comes? Of course, this would not occur to the ego-dead, just as it does not occur to species of a lower order that recycle themselves as nature bids them. The ego-dead would be back to where our race began—surviving, reproducing, dying. Nature's way would be restored in all its mindlessness and puppetry.

But even if ego-death is regarded as the optimum model for human existence, one of liberation from ourselves, it still remains a compromise with being, a concession to the blunder of creation itself. We should be able to do better, and we can. To have our egos killed off is second-best to killing off death and all the squalid byplay that flitters around it. So let all lands be small, and let them grow smaller and smaller until no lands are left where any human footstep need press itself upon the earth.

At the height of her ego-death, Segal was ecstatic twenty-four hours a day. She also began to speak of what she called the "vastness," a term that sounds as if it belongs in one of Lovecraft's tales of cosmic horror. To Segal, the vastness was a unitary phenomenon that comprised all existence. As she wrote, "The purpose of human life has been revealed. The vastness created these human circuitries in order to have an experience of itself out of itself that it couldn't have without them." Living in the vastness as she did, nothing was useless to Segal because it served the purposes of the vastness. For her, it also felt good once she had gotten over her initial fear of being a tool of the vastness rather than a person. However, toward the end of her life, as American psychotherapist and Buddhist Stephan Bodian recounts in his afterword to *Collision with the Infinite*, Segal began to have more intense experiences in which "the vastness became even vaster for itself." This new phase of the vastness both distressed her emotionally and sapped her physical energy until she died from her unsuspected brain tumor not long afterward.

Like Segal's vastness, Schopenhauer's Will has the same purpose in mind for human beings—to use our "circuitries" to acquire some kind of knowledge of its mindless self. For Schopenhauer, though, the self-seeking Will does not feel good to human beings except during moments when we temporarily satisfy its universal ravening as it emerges within us. Why the vastness or the Will should want to use us in this way is a mystery. Both of these meta-realities do serve the purpose of making sense of human life in their own way. But whether they make us feel good does not seem to matter to either of them. We are just vehicles; they are the drivers. And wherever we are going, as Segal and Schopenhauer have assured us, along with every other individual whose consciousness has been opened to the vastness by whatever name or nature, we must keep in mind that we are not what we think we are. Taking things a step further, Professor Nobody would teach us that neither is our world what we think it is, lecturing with a flamboyant dispassion on the omnipresence of the *infernal* in "The Eyes That Never Blink."

Mist on a lake, fog in thick woods, a golden light shining on wet stones—such sights make it all very easy. Something lives in the lake, rustles through the woods, inhabits the stones or the earth beneath them. Whatever it may be, this *something* lies just out of sight, but not out of vision for the eyes that never blink. In the right surroundings our entire being is made of eyes that dilate to witness the haunting of the universe. But really, do the right surroundings have to be so obvious in their spectral atmosphere?

Take a cramped waiting room, for instance. Everything there seems so well anchored in normalcy. Others around you talk ever so quietly; the old clock on the wall is sweeping aside the seconds with its thin red finger; the window blinds deliver slices of light from the outside world and shuffle them with shadows. Yet at any time and in any place, our bunkers of banality may begin to rumble. You see, even in a stronghold of our fellow beings we may be subject to abnormal fears that would land us in an asylum if we voiced them to another. Did we just feel some presence that does not belong among us? Do our eyes see something in a corner of that room in which we wait for we know not what?

Just a little doubt slipped into the mind, a little trickle of suspicion in the bloodstream, and all those eyes of ours, one by one, open up to the world and see its horror. Then: no belief or body of laws will guard you; no friend, no counselor, no appointed personage will save you; no locked door will protect you; no private office will hide you. Not even the solar brilliance of a summer day will harbor you from horror. For horror eats the light and digests it into darkness.

Sick to Death

Bleakness I

To salve the pains of consciousness, some people anesthetize themselves with sunny thoughts. But not everyone can follow their lead, above all not those who sneer at the sun and everything upon which it beats down. Their only respite is in the balm of bleakness. Disdainful of the solicitations of hope, they look for sanctuary in desolate places—a scattering of ruins in a barren locale or a rubble of words in a book where someone whispers in a dry voice, "I, too, am here." However, downcast readers must be on their guard. Phony retreats have lured many who treasure philosophical and literary works of a pessimistic, nihilistic, or defeatist nature as indispensable to their existence. Too often they have settled into a book that begins as an oration on bleak experience but wraps up with the author slipping out the back door and making his way down a shining path, leaving downcast readers more rankled than they were before entering what turned out to be only a façade of ruins, a *trompe l'oeil* of bleakness. *A Confession* (1882) by Leo Tolstoy is the archetype of such a book.

Having basked in his status as the author of *War and Peace* (1865–69) and *Anna Karenina* (1875–77), not to forget his station as a wealthy landowner, Tolstoy was ripe for a devastating reversal of some kind. This came in the form of a crisis of consciousness during which he became mightily disenchanted with human life. Naturally, he began casting about for something to ease his discomfiture. After turning to science for answers to the big questions that had lately begun to eat at him, he came up with this: "In general, the relation of the experimental sciences to life's questions may be expressed thus: Question: 'Why do I live?' Answer: 'In infinite space, in infinite time, infinitely small particles change their forms in infinite complexity, and when you have understood the laws of those mutations of form you will understand why you live on the earth.'"

Post-nineteenth-century discoveries and speculations aside (quantum mechanics, multiverses, panpsychism, simulated realities), those still inclined to query the various sciences will come upon much the same answer. It is a useless answer to a useless question. But Tolstoy did not think the question useless, only the answer, so he kept on digging until he read Schopenhauer, who only exasperated the Russian's crisis by answering, "Life is that which should not be—an evil; and the passage into Nothingness is the only good in life." Tolstoy was impressed with Schopenhauer as a thinker and tried to hold the plow steady as he made his way through the philosopher's daunting works.

At length, Tolstoy narrowed down the options that people like himself had available to them depending on whether they wanted to keep believing that being alive was all right or were ready to consider the alternative. (Please pardon the length of this quotation, but Tolstoy's four principal strategies by which his high-class circle managed the predicament of conscious existence deserve as much of a hearing as Zapffe's four principal strategies by which everyone manages the same predicament.)

I found that for people of my circle there were four ways out of the terrible position in which we are all placed.

The first was that of ignorance. It consists in not knowing, not understanding, that life is an evil and an absurdity. People of this sort . . . have not yet understood that question of life. . . . They see neither the dragon that awaits them nor the mice gnawing the shrub by which they are hanging, and they lick the drops of honey. But they lick those drops of honey only for a while: Something will turn their attention to the dragon and the mice, and there will be an end to their licking. From them I had nothing to learn—one cannot cease to know what one does know.

The second way out is Epicureanism. It consists, while knowing the hopelessness of life, in making use meanwhile of the advantages one has, disregarding the dragon and the mice, and licking the honey in the best way, especially if there is much of it within reach. Solomon expresses this way out thus: "Then I commended mirth, because a man hath no better thing under the sun, than to eat, and to drink, and to be merry: and that this should accompany him in his labor the days of his life, which God giveth him under the sun. Therefore eat thy bread with joy and drink thy wine with a merry heart. . . . Live joyfully with the wife whom thou lovest all the days of the life of thy vanity . . . for this is thy portion in life and in thy labors which thou takest under the sun. . . . Whatsoever thy hand findeth to do, do it with thy might, for there is not work, nor device, nor knowledge, nor wisdom, in the grave, whither thou goest." That is the way in which the majority of people of our circle make life possible for themselves. Their circumstances furnish them with more of welfare than of hardship, and their moral dullness makes it possible for them to forget that the advantage of their position is accidental, and that not everyone can have a thousand wives and palaces like Solomon, that for everyone who has a thousand wives there are a thousand without a wife, and that for each palace there are a thousand people who have to build it in the sweat of their brows; and that the accident that has today made me a Solomon may tomorrow make me a Solomon's slave. The dullness of these people's imagination enables them to forget the things that gave Buddha no peace—the inevitability of sickness, old age, and death, which today or tomorrow will destroy all these pleasures.

So think and feel the majority of people of our day and our manner of life. The fact that some of these people declare the dullness of their thoughts and imaginations to be a philosophy, which they call Positive, does not remove them, in my opinion, from the ranks of those who, to avoid seeing the question, lick the honey. I could not imitate these people; not having their dullness of imagination I could not artificially produce it in myself. I could not tear my eyes from the mice and the dragon, as no vital man can after he has once seen them.

The third escape is that of strength and energy. It consists in destroying life, when one has understood that it is an evil and an absurdity. A few exceptionally strong and consistent people act so. Having understood the stupidity of the joke that has been played on them, and having understood that it is better to be dead than to be alive, and that it is best of all not to exist, they act accordingly and promptly end this stupid joke, since there are means: a rope round one's neck, water, a knife to stick into one's heart, or the trains on the railways; and the number of those of our circle who act in this way becomes greater and greater, and for the most part they act so at the best time of their life, when the strength of their mind is in full bloom and few habits degrading to the mind have as yet been acquired.

I saw that this was the worthiest way of escape and I wished to adopt it.

The fourth way out is that of weakness. It consists in seeing the truth of the situation and yet clinging to life, knowing in advance that nothing can come of it. People of this kind know that death is better than life, but not having the strength to act rationally—to end the deception quickly and kill themselves—they seem to wait for something. This is the escape of weakness, for if I know what is best and it is within my power, why not yield to what is best? . . . I found myself in that category

So people of my class evade the terrible contradiction in four ways. Strain my attention as I would, I saw no way except those four. . . .[1] (Translation by Aylmer Maude)

Earlier in his life, Tolstoy had fought intrepidly in the Crimean War, and in *War and Peace* he used this experience for his rendition of Russian life during the reign of Napoleon. Courageous in battle, the literary master also flourished his fortitude in writing the words in the above quotation. Few men of such wealth and accomplishment have had the mettle to express sentiments of this nature within earshot of their peers and the general public. Naturally, Tolstoy expressed these sentiments only after he had moved to safer ground, which turned his "confession" into a handbook for survival, a trip guide with directions for skating around the pitfalls of consciousness that Zapffe would later outline in "The Last Messiah."

Tolstoy's salvation came about when he hit upon a way to disown coherence and sidle up to religion, even though it was not religion of the common sort and led to his excommunication from the Russian Orthodox Church. A titan of conceptual prestidigitation, he had rationalized his way into irrationality. Spending time with his serfs helped him to befuddle his consciousness. Like them—more nicely, like his perception of them—he began living not by his brain but by his "gut." Then he started reasoning with his gut, which showed him the way to recovery and spared him the ordeal of becoming a suicide. Later, though, his mind went to work again, and he was once more in crisis. He remained preoccupied with life and death and meaning for the rest of his days and as an author preached a brand of positive thought—as in the bathetic "Death of Ivan Ilyich" (1886)—in an ongoing crusade against the bleakness that dogged him.

Bleakness II

Having been betrayed by such works as Tolstoy's *Confession*, connoisseurs of bleakness may become shrewd readers. If they are mistrustful of a book, leery that the promise of its inaugural pages will be broken by its conclusion, they turn first to the ending. Many books promoted as vehicles of a "dark vision" finish up by lounging in a warm bath of affirmation, often doing a traitorous turnabout in their closing pages or paragraphs.[2] As every author, publisher, and carnival owner knows, lurid billing gets a patron in the door. And so we have innumerable books and magazine articles with such inquiring titles as *The Misadventure of Consciousness: Are Human Beings a Mistake of Evolution?* or "Should We Stop Having Children?" The answer is almost always "no," sometimes resounding in its declamation but more often qualified, which is even more vile. Searchers after bleakness would do well, then, to begin at the ending of books and magazine articles with doomful titles or angst-fraught openings if they are not to be chiseled by a bait-and-switch maneuver.

One of the finest curtain closers in fiction is that of Horace McCoy's short novel *They Shoot Horses, Don't They?* The protagonist of this story is a young woman named Gloria Beatty. Hoping to walk away with a sum of much-needed cash, and for lack of anything better to do, Gloria becomes an entrant in a grueling dance marathon during the Great Depression of the 1930s. A disconsolate loser from the start of the book, she begins the dance with an insight not habitually stressed in popular fiction. "It's peculiar to me," Gloria says to her partner in the marathon, "that everybody pays so much attention to living and so little to dying. Why are these high-powered scientists always screwing around trying to prolong life instead of finding pleasant ways to end it? There must be a hell of a lot of people in the world like me—who want to die but haven't got the guts."

After the dance marathon has taken its toll on Gloria and the other contestants, her once happy-go-lucky partner goes over to her side, and with more nobility than any high-powered scientist and more mercy than any god born of human imagination, he helps her to end it all. This liberation is effectuated in one of the most common and untidy ways the suicidal have been forced to use for so long—a bullet to the brain. The ending of McCoy's novel is what the average mortal would call bleak. Naturally, bleak-minded readers of *They Shoot Horses* swoon with relief when the gunshot has done its work. Yet even the consolations of bleakness have their limits for those who treasure philosophical and literary works of a pessimistic, nihilistic, or defeatist nature as indispensable to their existence. And should bleakness itself fail them, they have been failed indeed.

Pro-Life

They Shoot Horses, Don't They? was first published in 1935. Since that time, scientists have continued screwing around to draw out our days of pain and have done almost nothing on the other front. It is as if they have taken Victor Frankenstein as a role model and emulate him as they can. In his 1994 bestseller *How We Die: Reflections on Life's Final Chapter*, surgeon Sherwin B. Nuland recounts how he coaxed a ninety-two-year-old woman into having an operation that would wring from her a few more months or years of life. While she initially declined, content to die at what was already an advanced age, Dr. Nuland wore her down and got her into the operating room, figuring, as he states, that his patient was "one of those people to whom survival was not worth the cost." He admits that he withheld from her the exact nature of that cost as it would be extracted in the form of postoperative agonies should she survive the surgery. She did survive long enough to suffer those agonies and to let Nuland know what a villain she considered him to be.

Subsequent to some perfunctory hand-wrenching about his dishonorable ministration, the doctor tries to vindicate himself by confiding that, had he not performed this operation, he would be chastised by his peer group at the hospital's weekly surgical conference for not following standard operating procedure. Nuland's fellow surgeons, so he informs us, would have viewed his compliance with a patient's request to let her body die without further tampering as an ethical call. But that was not his call to make. He was not a moral philosopher. He was a technician entrusted to keep bodies beating with life. All his decisions, then, must comply with this trust or he would have to answer for why they did not. And to answer that his patient chose not to go under the knife would be unacceptable, since doctors should be the only ones to decide such things.[3]

In their actions, Nuland and his colleagues played out a mainstay of the horror genre: that of an experiment gone wrong. This convention became proverbial following the publication in 1818 of a novel that immortalized Mary Shelley. It is as if Nuland and his fellow mad doctors took the botched surgery in that book as their guiding light. "What protocol would Frankenstein follow?" they might have asked themselves. He was their mentor—the one for whom Life was the greatest show on earth. To boot, Nuland had already sized up the old woman as "one of those people."

Not as philosophically ahead of her years as McCoy's Gloria in *They Shoot Horses, Don't They?*, Nuland's patient did know when the time had come for her to bow out gracefully. She thought she might be allotted that much control over her life. What she did not know was that she was strapped down in Frankenstein's world, and by damn she would live and die by Frankenstein's Oath: "We, as licensed protectors of the species and members in good standing of the master-class of the race, by the power invested in us by those who wish to survive and reproduce, vow to enforce the fiction that life is worth having and worth living come hell or irreparable brain damage." How could an old woman who had been stigmatized as "one of those people" go up against such a juggernaut of chicanery?

Eventually euthanasia will be an elective procedure for the terminally ill, and perhaps for anyone who so chooses this sure cure. At this stage of social progress, however, those who reject Frankenstein and affirm McCoy's Gloria must take care of themselves . . . if they can work up the guts or get a little help. But standing in the way of their making the right move are some formidable obstacles. One of them is the conscience (archaic for "consciousness") that

Shakespeare's Hamlet avowed "makes cowards of us all." Another is the peer pressure that Dr. Nuland felt might squeeze him out of a job. There may also be a crew of friends and relatives whose lives are interwoven with those of suicides and who die with them though they live on after the "crime" of voluntary death has been committed.

If nature made a blunder by retching up creatures in which consciousness grew like a fungus, she still knew enough to implant in them an instinct that serves the species and spurs on its members to chew off a leg to escape capture and killing, whose dominant drives are survival and the spreading of themselves far and wide. Should any philosopher ever establish that life is not worth having and not worth living, the average mortal, as well as the average surgeon, would somehow preserve the fiction of its value, however meager that might be.

Thanatophobia

A philosophical bromide of the post-nihilistic era asserts that being alive has no value except within a limited framework. In the history of cinema, a well-worn storyline is that of a law-enforcement official who moves from a big city to a small town because in the big city his efforts to better his environment were ineffective or unnoticeable while those in a small town, he expects, will "make a difference." The plan here is to change frameworks in hopes of creating the illusion that one's life has value in itself. It is an atheistic plan, if not overtly so. Theists do not need limited frameworks to snatch some meaning for their lives because they believe they have an absolute framework in a Higher Power, even though they really do not. The veritable exclusion of a deity from both high and low cultural products testifies that theism is a rather weak framework of meaning for the majority of mortals, or at least for those who consume high and low cultural products. If this were not so, then movies and other types of entertainment in which meaning is found within the frameworks of romantic love, action in the world, and so on would be unnecessary, as they prove to be among certain Amish and Mennonite sects.

Outside of the movies, the plan of exchanging one framework for another is more difficult to pull off. And since these frameworks are made up by our minds, and not by a filmmaker, they may break up at any moment. Although one may believe in an ultimate frame in which our lives are lived out, the persistence of this belief is uncertain and not reliably consolatory. Faith in some absolute—or, alternatively, faith in some nontheistic framework of meaning— may go limp without advance notice. Once the frame falls in upon itself, we must fall back on our own resources and seek out another frame. None of these frames is constant in preserving our comfort of mind and assisting us in making sense out of our lives. Moving from frame to frame may afford us some comfort and sense for a good while, yet there still remains that final frame from which we will never break loose because it is a holding place waiting to be filled by pain and then, in some form, by death. This is not a frame one wants to explore for very long. All things considered, the happiest epitaph to have etched on one's headstone is this: "He never knew what hit him." On second thought, though, would dying without so much as a heads-up and in the blink of an eye really be the best way for us to go?

In his "Letter on Happiness" addressed to Menoeceus, Epicurus wrote: "Foolish . . . is the man who says that he fears death, not because it will pain when it comes, but because it pains in the prospect." This statement seems to affirm that there is nothing foolish about fearing the pain of death "when it comes." But when Epicurus himself was dying, he wrote a note to his friend Idomeneus, "On this blissful day, which is also the last of my life, I write this to you. My continual sufferings from strangury [due to kidney stones] and dysentery are so great that nothing could increase them; but I set above them all the gladness of mind at the memory of our past conversations." So Epicurus had all a mortal could want: to be fearless of dying, to be happy while dying, and to be unafraid of death.

Unflustered as he was by the process of dying, the founder of Epicureanism offered no logic for why others should not be terrorized by it. His only logical formula was for the relieving oneself of the fear of death: "Whatever causes no annoyance when it is present, causes only a groundless pain in the expectation. Death, therefore, the most awful of evils, is nothing to us, seeing that, when we are, death is not come, and, when death is come, we are not." Some persons may believe in Epicurus's logic and by it not suffer the "groundless pain in the expectation" of death. But how many can say the same about death's pain before it comes or "when it comes"? This question brings us back to our second thoughts on what would be the happiest epitaph to have etched on one's headstone.

Suppose that the pain of dying were taken out of our lives? Suppose that we all died without so much as a heads-up and in the blink of an eye, because if our deaths did not happen in this manner then dying would necessarily be painful. How else would you know you were dying without the presence of pain, the fear of which even Epicurus did not think was foolish? One second we are alive, and the next we are dead. Then all of us would never know what hit us, a gift that is now reserved only for a happy few. Ideally democratic, this system of mortality would equalize our ruination as one by one, or thousands in a stroke, we departed from this life without so much as a heads-up and in the blink of an eye. Every time we sat down in a chair, we could not be sure we would rise again before the reaper impalpably took our hand. We could bypass every pain that would lead to our death, which is not to say we would bypass pains that would not lead to our death. Being in pain would then mean that one was not dying. Everything would be as it is now except that we would succumb without so much as a heads-up and in the blink of an eye. We would never have to think about How we would die, only When. And when the When came, we would not even know we had died. Each breath could be our last. Under such an arrangement, we would either have to become Epicureans and not fear death or, more likely, we would divert from our consciousness the thought that we could die without so much as a heads-up and in the blink of an eye. The latter is more likely because this is our present approach to the inevitability of our death, only we would never have to fear the all but inevitable pain of dying. Some morbid citizens among us might become cataleptic with anxiety because their next breath may be their last, but most of us would not be wrecked by such unremitting worry. As a further bonus, we would have no grisly images about the How, since the How would be the same for all. So even on second thought, the happiest epitaph to have etched on one's headstone would be: "He never knew what hit him." We would still have to live our lives in shaky frameworks, but death would be nothing to us because dying would be nothing to us, or most of us, since some of us might be cataleptic with the morbid fear that our next breath may be our last. But at least most of us would have it all, as did Epicurus, and would not be the least bit pained about dying, as the Greek philosopher was not. Who among us would be so unrepentantly wayward as to want a painful heads-up that we are dying or to die in anything more than the blink of an eye? And only our most morbid citizens would feel anxious about death.

Be that as it may, there is a school of psychology that has us all figured as morbid citizens. Known as Terror Management Theory

(TMT), its principles were inspired by the writings of the Canadian cultural anthropologist Ernest Becker, who was one with Zapffe in wondering why a "damning surplus of consciousness" had not caused humanity to go "extinct during great epidemics of madness." In his best-known work, *The Denial of Death* (1973), Becker wrote: "I believe that those who speculate that a full apprehension of man's condition would drive him insane are right, quite literally right." Zapffe concluded that we kept our heads by "artificially limiting the content of consciousness." Becker stated his identical conclusion as follows: "[Man] literally drives himself into a blind obliviousness with social games, psychological tricks, personal preoccupations so far removed from the reality of his situation that they are forms of madness, but madness all the same." Outlawed truisms. Taboo commonplaces.

Synthesizing and expanding Becker's core ideas, three psychology professors—Sheldon Solomon, Jeff Greenberg, and Tom Pyszczynski—presented the concepts of TMT to the psychological community in the mid-1980s. In its clinical studies and research, TMT indicates that the mainspring of human behavior is thanatophobia, and that this fear determines the entire landscape of our lives. To subdue our death anxiety, we have trumped up a world to deceive ourselves into believing that we will persist—if only symbolically—beyond the breakdown of our bodies. We know this fabricated world because we see it around us every day, and to perpetuate our sanity we apotheosize it as the best world in the world. Housing the most cyclopean fabrications are houses of worship where some people go to get a whiff of meaning, which to such people means only one thing—immortality. In heaven or hell or reincarnated life forms, we must go on and on—*us* without end. Travesties of immortality are effected day and night in obstetrics wards, factories of our future that turn out a product made in its makers' image, a miracle granted by entering into a devil's bargain with God, who is glorified with all the credit for giving us a chance to have our names and genetics projected into a time we will not live to see.[4]

However, as TMT analyzes this scheme, getting the better of our death anxiety is not as simple as it might appear. If we are to be at peace with our mortality, we need to know that what we leave behind us when we die will survive just as we left it. Those churches cannot be just any churches—they must be *our* churches, whoever we may be. The same holds true of progeny and its stand-ins. In lieu of personal immortality, we are willing to accept the survival of persons and institutions that we regard as extensions of us—*our* families, *our* heroes, *our* religions, *our* countries.[5] And anyone who presents a threat to our continuance as a branded society of selves, anyone who does not look and live as we do, should think twice before treading on our turf, because from here to eternity it is every self for itself and all its facsimiles. In such a world, one might extrapolate that the only honest persons—from the angle of self-delusion, naturally—are those who brazenly implement genocide against outsiders who impinge upon them and *their* world. With that riff raff out of the way, there will be more room on earth and in eternity for the right sort of people and their fabrications.

That said, promulgators of TMT believe that a universal dispersion of their ideas will make people more tolerant of the alien worldviews of others and not kill them because those worldviews remind them of how ephemeral or unfounded their own may be. The paradox of this belief is that it requires everyone to abandon the very techniques of terror management by which TMT claims we so far have managed our terror, or some of it. As usual, though, there is an upbeat way out for terror management theorists in that they argue "that the best worldviews are ones that value tolerance of different others, that are flexible and open to modifications, and that offer paths to self-esteem minimally likely to encourage hurting others" (*Handbook of Experimental Existential Psychology*, ed. Jeff Greenberg et al.). Of course, this is just another worldview that brandishes itself as the best worldview in the world, meaning that it would agitate others with a sense of how ephemeral or unfounded their own may be and cause them to retaliate. But terror management theorists also have a backup plan, which is that in the future we will not need terror management and instead will discover that "serious confrontations with mortality can have positive, liberating effects, facilitating real growth and life satisfaction." There is no arguing that humanity may someday reap the benefits of a serious confrontation with mortality. While waiting for that day, we still have genocide as the ultimate insurance of our worldviews.

In categorical opposition to genocide on an as-needed basis are such individuals as Gloria Beatty. Without making too much of a mess, they quietly shut the door on a single life, caring not that they leave behind people who are not like them. Most of these antisocial types are only following the logic of pain to its conclusion. Some plan their last bow to serve the double duty of both delivering them from life and avenging themselves for some wrong, real or imagined, against them. Also worthy of mention is a clique among the suicidal for whom the meaning of their act is a darker thing. Frustrated as perpetrators of an all-inclusive extermination, they would kill themselves only because killing it all is closed off to them. They hate having been delivered into a world only to be told, by and by, "This way to the abattoir, ladies and gentlemen." They despise the conspiracy of Lies for Life almost as much as they despise themselves for being a party to it. If they could unmake the world by pushing a button, they would do so without a second thought. There is no satisfaction in a lonesome suicide. The phenomenon of "suicide euphoria" aside, there is only fear, bitterness, or depression beforehand, then the troublesomeness of the method, and nothingness afterward. But to push that button, to depopulate this earth and arrest its rotation as well—what satisfaction, as of a job prettily done. This would be for the good of all, because even those who know nothing about the conspiracy against the human race are among its injured parties.[6]

Tragedy

As we are all well aware, people often have seriously discrepant interests and desires. If this were not so, we would all be getting along with one another, which has never been and never will be the rule. Nothing in our history or our nature even hints that we will ever liquidate our differences, which can be anything from a good-natured divergence of opinion to a war-making contentiousness over property rights. Some people would like to have a little peace rather than the ever-sounding disharmony of bloodletting. But for that to happen, our myriad voices would have to dissolve into a single pitch—a unison that would bore to tears anyone who is not a saint or ego-dead.

Our common preference as a species is for difference rather than unity. (*Vive la différence. Vive la guerre.*) Nobody designed us to be this way—it just happens to be how we blundered into the nightmare of being. Life preys on life, per Schopenhauer and natural history. One organism's body is another organism's meal. As the title character of Stephen Sondheim's *Sweeney Todd* (1979) sings to his partner in manslaughter, one Mrs. Lovett: "For what's the sound of the world out there? It's man devouring man, my dear." To claim otherwise is a lie. Differences make all the difference to us. What we want is variety in our lives—a multitude of distractions to keep consciousness in its cage. What we want is the unheard-of, the nothing-like. And there is nothing like the screech of Sweeney's blade that we hear at the opening to Sondheim's musical tragedy about the Demon Barber of Fleet Street.

To entertain ourselves for a spell, let us proclaim that were it not for tragedy the human race would have gone extinct long ago. It keeps us on our toes and pushes us toward the future in a paradoxical search to purge the tragic from our lives. As the wise puppet said, "Better we should be inundated by tragedy than to have nothing meaningful to work toward." No one knows this better than the entertainers among us, those sublimating masters of artifice who could not forge their "great works" without the screams and sobs arising out of the pit where tremulous shadows run from themselves.

As decreed by its author, each action and consequence in *Sweeney Todd* flows out of and feeds into the tragic, artificially speaking. It is the pedal tone over which all other propellants of the drama—for instance, beauty and love—serve as passing grace notes that seem to suggest something other than the tragic, yet are actually as much a part of the piece as the unhomely horrors that stalk the stage. While Sondheim's musical inspires the pity and fear that Aristotle believed should be the affects induced by tragic drama, no Aristotelian purgation of emotion or catharsis is infused in us at the end. From the opening to the finale of Sondheim's tragedy there is only a perpetual agon among casualties of the human condition.

So Sweeney begins his tragic tale: "There was a barber and his wife." In the style of many a horror that has wormed its way from the muck of organic existence, *Sweeney Todd* has as its backstory a happy marriage and the propagation of a new life, in this case that of the child Johanna. ("Wake up, Johanna, it's another bright red day," sings Pater Todd.) And new life only rehashes old life in its pain when one offspring meets another. "I feel you, Johanna / I'll steal you, Johanna," croons Anthony to his beloved, who together compose a romantic pairing for the purpose of casting a ray of false hope onto the sooty stage set of the drama.

However, to anyone who has not fallen asleep during the

performance, this new Adam and Eve are only being readied for the meat grinder of existence, just as were a barber named Benjamin Barker and his wife Lucy, all because Judge Turpin lusted after Benjamin's spouse and got him out of the way by unjustly sentencing the haircutter to a long prison term in Australia. Deranged by her rape at a soirée presided over by the judge, Lucy kills herself, or tries to, by drinking poison, leaving her infant daughter in the hands of the dirty old jurist, who raises her as his ward and, despite his best efforts, drools to have her in his bed following a May-December marriage. When Benjamin returns after his escape from prison some decades later, all he wants is to be reunited with his wife and child. Alas, this is not to be, which is how Sweeney Todd, mad to avenge the wrongs against him and his wife, not to mention the abduction of his child, comes to be born. In league with Mrs. Lovett, an unscrupulous maker of meat pies, the tragedy begins in earnest as Sweeney begins slicing throats and his consort grinds his victims into tasty edibles to be sold at her shop.

As husband and wife raising a girl-child, Benjamin and Lucy would have been galloping bores. It is only when they have been driven in chains through the inferno of their lives that they are fit to slake our thirst for tragedy, motivator of both the masses and above-average mortals. They are positioned within the innermost circle of hell, while Mrs. Lovett, Judge Turpin, Tobias Ragg, and others radiate concentrically about them with their own fateful cravings (for beauty, love, and such like), edging them ever closer to the barber's blade and the fire-belching oven.

Ready or not, we all end up as filling for one of Mrs. Lovett's meat pies. In the reported last words of Thomas Lovell Beddoes, the Romantic poet called himself "food for what I am good for— worms." Even though worms do not dine on many of us in modernized nations, the point still resonates that our lives are fundamentally inglorious. It is as a counterweight to the blithering fatuousness of human life that *tragedy as entertainment* performs a crucial function—that of coating the spattered nothingness of our lives with a veneer of grandeur and style, qualities of the theatrical world and not the everyday one. This is why we are thrilled with the horror of Sweeney Todd and envy the qualities that he possesses and we lack. He is as edifying as any sage when he sings "We all deserve to die," given that none of us can unmake our making. He has a sense of mission that few who are made of flesh and blood rather than of music and poetry will ever know ("But the work waits / I'm alive at last / And I'm full of joy"). Most of all, he has the courage and bravado to do that which he knows needs to be done. "To seek revenge may lead to hell," he cautions, to which Mrs. Lovett answers, "But everyone does it and seldom as well . . . as Sweeney."

Nature is limited to Grand Guignol, spectacles of bloodlust and fests of slaughter. But we humans can reach for things more heady than the corpse. After murder and cannibalism have been played out in *Sweeney Todd*, the dead rise up for an encore, one of many they will make in a world where nature is not in charge—a world that spins in the supernatural, our world. Collectively, we are the undead, and for us the work will always be waiting, the devouring will never be done until someone or something performs the service of killing our rat race or we kill off ourselves. As in the beginning, so at the end, the dangling puppets sing: "Attend the tale of Sweeney Todd," a story that makes for a wonderfully tragic evening at the theater.

Whatever else we may be as creatures that go to and fro on the earth and walk up and down upon it, we are meat. A cannibalistic tribe that once flourished had a word to describe what they ate. That word translates as "the food that talks." Most of the food that we have eaten over the course of human history has not talked. But it does make other noises, terrible sounds as it is converted from living meat to dead meat on the slaughterhouse floor. If we could hear these sounds every time we sat down to a hearty meal, would we still be the wanton gobblers of flesh that most of us are now? This is hard to say. But as Farmer Vincent (Rory Calhoun) says in the movie *Motel Hell* (1980): "Meat's meat and a man's gotta eat." And it takes all kinds of critters to make Farmer Vincent's fritters.

Beef, pork, sometimes goat—they go into us and come out of us. This is part of the regimen of nonsense that nature forced upon us. But it is not all the nonsense we must endure as we go to and fro on the earth and walk up and down upon it. The nature nonsense, the God nonsense. How much nonsense can we take in our lives? And is there any way we can escape it? No, there is not. We are doomed to all kinds of nonsense: the pain nonsense, the nightmare nonsense, the sweat and slave nonsense, and many other shapes and sizes of insufferable nonsense. It is brought to us on a plate, and we must eat it up or face the death nonsense.[7]

But perhaps by lustfully consuming the worst nonsense of our lives, including the death nonsense, we may eat our way out of our all-consuming tragedy as a conscious species. Professor Nobody has something to say about this tactic in his lecture "Sardonic Harmony." Here he builds to a tone of undisguised acrimony unusual for the coolly didactic, self-styled savant. But that is no reason we should not listen to his nonsense once more.

> Compassion for human hurt, a humble sense of our impermanence, an absolute valuation of justice—all our so-called virtues only trouble us and serve to bolster, not assuage, horror. In addition, they are the least vital of our attributes, the least in line with life. More often than not, they stand in the way of one's rise in the welter of this

world, which found its pace long ago and has not deviated from it since. The putative affirmations of life—each of them based on the propaganda of Tomorrow: reproduction, revolution in its most wide-ranging sense, piety in any form you can name—are only affirmations of our desires. And, in fact, these affirmations affirm nothing but our propensity for self-torment, our mania to preserve a demented innocence in the face of gruesome facts.

By means of supernatural horror we may evade, if momentarily, the horrific reprisals of affirmation. Every one of us, having been stolen from nonexistence, opens his eyes on the world and looks down the road at a few convulsions and a final obliteration. What a weird scenario. So why affirm anything, why make a pathetic virtue of a terrible necessity? We are destined to a fool's fate that deserves to be mocked. And since there is no one else around to do the mocking, we will take on the job. Bent on a perverse self-gratification, let us indulge in cruel pleasures against ourselves and our pretensions, let us delight in the Cosmic Macabre. At least we may send up a few bitter laughs into the cobwebbed corners of this crusty old universe.

Supernatural horror, in all its eerie constructions, enables a reader to taste treats inconsistent with his personal welfare. Admittedly, this is not a practice likely to find universal favor. True macabrists are as rare as poets and form a secret society by the bad-standing of their memberships elsewhere, most being debarred at birth from the festivities of the social masque. But those who have gotten a good whiff of other worlds and sampled a cuisine marginal to stable existence will not be able to stay themselves from the uncanny feast of horrors that has been laid out for them. They will loiter in moonlight, eyeing the entranceways to cemeteries, waiting for some propitious moment to crash the gates and see what is inside.

Once and for all, let us speak the paradox aloud: "We have been force-fed for so long the shudders of a thousand graveyards that at last, seeking a macabre redemption, a salvation by horror, we willingly consume the terrors of the tomb . . . and find them to our liking."

The Cult of Grinning Martyrs

Institutionalized

Undeniably, one of the great disadvantages of consciousness—that is, consciousness considered as the parent of all horrors—is that it exacerbates necessary sufferings and creates unnecessary ones, such as the fear of death. Not having what it takes to take their own lives (ask Gloria Beatty), those who suffer intolerably learn to hide their afflictions, both necessary and unnecessary, because the world does not run on pain time but on happy time, whether or not that happiness is honestly felt or a mask for the blackest despondency. Every shrewd slave knows enough to be as perky as he is submissive in the presence of his master. And those seated in the head offices of the earth know that gales of gleeful talk must be blown the way of ordinary folk, who need to hear that things are all right all the time, or, if they are not all right, soon will be. Whether your ambition is to rule over your fellows or simply to maneuver among them, a show of jaunty optimism is requisite.

In a section of *The World as Will and Representation* where Schopenhauer argues that only pain is real while pleasure is an illusion, the philosopher writes: "I cannot here withhold the statement that *optimism*, where it is not merely the thoughtless talk of those who harbor nothing but words under their shallow fore-heads, seems to me to be not merely an absurd, but also a really *wicked*, way of thinking, a bitter mockery of the most unspeakable sufferings of mankind" (Schopenhauer's emphasis). Those who do not wholly endorse Schopenhauer's opinion of optimism can still gain some understanding of what he is talking about when they behold a spittle-chinned demagogue bawling out homilies and falsehoods to a rapt audience. It is on such occasions that optimism reveals itself as so noisome that even those who customarily prefer an optimistic spell to be cast upon them may become queasy with a sense of the wickedness that turns the gears of the world-machine. "Wickedness," we know, is a categorical term proper to philo-sophical systems of morality, for those who care about such fabrica-tions. Yet sometimes those who do not usually care a whit about such things are moved to bark out moral recriminations as the horribly clownish face of optimism brightens the sky the better to peruse the bodies and minds being mangled below.

Optimistically wicked or not, most people cannot afford to care, or to care too much, if they are living in the best or the worst of all possible worlds. They can care only about the one thing that, for anybody who likes to think of being alive as being all right, is worth caring about. And that one thing is this: *feeling good,* or as good as possible, no matter what "feeling good" might mean to a certain in-dividual at a certain time. For instance, whenever asked in so many words, "Hey, what are you doing there?," you might say, "I'm ham-mering a nail" or "I'm searching for absolute truth." Yet all you are really saying is this: "I'm trying to feel as good as I can." Of course, you may be caught in a tight spot where the best you can feel is not very good or is even very bad. These are situations in which the al-ternative, or the perceived alternative, is to feel worse. Ergo, you are still trying to feel as good as you can, though you might not see it that way as you mark time feeling not so good until you can once again feel good in the way you like most. But as evolution would have it, we seem to have a "negativity bias" that reins in those feelings which, when we feel them, are felt to be unquestionably good.

As one arm of evolutionary psychology hypothesizes, pleasurable emotions and sensations germinated because they were adaptive.[1] Example: In past ages, climactic release from the stress of carnal desire was an unarticulated catalyst for the generative survival of our species, the link between the two phenomena not yet being known. The illiteracy at issue now long gone, most of us are given to praise fleshly pleasure, though few celebrate the biological drive that leads to it, just as everyone praises a good meal but not the hunger that makes it so pleasurable. The analogy between these pleasures and others that are also appetite-driven, such as those of a drug addict, should be clear. Being freed of a desire is indeed a pleasure. But knowing the remorseless ways of nature, should anyone be thunderstruck that by mutation she has put a lid on the extent of our pleasure and a limit on how long it may last, not to mention favoring pain as the main inducement for our behavior?[2]

If human pleasure did not have both a lid and a time limit, we would not bestir ourselves to do things that were not pleasurable, such as toiling for our subsistence. And then we would not survive. By the same token, should our mass mind ever become discontented with the restricted pleasures doled out by nature, as well as disgruntled over the lack of restrictions on pain, we would omit the mandates of survival from our lives out of a stratospherically acerbic indignation. And then we would not reproduce. As a species, we do not shout into the sky, "The pleasures of this world are not enough for us." In fact, they are just enough to drive us on like oxen pulling a cart full of our calves, which in their turn will put on the yoke. As inordinately evolved beings, though, we can postulate that it will not always be this way. "A time will come," we say to ourselves, "when we shall remake this world in which we are battered between long burden and brief delight, and without disruption wallow in gladness all our days." The belief in the possibility of long-lasting, high-flown pleasures is a deceptive but adaptive flimflam. It seems that nature did not make us to feel too good for too long, which would be no good for the survival of the species, but only to feel good enough for long enough to keep us from complaining that we do not feel good all the time.

In the workaday world, complainers will not go far. When someone asks how you are doing, you had better be wise enough to reply, "I can't complain." If you do complain, even justifiably, people will stop asking how you are doing. Complaining will not help you succeed and influence people. You can complain to your physician or psychiatrist because they are paid to hear you complain. But you cannot complain to your boss or your friends, if you have any. You will soon be dismissed from your job and dropped from the social register. Then you will be left alone with your complaints and no one to listen to them gratis. Perhaps then the message will sink into your head: If you do not feel good enough for long enough, you should act as if you do and even think as if you do. That is the way to get yourself to feel good enough for long enough and stop you from complaining for good, as any self-improvement book can affirm. But should you not improve, someone must assume the blame. And that someone will be you. This is monumentally so if you are a pessimist or a depressive. Should you conclude that life is objectionable or that nothing matters—do not waste our time with your nonsense. We are on our way to the future, and the philosophically disheartening or the emotionally impaired are not going to hinder our progress. If you cannot say something positive, or at least equivocal, keep it to yourself. Pessimists and depressives need not apply for a position in the enterprise of life. You have two choices: Start thinking the way God and your society want you to think or be forsaken by all. The decision is yours, since you are a free agent who can choose to rejoin our fabricated reality or stubbornly insist on . . . what? That we should mollycoddle non-positive thinkers like you or rethink how the whole world transacts its business? That we should start over from scratch? Or that we should go extinct? Try to be realistic. We did the best we could with the tools we had. After all, we are only human, as we like to say. Our world may not be in accord with nature's way, but it did develop *organically* according to our consciousness, which delivered us to a lofty prominence over the Creation. The whole thing just took on a life of its own, and nothing is going to stop it anytime soon. There can be no starting over and no going back. No major readjustments are up for a vote. And no melancholic head-case is going to bad-mouth our catastrophe. The universe was created by the Creator, by damn. We live in a country we love and that loves us back. We have families and friends and jobs that make it all worthwhile. We are somebodies, not a bunch of nobodies without names or numbers or retirement plans. None of this is going to be overhauled by a thought criminal who contends that the world is not double-plus-good and never will be. Our lives may not be unflawed—that would deny us a better future to work toward—but if this charade is good enough for us, then it should be good enough for you. So if you cannot get your mind right, try walking away. You will find no place to go and no one who will have you. You will find only the same old trap the world over. Lighten up or leave us alone. You will never get us to give up our hopes. You will never get us to wake up from our dreams. We are not contradictory beings whose continuance only worsens our plight as mutants who embody the contorted logic of a paradox. Such opinions will not be accredited by institutions of authority or by the middling run of humanity. To lay it on the line, whatever thoughts may emerge from your deviant brain are invalid, inauthentic, or whatever dismissive term we care to hang on you, who are only "one of those people." So start pretending that you feel good enough for long enough, stop your complaining, and get back in line. If you are not as strong as Samson—that no-good suicide and slaughterer of Philistines— then get loaded to the gills and return to the trap. Keep your medicine cabinet and your liquor cabinet well stocked, just like the rest of us. Come on and join the party. No pessimists or depressives invited. Do you think we are morons? We know all about those complaints of yours. The only difference is that we have sense enough and feel good enough for long enough not to speak of them. Keep your powder dry and your pessimistic, nihilistic, and defeatist temperaments in check. Our shibboleth: "Up the Conspiracy and down with Consciousness."

Disillusionment

Antagonistic to any somber ideations, humankind has trained itself to ingest ever-increasing disillusionments and metabolize them without any impairment to its system. By means of self-mastery through conscious autosuggestion, or by whatever means, the biblical Genesis and all other fables of origination have been unproblematically reduced to mythic precursors of the Big Bang theory and the primordial soup. Pantheon after pantheon has been belittled into "things people used to believe in." And supplications to the Divine are murmured only inside the tents of faith healers or in the minds of the desperate.

The only constraint on disillusionment is the following: It must creep along so sluggishly that almost none can mark its movement. Anyone caught trying to accelerate the progress of disillusionment will be reprimanded and told to sit in the corner, if only in free-world nations where the Church and the State have lost the clout to kill or torture dissenters. A sign of progress, some would say. But sufferance of renegade minds should not lead us into premature self-congratulation. The rate at which our kind plods toward disillusionment is geologically slow, and humanity can be cocksure of its death by natural causes or an "act of God" before it travels very far toward that beatific day when with one voice it might exclaim, "Enough of this error of conscious life. It shall be passed down no longer to those innocents unborn."

In "The Last Messiah," Zapffe conjectures that with the passing of generations the more profligate will become humanity's means of hiding its disillusionments from itself: the more brainless and delusional its isolation from the actualities of existence; the more stupefying and uncouth its distractions from the startling and dreadful; the more heavy-handed and madcap its anchorings in unreality; and the more callous, self-mocking, and detached from life its sublimations in art. These developments will not make us any more paradoxical in our being, but they could make all manifestations of our paradoxical nature less effective and more aberrant. Speaking in terms of his time, and ours, Zapffe writes in "The Last Messiah" of our rising *spiritual unemployment.*

> The absence of naturally (biologically) based spiritual activity shows up, for example, in the pervasive recourse to *distraction* (entertainment, sport, radio—the "rhythm of the times"). Terms for anchoring are not as favorable—all the inherited, collective systems of anchorings are punctured by criticism, and anxiety, disgust, confusion, despair leaking in through the rifts ("corpses in the cargo"). Communism and psychoanalysis, however incommensurable otherwise, both attempt (as Communism also has a spiritual reflection) by novel means to vary the old escape anew; applying, respectively, violence and guile to make humans biologically fit by ensnaring their critical surplus of cognition. The idea, in either case, is uncannily logical.

But again, it cannot yield a final solution. Though a deliberate degeneration to a more viable nadir may certainly save the species in the short run, it will by its nature be unable to find peace in such resignation, or indeed find any peace at all. . . .

If we continue on these considerations to the bitter end, then the conclusion is not in doubt. As long as humankind recklessly proceeds in the fateful delusion of being biologically fated for triumph, nothing essential will change. As the numbers mount and the spiritual atmosphere thickens, the techniques of protection must assume an increasingly brutal character.

Rather than being a visionary or a prophet, Zapffe was an analyst of disaster, and his pessimism is nothing if not *down to earth*.

Pressurized

The Romanian-born French writer E. M. Cioran counted among his greatest accomplishments breaking himself of the habit of cigarette smoking and the fact that he never became a parent. Nothing in Cioran's file would lead one to think he was ever tempted to have children. His remark was a derision of people whose fecundity had swollen a world he would rather have seen in ashes. A maestro of pessimism, Cioran published several volumes of philosophical essays and aphorisms that assaulted what he considered the inexcusable crumminess of all creation. Contained in his works is an ample stock of quotable outbursts, any one of which could serve as a synopsis of his conviction that human existence was a wrong turn made by the universe. "Life," he wrote, "is an uprising within the inorganic, a tragic leap out of the inert—life is matter animated and, it must be said, spoiled by pain." But that was just his opinion.

Those who feel they have free will, meaning everyone, also feel they are free to have any opinion they want on any issue before them. They are like those "believers in anything" already mentioned who may have an opinion about whatever they believe to be true. As we know, the premier opinion that has held in all time and places is that there is some sure reason for the continuance of the human species. This opinion is so prevailing that it is usually assumed to be a fact and not an opinion. In *Reason's Grief: An Essay on Tragedy and Value* (2006), George W. Harris propounds this opinion most poignantly: "While we might . . . admit that the existence of human and animal suffering is itself a tragedy, it would be a greater tragedy still to end it all. How can we account for this tragic sense, the sense that something would be lost with such a termination?" That it would be a greater tragedy to end all animal and human suffering than to have it continue is an opinion stated as a fact. Granting that "something would be lost with such a termination," it remains to be established whether or not that "something" were better let go than kept going. And that this termination inspires in us a tragic sense for which we need to account is also only Harris's opinion—one that he later, with disarming honesty, concedes is reserved for those who are fortunate enough to have lives they believe are worth having; otherwise, what he calls the "apocalyptic option" would be all right.

Nothing definitive supports the opinion that humanity should persist in being, just as nothing definitive supports the opinion that humanity should cease to exist. In place of universally convincing reasons in this matter, or even commonsense thought, there is pressure. Thus, people who hold the opinion that the human race should go extinct are pressured by the bad opinion of almost all others to excoriate themselves as wrong in having this opinion. All said, the opinion of an antinatalist is not reckoned a praiseworthy one in this world, and antinatalists are cognizant of this fact. Dissimilarly, pro-natalists are not at all cognizant that their opinion that procreation is all right is not praiseworthy either.

Opinion: There are no praiseworthy incentives to reproduce. For pro-natalists, children are only a means to an end, and none of those ends is praiseworthy. They are the ends of people who already exist, a condition that automatically makes them prejudiced in favor of existence. (In his essay "Benevolent Artificial Anti-Natalism" [*EDGE*, 2017], Thomas Metzinger terms this baseless conviction "existence bias.") Yet even though these people think that being alive is all right, they are not at a loss to think of reasons why in some cases it would be better not to have been. They can only hope that their children will not be one of those cases, for their sake as well as for the sake of their offspring. To have a praiseworthy incentive for bearing a child, one would first have to prove that child's birth to be a good in itself, which no one can prove about anything, least of all about something that has no predictable outcome. You could *argue*, of course, that a child's birth is a good in itself. And you could go on arguing until the child ages to death or sickens to death or has a fatal vehicular misadventure. But you cannot prevail in an argument about any child's birth being a good in itself. You can only accept that someday the child who was born will come to an end that is an end in itself, which, as people sometimes say, may be for the best.

In place of arguments pro or con, pressure is brought to bear on breeders-in-waiting to be of the opinion that there is indeed a plethora of praiseworthy incentives for making more of us. The pressure put upon them, biology notwithstanding, takes the guise of the good opinion of others who want them to think, and who themselves think, they are right in having the opinion that procreation is all right. Some may resist this pressure, but they will not be roundly praised for doing so, although they may receive a dispensation if the product of their union is likely to be defective.

Among the least praiseworthy incentives to reproduce are parents' pipe dreams of posterity—that egoistic compulsion to send emissaries into the future who will certify that their makers once lived and still live on, if only in photographs and home movies. Vying for an even less praiseworthy incentive to reproduce is the sometimes irresistible prospect of taking pride in one's children as consumer goods, trinkets or tie-clips, personal accessories that may be shown off around town. But primary among the pressures to propagate is this: To become formally integrated into a society, one must offer it a blood sacrifice. As David Benatar has alleged in *Better Never to Have Been*, all procreators have blood-red hands, morally and ethically speaking.

Naturally, the average set of parents is able to conceive of less reprehensible, but still not praiseworthy, incentives for reproduction. Among these are the urgency to beat the biological clock or abandon all hope for the legendary enjoyments of the parental role; the desire to solidify a spousal relationship; the wish to please one's own parents with grandchildren; the need of an insurance policy that one's offspring will probably feel obligated to pay off once their begetters are in their dotage; the quelling of a sense of guilt or selfishness for not having done their duty as human beings; and the squelching of that pathos which is associated with the childless.[3]

Such are some of the non-praiseworthy incentives of those who would fertilize the future. And they are all pressures of one kind or another. These pressures build up in people throughout their lifetimes and cry to be released, just as our bowels cry to be released to avoid the discomfort of a fecal build-up. And who, if they could help it, wants the discomfort of a fecal build-up? So we make bowel movements to relieve this pressure. Similarly, quite a few people make gardens because they cannot withstand the pressure of not making a garden. Others commit murder because they cannot withstand the pressure building up within them to kill someone, either a person known to them or a passing stranger. And so on. Most of our days consist of pressures to make metaphorical as well as actual bowel movements. Releasing these pressures can have greater or lesser consequences in the scheme of our lives. But they are all bowel-movement pressures of some kind. At a certain age, children are praised for making a bowel movement in the approved manner. Later on, the praise of others dies down for this achievement and our bowel movements become our own business, although we may continue to praise ourselves for them. Yet pressures go on influencing our lives, including pressures to have some opinions rather than others, and even the proper release of these literal bowel-movement pressures may once more come up for praise, congratulations, and huzzahs of all kinds.

No different from other species on this planet, humanity will flourish while it can, even though there is no praiseworthy incentive to do so. Nevertheless, we cannot count out the possibility that with the passing of hundreds or thousands of years we will attain immortality, or something close to it, which would obviate our function as servants of our species whose primary interests are to survive and reproduce ourselves. Let us also presage that at this distant stage of human evolution we have fully fathomed all material matters of the universe—its beginning, its end, and all its workings. Having reached such an intellectual apex, we would need only to bar from our thoughts a single question, one to which there can be no positive answer in either material or metaphysical terms. The question takes various forms. We have already investigated one form of this question: "What use is it to exist?" Herman Tønnessen, in his essay "Happiness Is for the Pigs: Philosophy versus Psychotherapy" (*Journal of Existentialism*, 1967), cites another form of the question: "What is it all about?" He then explains the context and significance of the question.

Mitja (in *Brothers Karamazov*) felt that though his question may be absurd and senseless, yet he had to ask just that, and he had to ask it in just that way. Socrates bandied about that an unexamined life is not worthy of Man. And Aristotle saw Man's "proper" goal and "proper" limit in the right exercise of those faculties which are uniquely human. It is commonplace that men, unlike other living organisms, are not equipped with built-in mechanisms for automatic maintenance of their existence. Man would perish immediately if he were to respond to his environment exclusively in terms of unlearned biologically inherited forms of behavior. In order to survive, the human being must discover how various things around as well as *in him* operate. And the place he occupies in the present scheme of organic creation is the consequence of having learned how to exploit his intellectual capacities for such discoveries. Hence, more human than any other human longing is the pursuance of a *total* view of Man's function—or malfunction—in the Universe, his possible place and importance in the *widest conceivable cosmic scheme*. In other words it is the attempt to answer, or at least articulate whatever questions are entailed in the dying groan of ontological despair: *What is it all about?* This may well prove biologically harmful or even fatal to Man. Intellectual honesty and Man's high spiritual demands for order and meaning may drive Man to the deepest antipathy to life and necessitate, as one existentialist chooses to express it: "A *no* to this wild, banal, grotesque and loathsome carnival in the world's graveyard." (Tønnessen's emphases)

170

The quote at the end of this excerpt from Tønnessen's essay is taken from Zapffe's *On the Tragic*. While Tønnessen believes that "intellectual honesty" must lead to "ontological despair," ultimately his preference is for living the heroic life of a clear-eyed desperado of pessimism—after the existential stylings of Miguel de Unamuno, Albert Camus, William Brashear, Joshua Foa Dienstag, and others—rather than wallowing in the self-deceptive happiness of a human pig. In principle, there does seem to be a moral divide between the way of the desperado and that of the pig; practically, there is none. Both are spoiling for survival in a MALIGNANTLY USELESS world. And survival is for the pigs.

Ask Professor Nobody about reasoning the state of our lives to the limit. Tilting again toward stridency, here is what he has to say on the subject in "Pessimism and Supernatural Horror— Lecture Two."

Dead bodies that walk in the night, living bodies suddenly possessed by new owners and deadly aspirations, bodies without sensible form, and a body of unnatural laws in accordance with which tortures and executions are meted out—some examples of the logic of supernatural horror. It is a logic founded on fear, a logic whose sole principle states: "Existence equals nightmare." Unless life is a dream, nothing makes sense. For as a reality, it is a rank failure. A few more examples: a trusting soul catches the night in a bad mood and must pay a dreadful price; another opens the wrong door, sees something he should not have, and suffers the consequences; still another walks down an unfamiliar street . . . and is *lost* forever.

That we all deserve punishment by horror is as mystifying as it is undeniable. To be an accomplice, however involuntarily, in a reasonless non-reality is cause enough for the harshest sentencing. But we have been trained so well to accept the "order" of an unreal world that we do not rebel against it. How could we? Where pain and pleasure form a corrupt alliance against us, paradise and hell are merely different divisions in the same monstrous bureaucracy. And between these two poles exists everything we know or can ever know. It is not even possible to imagine a utopia, earthly or otherwise, that can stand up under the mildest criticism. But one must take into account the shocking fact that we live on a world that *spins*. After considering this truth, nothing should come as a surprise.

Still, on rare occasions we do overcome hopelessness or velleity and make mutinous demands to live in a real world, one that is at least episodically ordered to our advantage. But perhaps it is only a demon of some kind that moves us to such idle insubordination, the more so to aggravate our condition in the unreal. After all, is it not wondrous that we are allowed to be both witnesses and victims of the sepulchral pomp of wasting tissue? And one thing we know is real: horror. It is so real, in fact, that we cannot be sure it could not exist without us. Yes, it needs our imaginations and our consciousness, but it does not ask or require our consent to use them. Indeed, horror operates with complete autonomy. Generating ontological havoc, it is a mephitic foam upon which our lives merely float. And, ultimately, we must face up to it: Horror is more real than we are.

Autopsy on a Puppet:

An Anatomy of the Supernatural

Atmosphere

Billions of years had to pass following the formation of the earth before its atmosphere became . . . atmospheric. This transition could only have occurred with the debut of consciousness—parent of all horrors and the matrix of atmosphere. With our bodies bogged down in the ordure of this world, our new faculty instigated the genesis of other worlds, invisible ontologies that infiltrated appearances. Now we could feel the presence of things beyond the reach of our physical senses. The circumference of our fears dilated with further expansions of consciousness. Under the cover of atmosphere there seemed to be another side to the realm of being we knew, or thought we knew. Seeing shadows in the moonlight and hearing leaves rustling in the wind, our ancestors impregnated these sights and sounds with imaginings and apprehensions. Atmosphere had finally arrived, both foreshadowing horror and taking its substance from horror. Without this alliance, the first horror stories could not have been told.

As the horror story matured and branched out, so did the qualities of its atmosphere, most of all among the great names of this literary genre. For these writers, the atmosphere of their works is as unique as a signature or a fingerprint. It is the index of an identifiable consciousness that has been brewed from an amalgam of sensations, memories, emotions, and everything else that makes individuals what they are and predetermines what they will express as artists. Thus Lovecraft, in a 1935 letter to Catherine L. Moore, wrote these remarks on the weird story:

> It must, if it is to be authentic art, form primarily the *crystallization or symbolization of a definite human mood—not* the attempted delineation of *events*, since the "events" involved are of course largely fictitious and impossible. These events should figure *secondarily—atmosphere* being first. All real art must somehow be connected with truth, and in the case of weird art the emphasis must fall upon the one factor representing truth—certainly not the events (!!!) but the *mood of intense and fruitless human aspiration typified by the pretended overturning of cosmic laws and the pretended transcending of possible human experience.* (Lovecraft's emphasis)

The works in which Lovecraft most successfully put his theoretics of atmosphere into practice are paradigms of weird (or supernatural horror) fiction. Yet he wrote himself off as a failure in his pursuit to get on paper what he had in his head and strove to the end of his life to do what no other horror writer had done before him nor will ever do: lay bare his consciousness in an artifact. By the stress he placed on atmosphere, Lovecraft showed the way to an analysis of this element in horror literature, and, by extension, to an evaluation of the genre as a whole. While his personal use for atmosphere was to facilitate a sense of cosmic laws being overturned and human experience being transcended, he also defined the general purpose of atmosphere in horror stories: to give consistency (mood) to an imagined world in which we can at least pretend to escape from our mere humanity and enter into spaces where the human has no place and dies to itself either weeping or screaming or in awe at the horror of existence. Here lies the paradox of consuming horror as an escapist venture.

The secret of atmosphere in supernatural horror is simplicity itself. Already spoken of in the first paragraph of this chapter, it is here repeated and made categorical: Atmosphere is created by anything that suggests an ominous state of affairs beyond what our senses perceive and our minds can fully comprehend. It is the signature motif that Schopenhauer made discernible in pessimism—that behind the scenes of life there is something pernicious that makes a nightmare of our world. This something, this ominous state of affairs beyond what our senses perceive and our minds can comprehend, has previously been discussed in connection with Blackwood's "The Willows." In this story, Blackwood was careful not to dissipate with explanatory details the atmosphere he created. Lovecraft admired this work for its evocation of "nameless presences" that remain nameless and yet are powerfully felt. This is not a rule that Lovecraft himself often followed, as is particularly evident in his later stories. In such works as "The Dunwich Horror" and *At the Mountains of Madness*, Lovecraft details, analyzes, and, unlike Blackwood in the "The Willows," *names* the monstrosities at the center of these narratives. Nevertheless, there are always unparalleled images and ideas in Lovecraft's fiction that stay with the reader and instill a feeling of unknown horrors surpassing those that have been made known.

———

From the perspective of atmosphere, horror fiction may be dated only as far back as the novels of Ann Radcliffe, which contain enough visionary mood to make up for their bodice-ripper plots. Radcliffe's genius resided in turning a rage in the late eighteenth century for the picturesque in natural topographies into one that emphasized sublime dread as an aesthetic. Her works are known for the descriptions they contain of landscapes featuring mountains of intimidating height, valleys vast and deep, and moody twilights. Here quoted is such a view as witnessed by Emily St. Aubert, the heroine of Radcliffe's most popular novel, *The Mysteries of Udolpho* (1794). In this scene, Montoni, the story's malefactor, is delivering Emily and her aunt to his home. (Please bear with yet a few more long excerpts, ones from a long novel in which Radcliffe at length and often entertained her readers with sublimely thrilling carriage rides.)

> Towards the close of day, the road wound into a deep valley. Mountains, whose shaggy steeps appeared to be inaccessible, almost surrounded it. To the east, a vista opened, that exhibited the Apennines in their darkest horrors; and the long perspective of retiring summits, rising over each other, their ridges clothed with pines, exhibited a stronger image of grandeur, than any that Emily had yet seen. The sun had just sunk below the top of the mountains she was descending, whose long shadow stretched athwart the valley, but his sloping rays, shooting through an opening of the cliffs, touched with a yellow gleam the summits of the forest, that hung upon the opposite steeps, and streamed in full splendour upon the towers and battlements of a castle,

that spread its extensive ramparts along the brow of a precipice above. The splendour of these illumined objects was
heightened by the contrasted shade, which involved the
valley below.

"There," said Montoni, speaking for the first time in
several hours, "is Udolpho."

Emily's initial sighting of Udolpho elicits the same kind of tingling
sensation she feels for nature's mixed effects of minatory gigantism
and soul-striking splendor.

Emily gazed with melancholy awe upon the castle, which
she understood to be Montoni's; for, though it was now
lighted up by the setting sun, the gothic greatness of its
features, and its mouldering walls of dark grey stone, ren-
dered it a gloomy and sublime object. As she did, the light
died away on its walls, leaving a melancholy purple tint,
which spread deeper and deeper, as the thin vapour crept
up the mountain, while the battlements above were still
tipped with splendour. From those, too, the rays soon
faded, and the whole edifice was invested with the solemn
duskiness of evening. Silent, lonely, and sublime, it seemed
to stand the sovereign of the scene, and to frown defiance
on all, who dared to invade its solitary reign. As the twi-
light deepened, its features became more awful in obscurity,
and Emily continued to gaze, till its clustering towers were
alone seen, rising over the tops of the woods, beneath
whose thick shade the carriages soon after began to ascend.

The extent and darkness of these tall woods awakened
terrific images in her mind, and she almost expected to see
banditti start up from under the trees. At length, the

carriages emerged upon a heathy rock, and, soon after, reached the castle gates, where the deep tone of the portal bell, which was struck upon to give notice of their arrival, increased the fearful emotions, that had assailed Emily. While they waited till the servant within should come to open the gates, she anxiously surveyed the edifice: but the gloom, that overspread it, allowed her to distinguish little more than a part of its outline, with the massy walls of the ramparts, and to know, that it was vast, ancient and dreary. From the parts she saw, she judged of the heavy strength and extent of the whole. The gateway before her, leading into the courts, was of gigantic size, and was defended by two round towers, crowned by overhanging turrets, em-battled, where, instead of banners, now waved long grass and wild plants, that had taken root among the mouldering stones, and which seemed to sigh, as the breeze rolled past, over the desolation around them. The towers were united by a curtain, pierced and embattled also, below which ap-peared the pointed arch of a huge portcullis, surmounting the gates: from these, the walls of the ramparts extended to other towers, overlooking the precipice, whose shattered outline, appearing on a gleam, that lingered in the west, told of the ravages of war.—Beyond these all was lost in the obscurity of evening.

The horrid vicissitudes of Emily's stay at Udolpho further extend the spirit-stirring and densely atmospheric world in which she is immersed. To move along the plots of her essentially romantic nar-ratives, Radcliffe entrapped her heroines in castles so great and gloomy that their dungeons seem to have dungeons and their towers appear to the imagination to sprout supplementary towers into infinity. Within such gargantuan settings, Radcliffe's young women are terrorized by men of a wicked nature. They are also terrorized by simulacra of the supernatural that are later exposed as being natural in origin. Then they are rescued by their beloveds and, presumably, live gladsome lives unmarred by their traumatic experiences.

Some readers and critics disapprove of Radcliffe's ex post facto rationalizing of what seemed at the time to have been depictions of bona fide supernatural events, which for them dispels much of the frightful atmosphere she worked so diligently to create. The protest is that if she did not explain her way back to nature, her protagonists would have had to look into the face of a metaphysical horror that challenges one's concept of reality rather than the lesser horror of having to marry a man of bad character. It must seem a paradox, then, that Radcliffe is credited here as the parent of supernatural atmosphere when there are no supernatural happenings in her narratives. The resolution to this paradox is discussed in the section *Supernaturalism* later in this chapter. For now, let us listen to what Lovecraft had to say about Radcliffe as an author "who set new and higher standards in the domain of macabre and fear-inspiring atmosphere despite a provoking custom of destroying her own phantoms at the last through labored mechanical explanations."

To the familiar Gothic trappings of her predecessors Mrs. Radcliffe added a genuine sense of the unearthly in scene and incident which closely approached genius; every touch of setting and action contributing artistically to the impression of illimitable frightfulness which she wished to convey. A few sinister details like a track of blood on castle stairs, a groan from a distant vault, or a weird song in a nocturnal forest can with her conjure up the most powerful images of imminent horror; surpassing by far the extravagant and toilsome elaborations of others. Nor are these images in themselves any the less potent because they are explained away before the end of the novel. (*Supernatural Horror in Literature*, 1927; revised 1933–35)

The only real disappointment of Radcliffe's novels is that she did not follow through on the death threats to her main characters with their actual deaths, which, considering each of her novels in whole, burns off some of their atmospheric set-up with the resplendent sun of a happy ending. But to leave her heroines or heroes lying dead at the end of one of her narratives would have violated the terms of the genre of Gothic romance in which she wrote. And that would truly have been a blemish on her record as an adept storyteller. Atmospherically, death itself had not yet been added as an element to concentrate the effect of a horror tale.

The next innovation in atmosphere began with Poe in the early nineteenth century. Poe was familiar with Radcliffe's works, which laid the groundwork of the Gothic genre and registered brisk sales. Possibly in reaction to Radcliffe, he turned the world of scenic thrills and salvation upside down in "The Fall of the House of Usher." The story begins at evening as its narrator approaches on horseback a secluded mansion flanked by a swampy and putrid-looking tarn. While the House of Usher may at first seem to be oozing an enchanting Gothic atmosphere, the narrator goes out of his way to argue that this is not so. The dilapidated manse, which has a deep crack running across its façade, is not sublimely desolate in the manner of the ruined castles of Radcliffe's novels. It is rather a locus of indomitable despair. Here is how we see the Usher estate through the eyes of the character who has come to visit the old pile.

I know not how it was—but, with the first glimpse of the building, a sense of insufferable gloom pervaded my spirit. I say insufferable; for the feeling was unrelieved by any of that half-pleasurable, because poetic, sentiment, with which the mind usually receives even the sternest natural images of the desolate or terrible. I looked upon the scene before me—upon the mere house, and the simple landscape features of the domain—upon the bleak walls—upon the vacant eye-like windows—upon a few rank sedges—and upon a few white trunks of decayed trees—with an utter depression of soul which I can compare to no earthly sensation more properly than to the after-dream of the reveler upon opium—the bitter lapse into everyday life—the hideous dropping off of the veil. There was an iciness, a sinking, a sickening of the heart—an unredeemed dreariness of thought which no goading of the imagination could torture into aught of the sublime. What was it—I paused to think—what was it that so unnerved me in the contemplation of the House of Usher? It was a mystery all insoluble; nor could I grapple with the shadowy fancies that crowded upon me as I pondered. I was forced to fall back upon the unsatisfactory conclusion, that while, beyond doubt, there are combinations of very simple natural objects which have the power of thus affecting us, still the analysis of this power lies among considerations beyond our depth. It was possible, I reflected, that a mere different arrangement of the particulars of the scene, of the details of the picture, would be sufficient to modify, or perhaps to annihilate its capacity for sorrowful impression; and, acting upon this idea, I reined my horse to the precipitous brink of a black and lurid tarn that lay in unruffled lustre by the dwelling, and gazed down—but with a shudder even more thrilling than before—upon the re-modeled and inverted images of the grey sedge, and the ghastly tree-stems, and the vacant and eye-like windows.

However the narrator tries to relish rather than be distraught by the atmosphere of the house and its bedraggled grounds, he cannot do so. From the tenor of this beginning, the reader can expect no saving outcome. The atmosphere Poe created in the introductory section of his greatest tale is genuinely atmospheric because it bodes doom, which can mean only one thing—death. And in "The Fall of the House of Usher" such is the portion of Roderick and Madeline, the brother and sister who are the last of their family to occupy the hereditary domicile. Furthermore, the precarious con-dition of the house worsens to the point where the structure itself begins to cave. To thicken this climate of demise, the light of a blood-red moon shines through a widening breach in the masonry of the Usher abode as it sinks stone by stone beneath the still surface of the noxious tarn. Earlier the narrator told us of the identity that the local townspeople perceived between the House of Usher and its inhabitants. Admirably, Poe's tale culminates in the extinction of both. With this conclusion, Radcliffe's picturesque Gothic world had been supplanted by an atmosphere spilling out of death—the most ominous state of affairs with which we must deal.

In his tales, Poe created a world that is wholly evil, desolate, and doomed. These qualities give consistency to his imagined world. And there is no escape from this world, only a fall into it. Poe's enclosure of the reader in an environment without an exit distinguishes his works from those of earlier writers like Radcliffe. His characters do not take us from place to place looking at the scenery. They are inside a world that has no outside—no well-mapped places from which one can come and none to which one can go. The reader of Poe never has the sense that anything exists outside the frame of his narratives. What they suggest is that the only thing beyond what our senses can perceive and our mind can fully comprehend is blackness, nothing. It is the same in those most atmospheric of experiences we all know—dreams.

When you dream, you do not feel that anything exists which is not in your immediate surroundings. You cannot be anywhere in a dream except the place you are already in. Besides the psychological entrapment of dreams, there is also their fundamental strangeness, and Poe was expert at insinuating this phenomenon into his stories. Reading "The Fall of the House of Usher" is like having a lucid dream: we know that everything we see is unreal, yet there is paradoxically a heightened reality to it all. To awaken from such a dream is to lose your freedom from yourself and return to an onerous embodiment where consciousness is a tragedy and you cannot soar unscathed within an atmosphere of death. You can only die.

It was almost a century after the 1839 publication of "The Fall of the House of Usher" that Lovecraft took a giant step in the art of atmospherics with his "Call of Cthulhu." Well known as they may be to readers of horror fiction, the story's introductory sentences require transcription here.

The most merciful thing in the world, I think, is the inability of the human mind to correlate all its contents. We live on a placid island of ignorance in the midst of black seas of infinity, and it was not meant that we should voyage far. The sciences, each straining in its own direction, have hitherto harmed us little; but some day the piecing together of dissociated knowledge will open up such terrifying vistas of reality, and of our frightful position therein, that we shall either go mad from the revelation or flee from the deadly light into the peace and safety of a new dark age.

From Lovecraft's overture to this tale, the reader may surmise that besides the death of a character or two, the human race itself may go under by voyaging too far on the "black seas of infinity." While the above statement is abstract, it is all the more atmospheric for being so, and we are ardent to read what "dissociated knowledge," not a stunningly evocative phrase, has been pieced together by one Francis Wayland Thurston, who is displaced from his old reality and set into an ill-starred fictional world that makes all of his former days seem a heaven of naïveté.

"I have looked upon all that the universe has to hold of horror," F. W. Thurston writes after he has pieced together the puzzle, "and even the skies of spring and the flowers of summer must ever afterward be poison to me." In other words, he has done what no one has been in a position to do before him—sort out the worst of existence from any compensatory dividends, a process which leads him to conclude that life is a malignancy it were better not to know. This is Lovecraft's atmosphere—that of a world in which the "frightful position" he has placed all human existence could lead to universal madness or extinction at a moment's notice. Through this atmosphere, Lovecraft gives consistency to an imagined world where there is greatness in knowing too much of the horror of a planet in the shadow of Cthulhu and all that this implies about our existence. As for those people who still go about their ordinary, average business complacently enjoying the skies of spring and the flowers of summer, innocently unaware of the monstrosities with which they coexist—they are children. They have no idea that there is nothing worth living for in Lovecraft's world. They are not in its atmosphere. Yet at any time they could be. It must be remembered that the atmosphere of a supernatural world and its horror exists only in the human imagination. There is nothing like it in nature, nor can nature provoke it. It is a contrivance of our consciousness, and only we can know it among all the organisms of the earth. We are alone in our minds with the atmosphere of a supernatural world and its horror. We are both its creators and what it has created—uncanny things that have nothing to do with the rest of creation.

Theme

The literary world may be divided into two unequal groups: the insiders and the outsiders. The former are many and the latter are few. The placement of a given writer into one group or the other could be approached by assessing the consciousness of that writer as it is betrayed by various components of his work, including verbal style, general tone of voice, selection of subjects and themes, etc. As any reader knows, such things do vary among authors. To pin any of them down within a capricious or oneiric taxonomy of insiders and outsiders would then perforce become an experiment in uselessness.

Ernest Hemingway, William Faulkner, Jean-Paul Sartre, Samuel Beckett, T. S. Eliot, Knut Hamsun, Hermann Hesse: who is on the inside and who is on the outside? The brain reels when considering well-known works by these writers, as they seem to express sensibilities at several arms' length from those of average mortals. Immediately, we recall Hemingway's story "A Clean, Well-Lighted Place," which ends with a travesty of the Lord's Prayer: "Our nada who art in nada, nada be thy name." Then our thoughts turn to the collection of degenerates in Faulkner's novels, which do not seem intent on showing off the nobler side, if there is one, of the human race. Nor should we forget Eliot's homage to entropy, *The Waste Land* (1922), or the unbalanced protagonists who lead us through Hamsun's *Hunger* (1890), Hesse's *Steppenwolf* (1928), Sartre's *Nausea* (1938), and the entire output of Beckett. Conveniently, the status of these authors—insider or outsider—has been adjudicated for us by the Swedish committees that dispensed to each of them a Nobel Prize in literature, which is annually given out to authors who produce "the most outstanding work of an idealistic tendency."

But should these literary greats be classed as insiders exclusively because they received a *prize* from a panel of Swedish judges? Some would say "yes," but not entirely because of the Nobel. Some would say "no," despite the Nobel.[1] These conflicting opinions leave our job unfinished insofar as determining the consciousness of an author to be that of an insider or an outsider. To expedite this inquest, we could use a candidate whose credentials unambiguously place him in the latter group. To fill this position, any number of worthy outsiders could be named. One of them is Roland Topor, whose short horror novel *The Tenant* (1964) is a document that expresses the consciousness of an unimpeachable outsider. To discern with a modest confidence what places a writer on the inside or the outside, *The Tenant* will be compared with another short novel that shares its theme, *One, No One, and One Hundred Thousand* (1926) by the Nobel Prize-winning Luigi Pirandello. In itself, theme is no giveaway of an author's consciousness. What counts is how that theme is resolved. Pirandello's resolution parades the symptoms of "an idealistic tendency," while Topor's takes the anti-idealistic position.

The theme of *One, No One, and One Hundred Thousand* is explicitly that of the self as a falsehood born of our systems of perception and cognition. In contrast to the dogma of the many, as Pirandello's narrator and leading character Vitangelo Moscarda comes to appreciate, the self is an insubstantial construct invented to lend coherence and meaning to an existence that is actually chaotic and meaningless. However well we function as bodies, we also recognize—because we are so often forced to do so—that they are unstable, damage-prone, and disposable phenomena. Simultaneously, we believe—until a malignant brain lesion or some life-rending event causes us to question this belief—that our "selves" are more sturdy, enduring, and real than the deteriorating tissue in which they are encased.

In *One, No One, and One Hundred Thousand*, Moscarda is made aware of his misperception of his self, and by extension of the entire world of forms in which the self functions, by a misperception he has made about his body. Early in the story, he believes his nose to be evenly structured on its right and left sides. Then his wife tells him that his nose is not symmetrical but is lower on the left side than on the right. Being an incurably pensive individual, Moscarda is troubled by his wife's remark; being an intellectually honest individual, he has to admit it is true. That he misperceived this single feature of his appearance leads Moscarda to investigate what other delusions he has been entertaining about his appearance throughout his life. He ascertains a constellation of them. After scrupulous self-examination of his physical person, he grants that he is not the man he thought he was. Now he believes he is an outsider to himself—a figment in his own eyes and in the eyes of others.

Later, Moscarda is condemned to further revelations: "I still believed this outsider was only one person: only one for everybody, as I thought I was only one for myself. But soon my horrible drama became more complicated." This occurs when he discovers "the hundred thousand Moscardas that I was, not only for the others but also for myself, all with this one name of Moscarda, ugly to the point of cruelty, all inside this poor body of mine that was also one, one and, alas, no one. . . ." Fortunately for Moscarda, and ruefully for the reader (at least the reader who is an outsider), he comes to accept the unreality of everything he had conceived himself to be and becomes one with all that exists. He no longer thinks but simply *is*. "This is the only way I can live now. To be reborn moment by moment. To prevent thought from working again inside me. . . ." The last paragraph of the novel is an exaltation of his new state of existence.

> The city is far away. There comes to me occasionally, upon the vesper calm, the sound of its bells. I, however, no longer hear those bells within me, but without, ringing for themselves and perhaps trembling with joy in their re-sounding cavities, in a beautiful blue sky filled with a warm sun, to the twittering of swallows or swaying heavily to wind and cloud, so high, so high, in their aerial belfries. To think of death, to pray. It may be that there is one who yet has need of this, and it is to his need that the bells give voice. I no longer have any such need, for the reason that I am dying every instant, and being born anew and without memories: alive and whole, no longer in myself, but in ev-erything outside. (Translation by Samuel Putnam)

End of story. Things turn out all right for Moscarda. He is now an outsider who has been *saved*. In his loss of a self, he brings to mind U. G. Krishnamurti, John Wren-Lewis, and Suzanne Segal—those unwitting prodigies who recovered from shocks to their systems, following which the cognitive mechanisms which produce a fictive ego shut down. In these instances, the individual who loses himself is the beneficiary of a rapturous pay-off. This is truly a "good death" in which someone disappears as a purported self and is reborn as . . . no one. He is content just to exist, and equally content not to exist.

But does anyone really believe that Luigi Pirandello knew firsthand his protagonist's state of selfless beatitude? Or is it more likely that he just imagined this ending of a decidedly "idealistic tendency"? Yet whether Pirandello actually experienced or merely researched the ideal resolution to Moscarda's painful self-consciousness, it is not a resolution available to the reader, who could follow Moscarda's route to salvation step-by-step and never be delivered to the promised land of the ego-dead. If it were so, Pirandello would have discovered the most phenomenal cure ever known for the sufferings especially reserved for humankind. He would have solved every scourge we face as a species. As one might expect, though, he did no such thing. Instead, Pirandello resolved his fairy tale by lowering down a deus ex machina. His book is a moral scam with mystical transcendence standing in for the prayer Moscarda says he no longer needs. This is what the literary insider offers. In *The Tenant*, Roland Topor supplies the opposing view of the outsider.

When Pirandello's character Moscarda describes his escalating puzzlement over his identity as a "horrible drama," his words appear as a formality—a perfunctory gesture that fails to convey the uncanny nature of his situation. In *The Tenant*, on the other hand, Topor affectingly dramatizes the horror of his non-hero Trelkovsky as he traverses the same terrain as his Italian counterpart. A critical passage in Topor's novel begins with the following sentence: "'At what precise moment,' Trelkovsky asked himself, 'does an individual cease to be the person he—and everyone else—believes himself to be?'"

A Parisian with a Slavic name, Trelkovsky is an outsider and moves in a world where outsiders are persecuted, as they are in the real world. Hoping to move into a new apartment—one previously occupied by a woman named Simone Choule, who was critically injured and not expected to live—he is made to feel as if he is nobody by the landlord, Monsieur Zy, and then by the other residents of this sinister place. By flexing their self-appointed grandiosity, Trelkovsky's persecutors can maintain their own delusional status as somebodies, real persons who are well adapted to the hell they have created for themselves.

Anyone who is marked as being outside of the group is fair game for those who would assert *their* reality over all others. (Compare with the psychosocial devices of Terror Management Theory.) Yet they, too, are nobodies. If they were not, their persecutions would not be required: they could pass their lives with a sure mindfulness of their substance and value. But as any good Buddhist (or even Pirandello's Moscarda) could tell you, human beings have no more substance and value than anything else on earth. The incapacity to repose alongside both the mountains and the mold of this planet is the fountainhead of the torments we wreak on one another. As long as we deny a person or group the claim to be as right and as real as we are, so long may we hold this dreamlike claim for ourselves alone. And it is the duty of everyone to inculcate a sense of being empty of substance and value in those who are not emulations of them.

Without being consciously aware of it, Trelkovsky experiences an epiphany at the midpoint of the novel that is inspired by his neighbors' behavior toward him: "'The bastards!' Trelkovsky raged. 'The bastards! What the hell do they want—for everyone to roll over and play dead! And even that probably wouldn't be enough!'" He is more right than he knows. Because what they want is for everyone to roll over and play *them*.

Martians—they were all Martians. . . . They were strangers on this planet, but they refused to admit it. They played at being perfectly at home. . . . He was no different. . . . He belonged to their species, but for some unknown reason he had been banished from their company. They had no confidence in him. All they wanted from him was obedience to their incongruous rules and their ridiculous laws. Ridiculous only to him, because he could never fathom their intricacy and their subtlety.

Trelkovsky's neighbors cannot admit to themselves what he comes to realize: Everybody is nobody; no one is empowered to define who he or she is. But people do arrogate to themselves the authority to make a ruling on who *you* are, and you will stand mute before their bench. From the outset, Trelkovsky is manipulated to accept this verdict; finally, he pronounces it on himself. To his broken mind it seems that the only way to defy his neighbors' murderous conspiracy against him is to cooperate in it. He does this by allowing himself to fall from the window of his apartment and through the glass roofing over the courtyard below. The first time does not kill him, so he hauls his bloody anti-self back up the stairs, jeering at his neighbors who have come out to lunge at his body with sharp objects. He then falls a second time from the window. Following in the footsteps of Gloria Beatty, he decides to call it quits in the world's lugubrious game. Interestingly, *The Tenant* concludes with the same kind of leap beyond the mundane as does *One, No One, and One Hundred Thousand*. Sadly for Trelkovsky, it is a leap in the opposite direction. More accurately, it is a leap that does not deliver Topor's protagonist from his "horrible drama" but one that catapults him into the outermost nightmare of nobodies.

As an insider, Pirandello resolved the theme of *One, No One, and One Hundred Thousand* in a spirit-lifting mode. Imbued with a different consciousness, the outsider can only give us resolutions of a miserablist nature. For the past few slivers of human history, those of us living in what is termed the free world have been allowed to hold disparate worldviews, but only on the condition that they affirm, directly or indirectly, the survival of the species. They must not be pessimistic, nihilistic, or in any respect skeptical about the livability of human life. Such perspectives might well be valued by outsiders, but insiders, who form the preponderant division of humankind, will not incorporate the outsider's stark attitudes and unhappy endings into their philosophies, ideologies, national policies, or fraternal by-laws. Both Pirandello and Topor dealt with the identical theme: the transformative dissolution of one's self-concept. The former writer ended his story with a portrait of a man who joyously transcends himself by becoming the "no one" in the novel's title. This resolution has already been deplored as a put-up job. An insider might say as much about the ending of Topor's novel, which implies a descent into nightmare that Trelkovsky never saw coming.

In the epilogue to *The Tenant*, it turns out that Trelkovsky survives what should have been his death-plunge. But he does so in a strange way. Regaining consciousness in a hospital bed, he sees he has a visitor. And now everything comes home to him. (Anyone can tell where this is going.) The hospital bed where he now reclines is the same one that, at the beginning of the story, he stood beside as he looked over the bandage-hidden body of his apartment's former tenant, whom he wanted to see for himself was not going to recover from her injuries and try to reclaim her old lodgings. She, too, had fallen from the window of that shabby residence. The newly bed-ridden patient, like the one before, identifies to his horror the one who has come to visit him. It is himself. Immobilized by his injuries and his face dressed to expose only one eye and an opening for his mouth, he realizes that he has changed places with the woman whose apartment he once coveted. Perhaps not for the first time, as he might be caught in a loop of reincarnations, he has come to be at his own bedside. Realizing what has happened to him, the one in the bed, he already knows what is going to happen to the one standing over him, the one who is not him anymore, and yet is.

Trelkovsky has now solved his (and Moscarda's) riddle: "At what precise moment does an individual cease to be the person he—and everyone else—believes himself to be?" Answer: at the moment when an individual becomes conscious that he has been trapped in a paradox of identity and there is no way out for him as long as he believes himself to be something he is not. Ask any puppet that thinks it is a person.

As neither Pirandello nor Topor underwent the transformative dissolution of the self-concept that is the common theme of their stories—it would be the high point of each man's biography if they had—are they not equally disingenuous? The answer to that question would seem to turn upon which author's representation of the world you deem to be more symbolically well founded: ending one's days in serene communion with all that makes up the world . . . or trapped in a damaged body in a hospital bed, unable to do anything but scream at the sight of a clueless wraith, the nobody who was you in the dream that was your life. Whichever conclusion to these thematically analogous stories appears more faithful to human experience depends on who you are . . . or who you think you are. This is a very Pirandellian theme.

While Topor's vision seems empirically sturdier, Pirandello's is the crowd favorite. To receive the prize Pirandello awards Moscarda, if only for a moment before one's death, would make amends for a lifetime of lashings. Grievously, just because something is a desideratum does not mean that believing in it will save you. But Pirandello and his kind want you, and themselves, to die trying. All Topor and his kind have to say is that you should always have your affairs in order, which may bring you some peace of mind if you are confined to a hospital bed . . . or only looking for a new apartment.

Characters

In his essay "The Undelivered," Cioran wrote: "The more we consider the Buddha's last exhortation, 'Death is inherent in all created things; labor ceaselessly for your salvation,' the more we are troubled by the impossibility of *feeling* ourselves as an aggregate, a transitory if not fortuitous convergence of elements." Cioran could not have been more right about the impossibility of feeling oneself to be a thing of parts, a being made as it is made. Transporting ourselves to and fro on the earth and walking up and down upon it, we are doggedly believable *characters*, although we are not provably anything more than that. Yet we do seem to be more than that, and seeming is enough for us to get by as we have all these years.

In the course of our disillusionments, we have confessed to being bodies made of elementary particles just like everything else. But we must stop short of any tidings that would put us on a par with bacteria and beer mugs. That would be to skyrocket disillusionment out of the atmosphere, leaving us without a speck of our invaluable selves and the games they play. One game that most writers of horror fiction play with their characters is called Good versus Evil. And they play it as if it were the only game in town. Certainly it is the oldest game in town, the one we have relied on for much of our characterization from the time we first knew who we were, or thought we did. A few horror writers, though, play a different game, one in which, as Poe wrote, "Horror is the soul of the plot" rather than believable characters. The game of Good versus Evil is about horror *in* the world, and its players, its characters, are given a fighting chance. The other game is about the horror *of* the world, and none of its players has a chance, unless by pure chance.

For example, compare two horror novels that presume the reality of supernatural possession—William Peter Blatty's *The*

Exorcist (1971) and Lovecraft's *The Case of Charles Dexter Ward* (written 1927; published posthumously, 1941). In the world of Blatty's Good-versus-Evil novel, certain believable characters are dressed for doom and others for survival. (This is a formulaic element of nearly all popular horror novels.) Two priests, Frs. Karras and Merrin, give their lives to save Regan, a believable characterization of a young girl whose body, and perhaps her soul—the relationship between body and soul among Christian sects is not consistent—has been possessed by a demon or demons. The deaths of these priests are acceptable to readers as part of the story's formula, despite the fact that they are the sort of characters whom ordinary folk *care about*. Burke Dennings, the director of the movie in which Regan's actress mother Chris MacNeill stars, is murdered by the possessed Regan. He is not a terribly likeable fellow, being a profane and belligerent drunk, so the function he serves is that of a character who can be killed off to advance the narrative in a shocking direction, since the reader does not care much about him, however believable he may be. This is very acceptable to readers, who are within their rights to expect at least one person to be slain over the course of a horror novel. Such is the way that the greater part of those who patronize works of fiction like to see writers handle their characters—believably. They also want a finale in which Good wins out over Evil, which assures them that the formula "being alive is all right" is the right formula.

The Case of Charles Dexter Ward is in every way a negation of Blatty's *Exorcist*. In Lovecraft's novel, the universe cares nothing for human life, just as it is in the real world, and one does not care about the characters—they are only a perspective from which to view the horror of the plot. This is acceptable to very few readers. Good and Evil are rubrics of an existential code long gone, just as they are in the real world. Again, this is acceptable to very few readers. And the idea of human beings as creatures with souls is not an issue in *The Case of Charles Dexter Ward* because it was not an issue for Lovecraft. Everyone, not only the hapless protagonist of the book, exists in a world that is a wall-to-wall nightmare. In Lovecraft's *universe without a formula*, everyone is killable—and some kill themselves just ahead of the worse things waiting for them. Life as we conceive it, let alone a configuration of atoms that goes by the name Charles Dexter Ward, occurs in a context of permanent jeopardy which only remains to be discovered and from which there is no salvation. Lovecraft does not want to take you on an emotional roller-coaster ride, at the end of which he tells you to watch your step as your car comes to a stop and you settle back onto steady ground. He simply wants to say that we no longer have to stand back very far to see that the human race is what it always has been in this or any other world—irrelevant, which is as liberating to some as it is maddening to others, including Lovecraft's characters.

Lovecraft's employment of supernatural possession as a story-telling device in *The Case of Charles Dexter Ward* is so alien to Blatty's in *The Exorcist* that the two men might as well have been living in different centuries, or even different millennia. The narrative parameters of *The Exorcist* begin and end with the New Testament; those of *The Case of Charles Dexter Ward* could only have been conceived by a fiction writer of the modern era, a time when it had become safe not only to place humanity outside the center of the Creation but also to survey the universe itself as centerless and our species as only a smudge of organic materials at the mercy of forces that know us not, just as we are in the real world.

As for the special fate of the protagonist of Lovecraft's novel, his possession by his ancestor Joseph Curwen, a master of occult arts, is only a means to much larger ends that have been eons in the making. As previously imaged, he is just a configuration of atoms, not an ensouled creature of a god who has been toying with us for the past hundred thousand years more or less. Absolutely up-to-date—that is, post-*everything*—*The Case of Charles Dexter Ward* emerged from an imagination that was deferential to no traditions or dogmas, and its author went the distance of disillusionment in assuming the meaningless universe that became the starting point for later investigators in the sciences and philosophy (Ask the Nobel Prize-winning physicist Steven Weinberg, who notoriously said, "The more we know about the universe, the more meaningless it appears.") Although Lovecraft did have his earthbound illusions, at the end of the day he existed in a no man's land of disillusionment. As a fiction writer, he will ever be a contemporary of each new generation of mortals, because there will always be many a character in the real world for whom human life is not acceptable.

Uncharacters

In many horror stories there is an assortment of figures that appear as walk-ons or extras whose purpose is to lend their spooky presence to a narrative for atmosphere alone, while the real bogey is something else altogether. Puppets, dolls, and other caricatures of the human often make cameo appearances as shapes sagging in the corner of a child's bedroom or lolling on the shelves of a toy store. There are also dismembered limbs and decapitated heads of manikins that have been relegated to spare parts strewn about an old warehouse where such things are stored or sent to die. As backdrops or bit-players, imitations of the human form have a symbolic value because they seem connected to another world, one that is all harm and disorder—the kind of place we sometimes fear is the model for our own home ground, which we *must* believe is passably sound and secure, or at least not an environment where we might mistake a counterfeit person for the real thing. But in fiction, as in life, mistakes are sometimes made. When they are, one of those humanoid replicas may advance to the center of a story's action.

In E. T. A. Hoffmann's "The Sandman," for instance, the protagonist Nathanael discovers that the too perfect girl to whom he has proposed marriage is really just an automaton. This shakes him up so greatly that he is committed to an asylum until he recovers his senses. The incident with Nathanael's mechanical fiancée, a thing of parts who is the creation of two mysterious characters in the story, also shakes up others who are in love with dream girls. As Hoffmann's story goes, "Many lovers, to be quite convinced that they were not enamored of wooden dolls, would request their mistresses to sing and dance a little out of time, to embroider and knit, and play with their lapdogs, while listening to reading, etc., and, above all, not merely to listen, but also sometimes to talk in such a manner as presupposed actual thought and feeling." Toward the end of "The Sandman," Nathanael's madness returns, and he leaps to his death from a steeple after screaming, "Turn and turn about, little doll."

There are many abominable fates in horror stories, and among them is that of Nathanael. Worse still is when a human being becomes objectified as a puppet, a doll, or some other caricature of our species and enters a world that he or she thought was just a creepy little place *inside* of ours. What a jolt to find oneself a prisoner in this sinister sphere, reduced to a composite mechanism looking out on the land of the human, or one which we believe to be human by any definition of the word, and to be exiled from it. Just as we know that dreams are merely reflections of what happens in our lives, we are also quite sure that puppets, dolls, and other caricatures of our species are only reflections of ourselves. In a sane world, no correspondence could exist between those artificial anatomies and our natural flesh. That would be too strange and awful, for things to become confused in such a way. More strange and awful, of course, would be to find this a *living confusion*—life as the dream of a puppet.

Supernaturalism

When the narrator of Joseph Conrad's novel *Under Western Eyes* (1911) writes that "the belief in a supernatural source of evil is not necessary; men alone are quite capable of every wickedness," he seems to be speaking for the author, who shunned the supernatural in his fiction. Nevertheless, Conrad was a great depicter of what he felt was an ineffable deviltry that nests in the shadows of all that is. And any close reader of Conrad will perceive the impure breath of the supernatural in many of his works. In *Heart of Darkness* (1902), for example, he pulls at the collar of psychological realism, plying his genius for nuance and stealing up to the very border of supernaturalism. By proceeding thus, Conrad impresses upon his audience the consciousness of a horror that goes beyond the human and takes in all of being.

Conrad's odyssey into horror begins when the narrator of *Heart of Darkness*, Charles Marlow, acquires a position with a European business concern as the skipper of a steamboat. His first charge is to guide the vessel down a snaking African river to a remote outpost run by one the company's best men, Mr. Kurtz, a prolific supplier of goods to his employers. At every point, Marlow feels his journey is taking him farther and farther into an unholy land as he progresses toward his destination. Thus:

> Going up that river was like traveling back to the earliest beginnings of the world, when vegetation rioted on the earth and the big trees were kings. An empty stream, a great silence, an impenetrable forest. The air was warm, thick, heavy, sluggish. There was no joy in the brilliance of

sunshine. The long stretches of the waterway ran on, deserted, into the gloom of overshadowed distances. On silvery sandbanks hippos and alligators sunned themselves side by side. The broadening waters flowed through a mob of wooded islands; you lost your way on that river as you would in a desert, and butted all day long against shoals, trying to find the channel, till you thought yourself bewitched and cut off forever from everything you had known once—somewhere—far away—in another existence perhaps. There were moments when one's past came back to one, as it will sometimes when you have not a moment to spare to yourself; but it came in the shape of an unrestful and noisy dream, remembered with wonder amongst the overwhelming realities of this strange world of plants, and water, and silence. And this stillness of life did not in the least resemble a peace. It was the stillness of an implacable force brooding over an inscrutable intention. It looked at you with a vengeful aspect. I got used to it afterwards; I did not see it any more; I had no time. I had to keep guessing at the channel; I had to discern, mostly by inspiration, the signs of hidden banks; I watched for sunken stones; I was learning to clap my teeth smartly before my heart flew out, when I shaved by a fluke some infernal sly old snag that would have ripped the life out of the tin-pot steamboat and drowned all the pilgrims; I had to keep a look-out for the signs of dead wood we could cut up in the night for next day's steaming. When you have to attend to things of that sort, to the mere incidents of the surface, the reality—the reality, I tell you—fades. The inner truth is hidden—luckily, luckily. But I felt it all the same; I felt often its mysterious stillness watching me. . . .

This passage substantiates that you do not need the supernatural to invoke the supernatural. Reality fades more and more as Marlow approaches Kurtz, who embodies the horrible "inner truth" of things. On the level of narrative, this inner truth is outwardly made plain by one look at Kurtz's base of operations, where the barbarous means of his successful career are visible everywhere. But Kurtz is not just a bestial headman managing a trading post in Africa. His whole meaning as a character is much more than that. What the brutally atavistic Kurtz signifies to Marlow surpasses the "wickedness of men" and deposits the steamboat captain on the threshold of an occult truth about the underpinnings of the only reality he has ever known—the anchoring fictions of civilization.

If Kurtz is simply a man who has realized his potential for wickedness—which, by inference, is a potential for each of us—then he is merely another candidate for incarceration or the death penalty. But if he is a man who has probed the mysteries of something that is wicked in its essence, then he has crossed the point of no return, and his last words—"The horror! The horror!"—have prodigious implications. Not to say that the assorted overtones that literary critics have heard in the story—civilization is only skin deep, European colonialism was a bad business—are not horrors. But they are not *the* horror that every incident of the narrative prefigures. In *Heart of Darkness*, Conrad did not cede "the horror" a local habitation and a name (example: *The Creature from the Black Lagoon*), but artfully suggested a malignity conjoining the latent turpitude of human beings with that active in being itself.

As a species, we might have been saved both from our turpitude, latent or not, and from any notion of turpitude active in being itself. The real horror, the real tragedy, is that we were not saved. In an 1898 letter to the Scottish writer R. B. Cunninghame Graham, Conrad wrote:

Yes, egoism is good, and altruism is good, and fidelity to
nature would be the best of all . . . if we could only get rid
of consciousness. What makes mankind tragic is not that
they are the victims of *nature*, it is that they are conscious
of it. To be part of the *animal kingdom* under the conditions
of this earth is very well—but as soon as you know of your
slavery, the pain, the anger, the strife—the tragedy begins.
We can't return to nature, since we can't change our place
in it. Our refuge is in stupidity . . . There is no morality, no
knowledge, and no hope; there is only the *consciousness of
ourselves* which drives us about a world that . . . is always
but a vain and floating appearance. (Conrad's emphases)

Too conscious that *Heart of Darkness* was not the place for such
discourse, Conrad gave us Marlow's sensitivity to an "implacable
force brooding over an inscrutable intention" and Kurtz's resonant
last words. If our species was not saved from consciousness, at least
the above letter was saved so that we could know what horror was
in Conrad's heart.

Some horror writers are not the least concerned with the wickedness of men but exclusively attend to an "implacable force
brooding over an inscrutable intention," which is to say, something
pernicious behind the scenes of life that makes our lives a living
nightmare. For Lovecraft, this all-embracing nightmare became the
grounding for the supernaturalism of his writings, most famously
in his negative mythology of multidimensional horrors sometimes
collectively designated as the "Great Old Ones," who came to earth
from other worlds, much like the Body Snatchers and the Thing.
Their individual names alone, some of which were referenced

earlier in this book, convey their otherworldly demonism. Here are some other names: Dagon, Yog-Sothoth, and Shub-Niggurath the Goat with a Thousand Young. Lovecraft also wrote of unnamed beings that may be apprehended only by their sensory attributes, as with the eponymous entity in "The Colour out of Space" or the unobserved source of the "exquisitely low and infinitely distant musical note" that sounds in the blackness above the Rue d'Auseil in "The Music of Erich Zann."

In composing the latter work, Lovecraft came up with a model supernatural horror tale, one in which a subjective mind and an objective monstrosity shade into each other, the one projecting itself outward and the other reflecting back so that together they form the perfect couple dancing to the uncanny music of being. The mind in the story is that of the nervously afflicted narrator; the monstrosity is the unnamed and unnamable nemesis of the nervously afflicted Zann. With his viol playing, Zann battles to keep at bay this *thing* that would destroy an already tumble-down world as represented by the Rue d'Auseil, the street on which he lives and where he dies. In "The Music of Erich Zann," Lovecraft offers no sanity or system of meaning. What he does offer are Zann's "weird notes," which correspond to powers of disorder that scoff at our fabricated world and show us the horror of our lives.

Belief in the supernatural is only superstition. That said, a *sense of the supernatural*, as Conrad evinced in *Heart of Darkness*, must be admitted if one's inclination is to go to the limits of horror. It is the sense of what should not be—the sense of being ravaged by the impossible. Phenomenally speaking, the supernatural may be regarded as the metaphysical counterpart of insanity, a transcendental correlative of a mind that has been driven mad. This mind does not keep a chronicle of "man's inhumanity to man" but instead tracks a dysphoria symptomatic of our life as transients in a creation that is natural for all else that lives, but for us is anything but.

The most uncanny of creaturely traits, the sense of the supernatural, the impression of a fatal estrangement from the visible, is dependent on our consciousness, which merges the outward and the inward into a universal comedy without laughter. We are only chance visitants to this jungle of blind mutations. The natural world existed when we did not, and it will continue to exist long after we are gone. The supernatural crept into life only when the door of consciousness was opened in our heads. The moment we stepped through that door, we walked out on nature. Say what we will about it and deny it till we die—we are blighted by our knowing what is too much to know and too secret to tell one another if we are to stride along our streets, work at our jobs, and sleep in our beds. It is the knowledge of a race of beings that is only passing through this shoddy cosmos.[2]

As explained in an earlier section of the present contrivance, literary use of the supernatural may strikingly differ among the works of diverse authors or even within the output of a single author. A noteworthy example of the latter case displays itself in a comparison of two of Shakespeare's greatest plays, *Hamlet* (c. 1600–1601) and *Macbeth* (c. 1606). In *Hamlet*, the supernatural element is extraneous; in *Macbeth*, it is integral. While both dramas are patterned along the lines of a soap opera—complete with squabbles, schemes, betrayals, and deceptions in a world on the make—*Macbeth* is played out within a supernatural order that is reinforced throughout the play and gives it a terrible mystery that *Hamlet* lacks. The latter tragedy does have its ghost, but this apparition serves only as a dramatic device to get the plot moving, which could have been done without an otherworldly intervention that gives away the work's central secret from its commencement and in no sense tinctures the incidents of the play with a tenebrous and malefic presence, as is the case with *Macbeth*.

Without the three witches (aka Weird Sisters; Sisters of Fate), who officiate as masters of a power that reduces the characters of the story to the status of puppets, *Macbeth* would not be *Macbeth*. Without the ghost of Hamlet, Sr., *Hamlet* would still be *Hamlet*. As we all know, later in the drama Hamlet the Younger doubts the words of his father's presumptive spirit and double-checks them by having a troupe of actors stage a number called *The Murder of Gonzago*, so that the indecisive protagonist can see for himself how the new king, his uncle Claudius, responds to the play's reenactment of how he killed his brother. Hamlet needs earthly evidence, not just the words of a revenant, to confirm the crime. The play's the thing, not the ghost. It is just too much that after all the inside information thunderously told by the Hamlet the Elder in the first act, Hamlet the Younger would still feel the necessity to engage in his own detective work before making his move. Another setup could have been used to point the finger at Claudius's nefarious deed—a snoop in the shrubbery perhaps—and the paternal shade could have been edited from the play. Along with this excision there would be lost a side issue of interest to Shakespeare scholars—to wit, the Bard's treatment of Catholicism's doctrine of Purgatory—but nothing apposite to the story would have gone missing. And the matter of whether or not the ghost is truly that of Hamlet's father or a lying goblin is not kept so much in the reader or playgoer's mind to be a source of great suspense and would have derailed the course of *Hamlet*'s plot had it turned out to be the latter. All told, *Hamlet* is not a work that gains anything considerable from a supernatural intrusion.

In both *Hamlet* and *Macbeth* the title characters deliver a mass of majestic rhetoric concerning the mysterious matters of human life. However, there is a dimension of the unknowable in *Macbeth* that situates us in a world of cosmic misrule outside the boundaries of the natural order. *Hamlet* is a tragedy of human errors; *Macbeth*, an uncanny puppet show. The springboard of the earlier play is, once more, the treacherous murder of Hamlet's father. That of the later piece is a malicious witchery in the world, an unbodied agency that tugs Macbeth through motions that accurse him and his wife as much as they do their victims. The play is a ferment of fatality. Every action is choreographed by a supernaturalism that deracinates its main characters from their natural drives to survive and reproduce and leads Macbeth to the revelation, among others, that "Life's but a walking shadow"—that death is the thing that makes us uncanny things that have nothing to do with the rest of creation. Hamlet has bad dreams, as do we all. But Macbeth cannot dream. As contracted by fate, he has murdered sleep and knows only a waking nightmare.

Plot

In his *Idea of the Holy: An Inquiry into the Non-Rational Factor in the Idea of the Divine and Its Relation to the Rational* (1917), the German theologian Rudolf Otto writes of the "numinous," the wholly Other (that is, God), as a *mysterium tremendum et fascinans* ("a terrifying and fascinating mystery"). Confrontations with the numinous are uncommon outside the lives of religious mystics, who may be terrified by their supernatural assignations but are never undone by them. For these extremist believers, the supernatural is a terror of the divine, not a demonic horror. And it is the absolute reality. After conjuring up the wholly Other through prayer and meditation, cultists of the sacred feel themselves to be nothing in its presence, only a bit of crud stuck to the shoe of the numinous. Eventually, so says Otto, they make common cause with the numinous and are able to feel good about themselves. On Otto's say-so, these are encounters with the supernatural in its truest and most encompassing sense; any others, including those evoked by supernatural horror stories, are primitive or perverted. What else could a theologian say? What other kind of supernatural story would he have to tell? While *The Idea of the Holy* has some electrifying moments when things are touch and go, the ending is all blessedness and no harm done. But this is not what readers expect when the supernatural is the featured element. They expect death, good or not so good, and will feel swindled if they do not get it. Because death is what really terrifies and fascinates them. In the midst of their lives, they are deep in death . . . and they know it. They do not know the numinous, which hangs back from life and welcomes very few into its circle. Why things should be this way is the real mystery.

The context of Otto's tract is the nature and origins of religion, a respectable fixation for scholars, divines, and anyone else who has a few coins to throw in the pot. But paranormal researchers have written with as much conviction, investigative rigor, and personal experience about their own field of study; they, too, have tales to tell of the terrifying and fascinating, as if anyone could have a monopoly on these emotions or reserve their copyright for true believers only.[3] The supernatural is in the public domain, and, whatever the ontological angle, it is packaged with plots that are missing from the natural world. When we and our prototypes were part of that world, our lives had as little plot to them as the doings of earth's flora and fauna. Later, as our consciousness began to inflate, we strayed off from the natural. Our bodies stayed behind, but our minds searched for stories with better plots than just survival and reproduction. However, these stories could not be set in the natural world, where there are no stories—where things just happen willy-nilly and events have no meaning outside of material practicality. These stories had to have plots at a distance from biology.

Say what we like, we do not believe ourselves to be just organisms. Ask any medical researcher in his home-sweet-home if he thinks of himself and his wife and kids in the same way he does the animals he left back in the lab. That we are *critters* is only a scientific technicality. What we see in our mirrors are human beings, and what we need in our diet is the sustenance of stories telling us that we are more than the sum of our creaturely parts. And our supply of this provender comes from only one source—our consciousness, which dramatizes survival as storied conflicts between everyone and his brother and tricks up procreation as legends of courtly love, bedroom farces, and romantic fictions with or without laughs.

But such narratives are not really very far from nature, as we can confirm for ourselves. Those recitals of physical or psychological strife among us: Are they really so removed from survival in the natural kingdom? No, they are not. They are still nature, red in tooth and claw. Masked by our consciousness and its illusions to seem uniquely human, our war stories, success stories, and other bio-dramas are not qualitatively different from their analogues in the wilderness. This goes doubly for romance yarns, those dolled-up variations on mating rituals as seen in nature documentaries. They are not detached from the procreative dog-and-pony show as observed by zoologists and would be dramatically incomplete without a sexual union as their chief motive. Properly considered, they are an ornate pornography, with oft-repeated plots having their climax in a release of tension between two parties and their falling action in what cinematic pornographers term a "money shot," which in conventional filmic products is replaced by a kiss or a marriage by way of consummation.

As survivors and procreators, we unravel stories that at their root are not dissimilar from the habitual behaviors seen in nature. But as beings who know they will die we digress into episodes and epics that are altogether dissociated from the natural world. We may isolate this awareness, distract ourselves from it, anchor our minds far from its shores, and sublimate it as a motif in our sagas. Yet at no time and in no place are we protected from being tapped on the shoulder and reminded, "You're going to die, you know." However much we try to ignore it, our consciousness haunts us with this knowledge. Our heads were baptized in the font of death; they are doused with the horror of moribundity.

Death—do we really believe it is part of the order of our lives? We say that we do. But when it becomes lucent to our imagination, how natural does it feel? W. A. Mozart's attributed last words are apropos here: "The taste of death is on my tongue. I feel something which is not of this world" (Quoted in Jacques Choron, *Death and Modern Man*, 1964). Death is not like survival and procreation. It is more like a visitation from a foreign and enigmatic sphere, one to which we are connected by our consciousness. No consciousness, no death. No death, no stories with a beginning, middle, and an end. Animal stories of survival and procreation have no comparable structure because animals have no consciousness of death.

Obviously, not all fictional plots end in death, only those which follow a character's life until it can be followed no more. However, in the world of nonfiction where we are making a go of it on our own, we know how far we will be followed. What we can never know is How and When the following will end. But suppose we did know How and When the ending would take place? What then? How could we go on? Who could *live* through a story whose ending he or she knew from page one—not in a general sense but as to the How and When of that ending, which may be a crucifixion and not an easeful cessation? Only because we do not know How or When our life stories will finish can we keep going. We remain in suspense about these details, making it possible for us to follow attentively the twists and turns of our personal plot. And so the story holds our interest for as long as it lasts.

Yet everyone knows *What* is going to happen at the end. We just do not know what it will be like when what is going to happen actually happens. One would think that would be enough to ruin the story, knowing *What* is going to happen—that no one is going to make it through. Somehow, though, it does not. Our crafty minds have taken care of that. They have thought a thousand different endings, most prominently that of dying in one's sleep, or not thought about the ending at all. But when it comes, it comes. Nothing will turn away that distinguished visitor. After being long refused admittance into our lives, death materializes outside our door and begins pounding to be let in. Now everything quivers with an aura of the uncanny, and nameless shapes begin to form. As the end nears, consciousness surges and the pieces fall together. Being alive is all right, or so most of us say. But when death walks through the door, nothing is all right. As some believe that life is that which *should not be*, the bulk of the rest of us believe the same of death. That is its terror and its fascination. Everyone knows that we are all the dead-to-be. There are gewgaws and knickknacks that stay in shape far longer than our mortal forms. If we called ourselves dead from the time we are born, we would not be far from the truth. But as long as we can walk or crawl or just lie abed sucking tubes, we can still say that being alive is all right.

Without death—meaning without our consciousness of death—no story of supernatural horror would ever have been written, nor would any other artistic representation of human life have been created for that matter. It is always there, if only between the lines or brushstrokes, or conspicuously by its absence. It is a terrific stimulus to that which is at once one of our greatest weapons and greatest weaknesses—imagination. Our minds are always on the verge of exploding with thoughts and images as we ceaselessly pound the pavement of our world. Both our most exquisite cogitations and our worst cognitive drivel announce our primal torment: We cannot linger in the stillness of nature's vacuity. And so we have imagination to beguile us. A misbegotten hatchling of consciousness, a birth defect of our species, imagination is often revered as a sign of vigor in our make-up. But it is really just a psychic overcompensation for our impotence as beings. Denied nature's exemption from fictitious designs, we are indentured servants of the imaginary until the hour of our death, when the final harassments of imagination will beset us.

Apart from vulgar mortality, supernatural literature also centers on the death of sanity, identity, ideals, abilities, passions, and hand-me-down conceptions about the universe and everything in it. Death is accepted in horror stories because a plot that did not ignite its terrors—in a fictional world, that is—would be a narrative miscarriage. But in real life few of us hang out in morgues and mausoleum chambers, and even those who do are only perversely inuring themselves to the graphic details of what puts us in these places. Being alive is supposed to be all right, but not when you have *no choice* but to consider the alternative. An example of how this might happen, one with which most of us are conversant, is the prosaic plot of a vehicular misadventure, a mischance that is ordinarily experienced as a dreamlike ramble with unforeseen stops along the way.

Imagine: You may be traveling on a slippery road when, without warning, your vehicle begins sliding across several lanes of oncoming traffic. You know that such things happen. They may even have happened to you on a prior occasion. You know that they happen to other people all the time. Nevertheless, this accident was not in your plans, which is why it is called an accident. In principle, it could be plotted as a cause-and-effect confluence of circumstances, although you would never be able to trace them to their originating source, not even if you went back to the beginning of time. It might occur to you, though, that the responsibility for your accident-to-come lay with a friend or relative who called and asked you to come over and lend a hand in some fix-it project, because you would not even be out of the house except for that untimely request. Yet you would be just as right to hold other factors responsible: the slippery road on which you were driving, the weather that made the road slippery, all the things that determined the weather, the length of time you spent looking in your clothes closet for the shoes that would be most proper to wear for the fix-it project in question—that interval of perfect extent which made sure you would be just where you needed to be so that you would not be too early or too late to become involved in a vehicular misadventure.

But whatever the proximate or remote causes of your vehicular misadventure might have been, you had an idea of how things were to happen that day, as you do every day, and spinning out of control in your car while other vehicles try to circumvent a collision with you was not on your schedule. One second ago you had a firm grip on things, but now you are veering toward who knows where. You are not filled with horror, not yet, as you career along the pavement that is slick with rain or snow glistening in the moonlight, the wind wailing and shadows scattering. At this point everything is all strangeness. You have been taken to a different place from where you were just a moment before.

Then it begins. *This can't be happening*, you think—if you can think at all, if you are anything more than a whirlwind of panic. In reality, though, anything can happen now. This is the whispering undercurrent that creeps into your thoughts—nothing is safe and nothing is off limits. All of a sudden something was set in motion that changed everything. Something descended upon you that had been circling above your life from the day you were born. And for the first time you feel that which you have never felt before—the imminence of your own death. There is no possibility for self-deception now. The paradox that came with consciousness is done with. Only horror is left. This is what is real. This is the only thing that was ever real, however unreal it may have seemed. Of course, bad things happen, as everyone knows. They have always happened and always will happen. They are part of the natural order of things. But this is not how we would have it. This is not how we think things should be for us. This is how we think things should *not* be. And all supernatural horror, as we remember, derives from what we believe should be and should not be.

Yet might we have avoided this horror by warding off our belief in what should be and what should not be, by believing only in what is? No, we could not. We were doomed to hold this belief and to suffer what looms out of it. What doomed us (if one will forgive another imperious repetition of this theme) was consciousness—parent of all horrors and author of all we believe should be and should not be. While consciousness brought us out of our coma in the natural, we still like to think that, however aloof we are from other living things, we are not in essence wholly alienated from them. We do try to fit in with the rest of creation, living and breeding like any other animal or vegetable. It is no fault of ours that we were made as we were made—experiments in a parallel being. This was not our choice. We did not volunteer to be as we are. We may think that being alive is all right, especially when we consider the alternative, but we think about it as infrequently as possible, for this very thought raises the spirits of the dead and all the other freaks of nature.

No other life forms know they are alive, and neither do they know they will die. This is our curse alone. Without this hex upon our heads, we would never have withdrawn as far as we have from the natural—so far and for such a time that it is a relief to say what we have been trying with our all not to say: *We have long since fallen from Nature's arms.* Everywhere around us are natural habitats, but within us is the shiver of startling and dreadful things. Simply put: *We are not from here.* If we vanished tomorrow, no organism on this planet would miss us. Nothing in nature needs us. We are like Mainländer's suicidal God. Nothing needed Him either, and His uselessness was transferred to us after He burst out of existence. We have no business being in this world. We move among living things, all those natural puppets with nothing in their heads. But our heads are in another place, a world apart where all the puppets exist not in the midst of life but outside it. We are those puppets, those *human* puppets. We are crazed mimics of the natural prowling about for a peace that will never be ours. And the medium in which we circulate is that of the supernatural, a dusky element of horror that obtains for those who believe in what should be and should not be. This is our secret quarter. This is where we rave with insanity on the level of metaphysics, fracturing reality and breaking the laws of life.

Deviations from the natural have whirled around us all our days. We kept them at arm's length, abnormalities we denied were elemental to our being. But absent us there is nothing of the supernatural in the universe. We are aberrations—beings born undead, neither one thing nor another, or two things at once . . . uncanny things that have nothing to do with the rest of creation, horrors that poison the world by sowing our madness everywhere we go, glutting daylight and darkness with incorporeal obscenities. From across an immeasurable divide, we brought the supernatural into all that is manifest. Like a faint haze it floats around us. We keep company with ghosts. Their graves are marked in our minds, and they will never be disinterred from the cemeteries of our remembrance. Our heartbeats are numbered, our steps counted. Even as we survive and reproduce, we know ourselves to be dying in a dark corner of infinity. Wherever we go, we know not what expects our arrival but only that it is there.

With eyes that see through a translucent veil shimmering before us, we look at life from the other side. There, something escorts us through our days and nights like a second shadow that casts itself into another world and fastens us to it. Leashed to the supernatural, we know its signs and try to tame them by desensitization and lampoonery. We study them as symbols, play games with them. Then an eerily hued light bathes them, and they become real in a peculiar modality: the grinning skull, the curving scythe, the moldy headstone, all the dark creatures of the earth and air, every memento mori we have hidden within us. These skeletons of ours—when will they come out and show themselves? They groan more loudly with each passing year. Time breezes by with chilling haste. Is the child in that old photograph really an erstwhile version of you, your little hand waving farewell? The face of that child is nothing like the face you have now. That child's face is now melding with the blackness behind you, before you, around you. The child is waving and smiling and fading as your car keeps skidding toward your abruptly curtailed future. Bye-bye.

Then another face appears. It has displaced the one you are used to seeing when your rearview mirror goes crooked, as it has now, and confronts you. You cannot look away, because the other face is lit up like a full moon, which both terrifies and fascinates you. And nothing about it looks natural. It seems rigid—the face of something that belongs in a toy chest. The face is smiling, but too much and too long to be real. And its eyes do not blink. The scene shifts moment by moment. People, places, and things appear and disappear. You appeared as others expected *but not as you chose*. You will disappear as if you had never been, having taken your turn in this world. You always told yourself that this was the natural way of things and that you could submit to it because you belonged to nature . . . MALIGNANTLY USELESS nature, which coughed you up like a little phlegm from its great lungs. Yet the supernatural has cleaved to you from the beginning, working its oddities into your life while you waited for death to begin beating on your door. It has not come to save you, but to bring you into its horror. Perhaps you hoped to make it through this horror that sat like a gargoyle upon your life. Now you find there is no way through. Only seconds are left, each one strangling you a little more tightly. Incantations are spoken all around. They have lost their power. The living and the dead jabber inside you. You cannot understand them. Dreams become more lustrous than memories. Darkness is shoveled over dreams.

Those unblinking eyes are still gleaming in the mirror, the eyes of that face, smiling too much and too long. And you can feel your own face smiling, too, your eyes not blinking. Now that secret you never wanted to know comes into your head—that you were made as you were made and manipulated to behave as you behaved. And as this secret comes into your head, the smile of that face in the mirror pushes up at its edges. So does yours, doing as it is bidden. Both faces at once are smiling the same smile. It widens past all sane proportion. At last a long-restrained voice cries out: *What is this life!* But only silence answers, and it mocks every mad hope you ever held.

No self now, consciously speaking.

No feeling your old self or new self, false imaginings if you think about it, self-conscious nothings everywhere you look.

No one to hear you weep or scream, making a go of it on your own, bye-bye.

No arms of nature, abandoned on the doorstep of the supernatural, minds full of flagrantly joyless possibilities, a real blunder that was, the human tragedy.

No reality to speak of, nobody here but us puppets, contradictory beings, mutants who embody the contorted logic of a paradox. No immortality, ordinary folk and average mortals coming and going, can't stay long, got an appointment with nonexistence, no alternative to consider, being alive was all right while it lasted, so they say.

No life story with a happy ending to tell, only a contrivance of horror, then nothingness—and nothing else.

No Free Will-to-live, no redemption by a Will-to-die, how depressing.

No philosophies to peddle, pessimism a no-sale, optimism had to close its doors, too wicked to pass code.

No meanings or mind-games, repressional mechanisms broke down, self-deception shuttered its windows.

No awakening from a dream within a dream, mutation of consciousness—parent of all horrors, best not mess with it, extinction looking better all the time.

No more pleasure, what there was of it, a few crumbs left by chaos at feast, still a good supply of pain, though.

No praiseworthy incentives, just bowel-movement pressures, potato-mashing relativism.

No euthanasia, bad for the business of life, you're on your own there, but watch out for the eternal return, most horrible idea in the universe.

No loving God, omnipotence off duty and omniscience on leave, the deity He dead—the horror, the horror, even the skies of spring and the flowers of summer must ever afterward be poison, blame it on the piecing together of dissociated knowledge.

No compassionate Buddha, Body Snatchers got him, heard tell, or some kind of thing, maybe next lifetime.

No Good-versus-Evil formulas around here, Azathoth running the show, human beings a mistake or a joke, something pernicious making a nightmare of our world.

No being normal and real, the uncanny coming at you full speed, startling and dreadful.

No ego-death—enlightenment by accident.

No way out of harm's way, better never to have been, worst saved for last.

No Last Messiah, buried in the fingernails of midwives and pacifier makers, gone the way of messiahs past.

No bleakness either, a failure indeed.

No terror management by isolation, anchoring, distraction, sublimation.

No tragedies to read or to write, death kept at a safe distance past the vanishing point down the road.

No escape routes into a useless bliss, useless existence, malignantly so. . .

What now? Now there is only that unnaturally spreading smile—a great gaping abyss where blackness reaches out to blackness, nothing. Then: the sense of being swallowed. The story is done; the plot complete.

Endgame

To contest Zapffe's philosophy, or any philosophy like it, would be as facile as to contest that of any other philosopher whose reasoning does not suit your predilections. If his analysis of human existence appears secure in a certain light, it may be flouted with little exertion by anyone thus motivated. Zapffe did not discover the New World, with a handful of dirt to prove it. He was someone who thought he had worked out why humankind should go extinct, knowing that we would never make that choice, whatever he and his Last Messiah had to say. Whether we are sovereign or enslaved in our being, what of it? Our species will still look to the future and see no need to abdicate its puppet dance of replication in a puppet universe where the strings pull themselves. What a laugh that we would do anything else, or could do anything else. That our lives might be a paradox and a horror would not really be a secret too terrible to know for minds that know only what they want to know. The hell of human consciousness is only a philosopher's bedtime story we can hear each night and forget each morning when we awake to go to school or to work or wherever we may go day after day after day. What do we care about the horror of being insufferably aware we are alive and will die . . . the horror of shadows without selves enshrouding the earth . . . or the horror of puppet-heads bobbing in the wind and disappearing into a dark sky like lost balloons? If that is the way you think things are, go shout it from the rooftops and see where it gets you. We are staying put, but you can go extinct if you like. We can make more little puppets like you, but we do not call them that. We call them people who have indivisible selves and stories that are nothing like yours.

Being somebody is rough, but being nobody is out of the question. We must be happy, we must imagine Sisyphus to be happy, we must believe because it is absurd to believe. Day by day, in every way, we are getting better and better. Positive illusions for positive persons. They shoot horses, don't they? But as for shooting ourselves—ask Gloria Beatty, ask Michelstaedter, ask Weininger, ask Hemingway. But do not ask Mainlander or Bjørneboe, who hanged themselves. And do not ask Jean Améry, author of *Suicide:*

A Discourse on Voluntary Death (1976), who made his exit with a drug overdose. Améry survived Auschwitz, but he did not survive his survival. No one does. With our progenitors and the world behind us, we will never hold this life to be MALIGNANTLY USELESS. Almost nobody declares that an ancestral curse contaminates us in utero and pollutes our existence. Doctors do not weep in the delivery room, or not often. They do not lower their heads and say, "The stopwatch has started." The infant may cry, if things went right. But time will dry its eyes; time will take care of it. Time will take care of everyone until there are none of us to take care of. Then all will be as it was before we put down roots where we do not belong.

There will come a day for each of us—and then for all of us—when the future will be done with. Until then, humanity will acclimate itself to every new horror that comes knocking, as it has done from the very beginning. It will go on and on until it stops. And the horror will go on, with generations falling into the future like so many bodies into open graves. The horror handed down to us will be handed down to others like a scandalous heirloom. Being alive: decades of waking up on time, then trudging through another round of moods, sensations, thoughts, cravings—the complete gamut of agitations—and finally flopping into bed to sweat in the pitch of dead sleep or simmer in the phantasmagorias that molest our dreaming minds. Why do so many of us bargain for a life sentence over the end of a rope or the muzzle of a gun? Do we not *deserve* to die? But we are not obsessed by such questions. To ask them is not in our interest, nor to answer them with hand on heart. In such spirit might we not bring to an end the conspiracy against the human race? This would seem to be the right course: the death of tragedy in the embrace of nonexistence. Overpopulated worlds of the unborn would not have to suffer for our undoing what we have done (just so that we might go on as we have all these years). That said, nothing we know would have us take that step. What could be more unthinkable? We are only human beings. Ask anybody.

Notes

The Nightmare of Being

1. The nativity of human consciousness as depicted in this paragraph may be seen as (1) a fable of humanity's "loss of innocence" and alienation from a "natural" way of being in the world; (2) a speculative moment with a loose footing in evolutionary psychology.

2. "The Last Messiah," *Wisdom in the Open Air: The Norwegian Roots of Deep Ecology* (1993), ed. Peter Reed and David Rothenberg (translators Sigmund Kvaløy with Peter Reed); *Philosophy Now*, March–April 2004 (translator Gisle R. Tangenes). Regrettably, Zapffe's philosophical masterwork, *On the Tragic* (1941), has not appeared in any major language at the time of this writing. However, abstracts of its substance, as well as excerpts from this treatise and other writings by Zapffe as translated into English by Tangenes, confirm that throughout his long life he did not abandon or dilute the pessimistic principles of *On the Tragic* as they appear in miniature in "The Last Messiah." While it may seem strange or ludicrous for any book to place so much of the weight of its discourse on a short essay written by an obscure

223

European philosopher in the early 1930s, one must start some-where.

3. Under the collective designation of "constructivists," philoso-phers, sociologists, and other authorities working in a range of fields have variously deliberated on the fabricated nature of our lives. Examples: P. L. Berger and T. Luckman, *The Social Con-struction of Reality*, 1966; Paul Watzlawick, ed., *Invented Re-ality: How Do We Know What We Believe We Know?*, 1984; Ernst von Glasefeld, *Radical Contructivism: A Way of Learning*, 1996. For book-reading intellectuals, this idea is just one of many that fill their days. Its import, however, is not often shared with the masses. But sometimes it is in no-nonsense ways. An in-stance in cinema where fabrication is hypothesized to be the cornerstone of our lives occurs at the end of *Hero* (1992) when the character referred to in the title, Bernard LaPlante, passes on some words of wisdom to his previously estranged son. "You remember where I said I was going to explain about life, buddy?" he says. "Well, the thing about life is, it gets weird. People are always talking to you about truth, everybody always knows what the truth is, like it was toilet paper or some thing and they got a supply in the closet. But what you learn as you get older is, there ain't no truth. All there is, is bullshit. Pardon my vulgarity here. Layers of it. One layer of bullshit on top of another. And what you do in life, like when you get older, is— you pick the layer of bullshit you prefer, and that's your bullshit, so to speak. You got that?" Despite the cynicism of LaPlante's words, the object of his fatherly lesson is to create a bond be-tween him and his son. (Hollywood is heavily invested in plot-lines in which a broken family is "healed.") This bond is reliant on the exposure of life as bullshit and is itself bullshit—since one can have no basis for preferring one layer of bullshit over

another without already being full of bullshit. The logic here employed makes LaPlante's case that "all there is, is bullshit" without his being aware of it, which is how bullshit works. This is not the message the moviegoer is meant to take away from the mass-audience philosophizing of *Hero*, but there it is anyway.

4. It was also no impediment to Weininger's posthumous reputation—after he killed himself by gunshot at the age of twenty-three—that he was an anti-Semitic Jew who converted to Christianity, a life-path that looked good on one's resume before the Second World War, and one that will always look good to the average Christian extremist until Judgment Day. (Naturally, Weininger's works have been widely translated and critically examined.) The libelous profile of Jews in *Sex and Character* must have filled someone like Adolf Hitler with a self-satisfied sense of being a real human and not a Jew, even a converted one. In regard to the Führer's own reputation, what we have is a biography of a bungler whose genocidal predisposition did not cause the way of life of his target group to falter. This is quite in contrast to the U.S. government's expertise in reducing indigenous peoples to internees on their own home ground and freely claiming their land. What they were is gone forever. To thwart suspicions to the contrary, the intent here is not to sympathize with any person or people but only to play up historical facts that live most vividly in the memory of their victims and must be repressed in the conscience of their perpetrators if the latter are to retain a good opinion of themselves, their god, their nation, their families, and the human race, or that part of the human race with whom they believe themselves to share a destiny. Such facts of life and death are just that—facts. To the extent they are submitted as an

indictment of humanity, a blunder has been made. What has been called "man's inhumanity to man" should not entice us into a misanthropy smarting for our species to come to an end. That deduction is another blunder, as much as it would be a blunder to tub-thump for our survival based on the real abundance of what is valued as "humane" behavior. Both the "inhuman" and the "humane" movements of our species are without relevance. None of us are at the helm of either of these movements. We believe ourselves to be masters of our behavior—that is the blunder. We believe ourselves to be something we are not—that is the blunder. To perpetuate these blunders, to conspire in the suffering of future generations, is the only misconduct to be expiated, not that we will ever be ready or able to rectify our incorrigible nature. That we were naturally or divinely made to collaborate in our own suffering and that of human posterity is the blunder. Ask Adam and Eve, symbols of the most deleterious blunder of all, one which we reenact every day.

5. For a study that reaches the conclusion that one's subjective well-being is approximately fifty percent determined by genetic lottery and fifty percent by life experiences, rather than something that a self-help book can instruct an individual to achieve, see "Happiness Is a Stochastic Phenomenon" by David Lykken and Auke Tellegen, *University of Minnesota Psychological Science*, 1996. The equal percentages of genetic and experiential factors in Lykken and Tellegen's study results in their conclusion that happiness is a "matter of chance" and is not a phenomenon genetically determined in whole. A full genetic determinism of one's happiness, and every other trait of ours, is known as "puppet determinism," although why

genetics should be the lone string-puller and not genetics coupled with events in one's existence, which would leave nothing of what we are to chance, seems curious. (For more on determinism, see the section *Actors* in the chapter "Who Goes There?")

6. The précis of Mainländer's philosophy in this chapter in based in several sources: Thomas Whittaker's *Essays and Notices Philosophical and Psychological*, 1895; H. P. Blavatsky's "The Origin of Evil" in the October 1897 issue of the journal *Lucifer*; Rudolph Steiner's *The Riddles of Philosophy*, 1914, and *Evil: Selected Lectures*, 1918; Radoslav Tsanoff's *The Nature of Evil*, 1931; Francesca Arundale's *The Idea of Rebirth*, 1942; Aleksander Samarin, "The Engima of Immortality," May 2005 (http://www.thebigview.com); Johann Joachim Gestering's *German Pessimism and Indian Philosophy: A Hermenuetic Reading*, 1986; and Henry Sheldon's *Unbelief in the Nineteenth Century*, 2005. A more conventionally philosophical working out of why the human race should be discontinued is contained in the section *Undoing III* later in this chapter.

7. Zapffe's solution to nature's sportive minting of the human race may seem the last checkpoint of pessimism. In his *Philosophy of the Unconscious* (1869), the German philosopher Eduard von Hartmann thinks further ahead: "What would it avail, *e.g.*, if all mankind should die out by sexual continence? The world as such would continue to exist." This endurance of the organic would allow the restive forces of life to set up "*a new man or similar type*, and the whole misery would begin over again" (Hartmann's emphasis). For Hartmann, the struggle for deliverance will not end until a super-potent force exterminates

every scintilla of the Creation. While Hartmann's vision is lunacy, so is the idea that humanity will ever leave off breeding. Between two uproarious implausibilities, why distinguish one as more implausible than the other?

8. The notion that human beings are caught in a paradox that affects no other creatures in this world reemerges in John Gray's *Straw Dogs: Thoughts on Humans and Other Animals* (2002). At the end of this work, the author echoes Zapffe's conceptualization of humanity when he writes: "Other animals do not need a purpose in life. A contradiction to itself, the human animal cannot do without one." While observing this contradiction, however, Gray never gives a moment's regard to the possibility that it might render human existence a paradox that only voluntary extinction can bring to an end. Even though Gray sees our involuntary extinction as probable and not far off, he is still open to solutions short of the cooperative cessation of the human race. The one that he suggests, which he seems not to have noticed is already in place, is that humanity should do what it can to get by in this world while living in a state of irremediable delusion. Following the previously quoted sentences is the parting sentiment of *Straw Dogs*: "Can we not think of the aim of life as being simply to see?" This query rests on the premise that there is a better way for the human race to live, and that we could live that way if we wanted to. Irrespective of the optimistic spirit of Gray's concluding question, *Straw Dogs* has been deprecated by many as a breviary of pessimism. Without cavil, it is a contrarian work that has rejuvenated for the common reader some of the most basic and neglected difficulties of human life. But to label it as pessimistic is an overreaction on the part of those who would remain mere dabblers in actuality.

9. For a supporting view of James's non-logical exoneration of the faithful, see Ellen Kappy Suckiel, "William James on Cognitivity of Feelings, Religious Pessimism, and the Meaning of Life," *The Journal of Speculative Philosophy*, 2004.

10. Included among these works are Herbert Fingarette's *Self-Deception* (2000), Alfred R. Mele's *Self-Deception Unmasked* (2001); Eviatar Zerubavel's *The Elephant in the Room: Silence and Denial in Everyday Life* (2006); *Perspectives on Self-Deception* (1988), Brian P. McLaughlin and Amelie Oksenburg Rorty, eds.; *Denial: A Clarification of Concepts and Research* (1989), E. L. Edelstein, D. L. Nathanson, and A. M. Stone, eds.; and *Lying and Deception in Everyday Life* (1993), Michael Lewis and Carolyn Saarni, eds.

Who Goes There?

1. Galen Strawson explains this experience in similar terms: For most people, "their personality is something that is unnoticed, and in effect undetectable in the present moment. It's what they look through, or where they look from; not something they look at; a global and invisible condition of their life, like air, not an object of experience" ("The Sense of Self" in *From Soul to Self*, ed. M. James Crabbe, 1999).

Freaks of Salvation

1. One's "sense of meaning" functions as an autonomic system, something that is noticed when it goes on the fritz but not when it is in working order. It is part of the cog-and-wheel

functioning of our psychological machinery and would perhaps be better characterized as a set of stored-up assumptions than a sensation or emotion. When one or more of these assumptions is threatened by someone or something, their meaning-system will come to the fore and face off with its foe. After the threat is dealt with, this system once again returns to its autonomic functioning. Only a tiny percentage of humans consciously fixate on meaning without an adversarial provocation. If for most of our race meaning comes straight from a handbook that may be referenced by page and paragraph, chapter and verse—"God exists," "I have a Self," "My country is the best in the world"—for this small percentage meaning is principally received from one source: a *sense of mystery.* In his essay "The Wall and the Book," the twentieth-century Argentine writer Jorge Luis Borges wrote: "Music, states of happiness, mythology, faces belabored by time, certain twilights and certain places try to tell us something, or have said something we should not have missed, or are about to say something; *this imminence of a revelation which does not occur* is, perhaps, the aesthetic phenomenon" (emphasis added). Lovecraft's "Notes on the Writing of Weird Fiction" opens with this sentence: "My reason for writing stories is to give myself the satisfaction of visualising more clearly and detailedly and stably the vague, elusive, fragmentary impressions of wonder, beauty, and *adventurous expectancy* which are conveyed to me by certain sights (scenic, architectural, atmospheric, etc.), ideas, occurrences, and images encountered in art and literature" (emphasis added). This sense of mystery that is never dissipated by express knowledge but is forever an *imminence* or *expectancy* explains much of the attraction of supernatural stories (Blackwood's "The Willows," Lovecraft's "The Colour out of Space," Poe's "The Fall of the House of Usher"). For Borges and

Lovecraft, the experience that a meaningful mystery was *about* to be revealed to them was stirred by works of art or by an aesthetic vision of things in the world. For others, the experience of meaning through mystery may not take place because of a crudeness of character or a mystery-killing condition such as depression, a disease that trumps everything that might mean something. But when a sense of mystery arises, it does so most potently on the threshold of realization. Should the mystery ever be revealed, it will crumble and lie in pieces upon the earth. Afterward, there will be an incursion of scriptures, doctrines, and narratives that specify the mysterious as an object or a datum. To say that some kind of god *might* exist is to vivify its being with mystery. To define a god into existence because it meets certain criteria for godhood is to kill that god by turning it into a cheapjack idol with a publicity team of theologians behind it. This would explain why so many deities—all of them, in fact—have fallen apart or are in the process of doing so: eventually every god loses its mystery because it has become overqualified for its job. After a god's mystery is gone, arguments for its reality begin. Logic steps in to resuscitate what has been bled of its healthful vagueness. Finally, another "living god" is consigned to the mortuary of scholars.

2. Borges's essay "The Doctrine of Cycles" both cites and conceives several refutations catastrophic for the ancient concept of the eternal return, which posits the identical recurrence of all beings and events forever and ever and ever. In the words of the bookish Argentine, the "eternal return of the same" is "the most horrible idea in the universe." To Borges, this idea was a nightmare born of bad philosophy; to Nietzsche, it was a nightmare fathered by his need to be joyful, or to believe he

would be joyful no matter what horror befell him. In Nietzsche's world, coming to terms with this idea *as a reality* was a must for affirming one's life and life itself, thus recalculating the horrors of existence into a fate, or an unceasing series of fates, that would somehow inspire love rather than alarm. Given the antinomy on this issue between Borges and Nietzsche, should one writer be heralded over the other as genuine, authentic, or whatever term of approval one cares to wield? This is a moot question. Each man was handling the stress of a hyper-diligent consciousness in his own style and not in one pressed upon him by cognitive meddlers.

3. How vapid is the rhetoric of insolence when used by infidels. Only the blasphemies of the faithful who feel themselves ill used by their deity carry the music of hatred that the unbeliever attempts in vain. Take the Book of Job. Were its protagonist an actual man and not a lesson in fearful obeisance, the Old Testament might contain a symphony of rancor greater than any this world has known. But Job turns legalistic rather than abusive; he wants to *argue* why he should be spared his hellish trials. No good can come of that. Any argument can go on interminably . . . or until one party gives in, which is what Job does because God will not argue with him and, being almighty, can say and do whatever he likes without question. One thing that Job's tale has conferred upon worshippers down through the ages is a compulsory workout in rationalization known as theodicy—a genre of Christian apologetics that endeavors to square an all-knowing, all-powerful, and all-loving god with the evils of existence. *Pace* Chesterton, reconciling a good Creator with a bad creation makes for a problem that believers cannot solve with or without logic. And anyone who believes this problem will ever go away will believe anything.

4. Some quotes from U. G. may be useful here. The likeness between U. G.'s contentions and those of Zapffe, as well as to others made or to be made by the author of the present work, are fairly blatant. Because of these conceptual affinities, skepticism regarding the experiences and ideas of U. G. and others in this section is wanting, for whatever fosters insights we are eager to dispense is always given a shameful leeway. But as U. G. once said, "All insights, however extraordinary they may be, are worthless. You can create a tremendous structure of thought from your own discovery, which you call insight. But that insight is nothing but the result of your own thinking, the permutations and combinations of thought. Actually there is no way you can come up with anything original." The following selection is taken from interviews with U. G. collected as *No Way Out* (1991).

> The problem is this: Nature has assembled all these species on this planet. The human species is no more important than any other species on this planet. For some reason, man accorded himself a superior place in this scheme of things. He thinks that he is created for some grander purpose than, if I could give a crude example, the mosquito that is sucking his blood. What is responsible for this is the value system that we have created. And the value system has come out of the religious thinking of man. Man has created religion because it gives him a cover. This demand to fulfill himself, to seek something out there was made imperative because of this self-consciousness in you which occurred somewhere along the line of the evolutionary process. Man separated himself from the totality of nature.

*   *   *

Nature is interested in only two things—to survive and to reproduce one like itself. Anything you super-impose on that, all the cultural input, is responsible for the boredom of man. So we have varieties of religious experience. You are not satisfied with your own religious teachings or games; so you bring in others from India, Asia or China. They become interesting because they are something new. You pick up a new language and try to speak it and use it to feel more important. But basically, it is the same thing.

*   *   *

Somewhere along the line in human consciousness, there occurred self-consciousness. (When I use the word "self," I don't mean that there is a self or a center there.) That consciousness separated man from the to-tality of things. Man, in the beginning, was a frightened being. He turned everything that was uncontrollable into something divine or cosmic and worshiped it. It was in that frame of mind that he created, quote and unquote, "God." So, culture is responsible for whatever you are. I maintain that all the political institutions and ideologies we have today are the outgrowth of the same religious thinking of man. The spiritual teachers are in a way responsible for the tragedy of mankind.

*   *   *

Your own death, or the death of your near and dear ones, is not something you can experience. What you actually experience is the void created by the disappearance of another individual, and the unsatisfied demand to maintain the continuity of your relationship with that person for a nonexistent eternity. The arena for the continuation of all these "permanent" relationships is the tomorrow—heaven, next life, and so on. These things are the inventions of a mind interested only in its undisturbed, permanent continuity in a "self"-generated, fictitious future. The basic method of maintaining the continuity is the repetition of the question, "How? How? How?" "How am I to live? How can I be happy? How can I be sure I will be happy tomorrow?" This has made life an insoluble dilemma for us. We want to know, and through that knowledge we hope to continue on with our miserable existences forever.

* * *

I still maintain that it is not love, compassion, humanism, or brotherly sentiments that will save mankind. No, not at all. It is the sheer terror of extinction that can save us, if anything can.

* * *

I am like a puppet sitting here. It's not just I; all of us are puppets. Nature is pulling the strings, but we believe that we are acting. If you function that way [as puppets], then the problems are simple. But we have superimposed on that [the idea of] a "person" who is pulling those strings.

5. Ask Charles Whitman, who left a written request that an autopsy be done on him that might explain why he ascended a

tower at the University of Texas to shoot at and kill strangers before he himself was shot and killed by policemen. Whitman did have a brain tumor, but neurologists could not connect this malignancy to his actions, possibly because he was dead. In a note written a few days preceding his murderous rampage on August 1, 1966, Whitman stated that in March of that year he had consulted with one Dr. Jan Cochrum, to whom he confided his "unusual and irrational thoughts" and "overwhelming violent impulses." Cochrum gave Whitman a script for Valium and referred him to a psychiatrist, Dr. Maurice Dean Heatly. In his one session with Heatly, Whitman said that he had an urge to "start shooting people with a deer rifle." While no causal association was established between Whitman's brain tumor and his bloody actions, he probably should have had his brain checked out sooner, or at least "chosen" not to destroy so many lives. In a determinist court of justice, perhaps Cochrum and Heatly would have been tried as collaborators in the killings. But why be solicitous about such legal intricacies when the law could put it all on Whitman's head?

Sick to Death

1. At this point in his life, Tolstoy was running low on each of Zapffe's four methods for befogging one's consciousness— isolation, distraction, anchoring, and, most toweringly, sublimation through his work as a literary artist. As Zapffe may have borrowed some of his central propositions from Nietzsche's *Birth of Tragedy*, he may also have gone to school on Tolstoy's *A Confession*. In naming the self-deceitful ways of human beings, original ideas are hard to come by. Zapffe's

thought in "The Last Messiah" is indeed based on "taboo commonplaces" and "outlawed truisms," which average mortals may not like to hear but which they cannot rebuff once they hear them.

2. A cinematic exemplification of this betrayal is the closing voiceover of *Se7en* (1995), which was indeed a work of dark vision in which chaos triumphs over order until, at the last minute, the actor Morgan Freeman saves the day with a laconic voiceover: "Ernest Hemingway once wrote, 'The world is a fine place and worth fighting for.' I agree with the second part." This quote is taken from Hemingway's 1940 novel *For Whom the Bell Tolls*. The words are those of the hero of the book, Robert Jordan, who sacrifices his life in war for what he considers a good cause. Not minding being killed by the enemy, Jordan is also willing to commit suicide in order to avoid capture. But he would rather not kill himself. His father had done that, as Hemingway's had, and Jordan judged him a coward for this act. Could Hemingway have also thought himself a coward when he adjourned this life by suicide some decades after writing *For Whom the Bell Tolls*? What a triumph of order over chaos that would have been—a terrible but heroic integrity.

3. During the 1970s, Nuland himself almost became the victim of a pack of doctors who wanted to treat a severe psychological disorder that was overwhelming his mind using the technique of a pre-frontal lobotomy. If things went as well as they possibly could with this procedure, Nuland would have been turned into an emotionless thing with only enough residual intellect to clean the toilets at the hospital where he once

performed surgeries. At the last moment, a doctor friend of his intervened. In his friend's minority opinion, the lobotomy should be postponed until Nuland was first put through a succession of electro-convulsive treatments. This therapy did the trick. Later Nuland became a writer with a mystical worship of the "human spirit" and its Will-to-live, though not in a Schopenhauerian sense. At the close of *How We Die*, Nuland writes: "The art of dying is the art of living." What he does not write is that to practice the art of living it helps if you have a doctor friend who will keep you from having an unnecessary lobotomy, or a needless surgery.

4. The human instinct to have one's own "way of life" outlast those of others is risibly skewered in Stanley Kubrick's *Dr. Strangelove or: How I Learned to Stop Worrying and Love the Bomb*. Faced with the extinction of humanity at the hands of a doomsday device created by the Russians and programmed to be tripped by a nuclear attack from the United States, American politicians and military officials, at the urging of ex-Nazi scientist Dr. Strangelove, plan to survive by living in mineshafts for the next hundred years, after which they would emerge and, in Strangelove's estimation, "work their way back to the present gross national product within, say, the next twenty years." Worried that the Russians could have the same plan, Gen. Buck Turgidson, with all the foresight one would expect from a man of his position, speculates, "I think we should look at this from a military point of view. I mean, supposing the Russkies stashed away a big bomb, see. When they come out in a hundred years, they could take over!" Another general agrees with Turgidson, who rambles on, "Yeah, I think it would be extremely naïve of us, Mr. President, to imagine that these new developments are going to cause any change in Soviet expan-

sionist policies. I mean, we must be increasingly on the alert to prevent them from taking over mineshaft space, in order to breed more prodigiously than we do, thus knocking us out in superior numbers when we emerge!" The goofball insanity played out in this scene has had audiences soaking their drawers since Kubrick's film was released in 1964. The characters seem to be such funny little puppets as they draw up a survival plan, the success or failure of which they will not live to see. All they request is the hope that succeeding generations will carry on the same goofball insanity that they did. In Zapffe's terms, *Dr. Strangelove* is a work of artistic sublimation. Its audiences can bust a gut watching it and still go on propagating to secure the way of life it parodies. Should the events of this movie ever be realized, those who emerge from the mineshafts will yelp with glee at its goofball insanity no less than those who went in. George Santayana's epigram "Those who cannot learn from history are doomed to repeat it" is one big hoot. Only by repeating history every second of every day can human beings survive and breed. How out of keeping with this fact is the idea that anyone among us would not *want* to be doomed to repeat history. Or that any mortal could possibly learn anything from it that would change our "way of life." That would be the doomsday scenario, the prologue to a melodrama that ends with the entrance of the Last Messiah.

5. Consciousness studies sometimes draw attention to the phenomenological view that at your death the whole world dies because the representation of it that you have inside your head *is* the world, a solipsistic dreamland of your own making. Consequently, there is no possibility of enshrining the world *as you know it* or partaking by proxy—for instance, by sexual reproduction—in the future.

6. In her 1995 book *Touched with Fire: Manic-Depressive Illness and the Artistic Temperament*, Kay Redfield Jamison cites an identical apocalyptic sentiment contained in the letters of the French composer Hector Berlioz, who remarked that in his frequent moments of depression he felt as if he could without hesitation light a bomb that would blow up the earth. Antecedents of Jamison's work are *The Anatomy of Melancholy* (1621) by Robert Burton; *Born under Saturn: The Character and Conduct of Artists: A Documented History from Antiquity to the French Revolution* (1963) by Rudolf and Margot Wittkower; *Voices of Melancholy: Studies in Literary Treatments of Melancholy in Renaissance England* (1971) by Bridget Gellert Lyons; and *The Demon of Noontide: Ennui in Western Literature* (1976) by Reinhard Kuhn.

7. One of the least solid rationalizations ever pitched to the world to soothe our fear of death was made by the Roman philosopher Lucretius, a disciple of Epicurus. Lucretius's rationalization to terminate death-fear is as follows: We accept with great aplomb that we did not exist before we were born; therefore, there is no reason to fear not existing after our death. Neither of the two parts of this proposition is sound. (They would be sound if human beings were consummately rational, but we are not; if we were, then the rationalization under discussion would not need to be put before us.) It may be out of the ordinary to experience fear in connection with the time when we did not exist, but nothing dictates that we cannot look upon it with fear, just as nothing dictates that we must look upon it with fear. We may or may not look upon anything with fear—as Pascal was terrified of the "infinite immensity of spaces" while other people, in the tradition of Lovecraft, do not

feel this terror—or we may fear something at one time but not another. As for experiencing fear in connection with the time when we will not exist, no one can dictate by reason that we are mistaken to experience this fear. Like every other emotion, fear is irrational; it is not subject to calculation and cannot be entered into philosophical equations. And whether or not you fear death has nothing to do with what some philosopher thinks is rational or irrational. Epicurus ingenuously believed that you could "accustom yourself to believing that death is nothing to us." While some people can short-circuit their jitters about speaking in public by repeatedly putting themselves in situations where they must do so, no mortal can *practice* overcoming the fear of death in this or any other manner. (This note need not be read beyond this point, the point having been made.) Rationality is irrelevant to our being afraid or not afraid of anything. Those who say that rationality has or can have any relevance in this regard do not know what they are talking about, perhaps most of all when they are talking about the fear of death. One reason among many for this fear is that we are perfectly capable of visualizing what it is like to be a stiff just like any other stiff we have witnessed in repose while loved ones wept and mere acquaintances checked their watches because they had places to go and people to see who had not been embalmed. This "being-towards-being-a-stiff," as the twentieth-century German philosopher Martin Heidegger might say, is an unpleasant prospect, if only in our imaginations. Another ugly prospect, and one we will be around to experience, is the How and When of our dying. That philosophy is useless in tackling these ultimate issues is a sufficient, though not a necessary, reason for not bothering with philosophy . . . except possibly to distract or sublimate our consciousness with reference to the How and When of our dying. This fact goes without saying, which is why we do not often say anything about it. When we do say something about it, we say that dying is part of life and let it go at that. Naturally, nothing dictates that we need to fear dying, or nothing that we know of. There are many, many things that nothing dictates we need to fear, and the fact that few people are fearful of these things makes the point. Nothing dictates that we should fear becoming paralyzed below our necks. Nothing dictates we should fear having our legs amputated because they, or some other part of our bodies, might be damaged in a vehicular mis-adventure. Nothing dictates we should fear having horrible nightmares before we go to sleep or that we should fear waking up with an irritating speck in one of our eyes. Nothing dictates that we should fear going mad or becoming so unbearably de-pressed we want to kill ourselves. Nothing dictates that we should fear bearing children with cystic fibrosis or some other congenital disease. Nothing dictates that parents should have the least fear that their child might be abducted by a psy-chopath and tortured to death or that they should fear their child may grow up to be psychopath who abducts children and tortures them for his pleasure because that is the kind of indi-vidual his psychology dictates he must be. Obviously and ab-solutely, nothing dictates that we need fear these contretemps or millions of others like them. If anything did dictate our fearing these things, why would we go on living? The answer is that if it were dictated that we should fear the millions of horrors that may befall us, we would go on living because we *already exist*. And as long as we exist, there will be a noisy klatch of philosophers haranguing us with reasons why nothing dictates we should fear death and why everything dic-tates that we should go on living.

The Cult of Grinning Martyrs

1. No scientist actually knows why or how sexual reproduction came to be, since it is a cumbersome and inefficient means of procreation, or it used to be. The pleasure theory is here emphasized because that is the way things are now, and scientific theories in this area have little existential relevance. It is possible that in the future non-orgasmic pregnancies will become the reproductive method of choice, perhaps for the reason that they may come to yield the best results, genetically speaking. Yet it seems a long shot that sexual activity among human beings will be relinquished, since without such activity there would be no reason for opposite or same-sex genders to bond in a "loving relationship." And that would be the end of the species.

2. For a two-sided view of this topic and a bountiful bibliography on the pain issue, see Roy F. Baumeister, Ellen Bratslavsky, et al., "Bad Is Stronger than Good," *Review of General Psychology*, 2001. For an expanding universe of debate on what may or may not be valid regarding these topics, see all books and essays on sociobiology, evolutionary psychology, and related studies.

3. Contradicting the positive image that is propagated by society, studies cited by Daniel Gilbert—author of the best-selling *Stumbling on Happiness* (2007)—have revealed that, whatever a couple's rationale may be for having children, they can expect newborns in their household to have a negative effect on their well-being or, best case, no effect. It seems that the two happiest days in parents' lives are the day their children are born and the

day they leave home. Naturally, the parents of the world will deny this determination, and well they should. When researchers report that children are not really a source of happiness for their parents, skepticism does seem in order. Mutatis mutandis, the same has been said about people who buy recreational boats, which anecdotally deliver a worse than neutral payback for the pleasures they bring due to the incommensurate effort of their upkeep. The reader is invited to reflect to no avail on any pursuit that is not more trouble than it is worth. As for procreation, no one in his right mind would say that it is the only activity devoid of a praiseworthy incentive. Those who reproduce, then, should not feel unfairly culled as the worst conspirators against the human race. Every one of us is culpable in keeping the conspiracy alive, which is all right with most people.

Autopsy on a Puppet:
An Anatomy of the Supernatural

1. Hemingway thought that Pío Baroja, a Basque writer whose works are of a pessimistic, cynical, and atheist bent, was more worthy of the Nobel than he was. As Baroja lay dying in a hospital bed, he was visited by Hemingway. It seems that the well-awarded American wanted to express personally his veneration for Baroja's work before the foreign writer made his final exit. The author of the 1911 novel *The Tree of Knowledge*, a meditation on the uselessness of both knowledge and life, simply sighed "Ay, caramba" at Hemingway's piety.

2. One cringes to hear scientists cooing over the universe or any part thereof like schoolgirls overheated by their first crush. From the studies of Krafft-Ebbing onward, we know that it is

possible to become excited about anything—from shins to shoehorns. But it would be nice if just one of these gushing eggheads would step back and, as a concession to objectivity, speak the truth: THERE IS NOTHING INNATELY IMPRESSIVE ABOUT THE UNIVERSE OR ANYTHING IN IT.

3. For one of the best accounts by a respected Psi researcher of her long dedication to making a tenable case for paranormal phenomena, see Susan Blackmore's *In Search of the Light: Adventures of a Parapsychologist*, 1987; revised edition, 1996. For a debunking of paranormal phenomena, see the same book.

Songs of a Dead Dreamer *and* Grimscribe

Foreword by Jeff VanderMeer

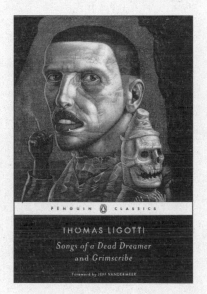

Thomas Ligotti's debut collection, *Songs of a Dead Dreamer*, and his second, *Grimscribe*, permanently inscribed a new name in the pantheon of horror fiction. Influenced by the strange terrors of Lovecraft and Poe and by the brutal absurdity of Kafka, Ligotti eschews cheap, gory thrills for his own brand of horror, which shocks at the deepest, existential, levels.

"Full of inexplicable and alarming delights . . .
Put this volume on the shelf right between H. P. Lovecraft
and Edgar Allan Poe. Where it belongs."
—*The Washington Post*